CHANGE THE WAY YOU COMMUNICATE
WHY YOU SHOULD. HOW YOU CAN.

KEN HASELEY

MISSION POINT PRESS

All rights reserved.
Copyright © 2021 by Ken Haseley

No part of this book may be reproduced, stored in a retrieval system, or transmitted in any form or by any means electronic, mechanical, photocopying, recording or otherwise, without the prior consent of the publisher.

ISBN: 978-1-954786-08-0
Library of Congress Control Number: 2021904063

Published by Mission Point Press
2554 Chandler Road
Traverse City, Michigan 49696

Printed in the United States of America

For information on obtaining bulk copies, please visit CornerSuiteCommunications.com.

CHANGE THE WAY YOU COMMUNICATE
WHY YOU SHOULD. HOW YOU CAN.

KEN HASELEY

CONTENTS

VIII	ACKNOWLEDGMENTS
IX	INTRODUCTION
1	**CRAFTING AND DELIVERING A TOP-FLIGHT PRESENTATION**

1	What's Your PQ (Presentations Quotient)?
6	Oh No! I Have to Give a Speech
9	Questionable Cures for Stage Fright
11	A Lesson from LSU
12	How to Craft a Winning Presentation
17	Let's Talk Framing
19	Presentations That Rock: What Business Leaders Can Learn from Rock Concerts
23	Hero in the Balcony
23	Analogies: Powerful Change Agents
25	Stories: Not Just for Kids Anymore
26	e.g. (exempli gratia)
27	Emotion: That Elusive but Necessary Component of a Presentation
28	Aim for the Amygdala
29	Give Those Students an "A"
30	How to Incorporate Humor
32	The Twenty-minute Rule
33	Please, Not Another PowerPoint Presentation
39	PowerPoint's Role in the Space Shuttle Disaster
41	Oops! Where's the Last Page of My Speech?

42	Practice Makes Perfect
44	Memo to Self: Talk to Self
46	Q&A: Not as Hard as You May Think
48	First Impressions Do Matter
49	Smile!
50	Another Reason to Gesture
52	How to (Correctly) Use a TelePrompter
53	The Presentation Genius of Steve Jobs
56	To Develop Executive Presence, Observe and Learn from the Best
58	Plan B: What to Do When Things Go Wrong
60	Why the Deck Is Stacked Against You

62 COMMUNICATING WITH THE NEWS MEDIA

62	The News Media Today
64	Corporate Media Relations—Then and Now
67	Who Speaks for Your Industry?
69	Due Diligence and the News Media
71	The Early Bird Catches the Worm (Or How You Can Benefit from a Change in Local TV News)
73	How to Meet the Press
78	Q = A+1
80	To Succeed with a Reporter, Think like a Reporter
82	The Power of a Good Quote
84	How to Answer the Question, "What if … ?"
85	How to Avoid an Off-the-Record Problem
87	"There are no guarantees." Ouch!
88	The Perils of a Personal Opinion
89	"No comment!"
90	Mastering the Remote … Interview
93	Some Advice for Email Interviews
94	Press Briefings and News Conferences
96	Peyton Manning: Superstar ~~Quarterback~~ Communicator
98	How to Handle Errors in Reporting
99	What to Do When the CEO Can't Cut It
101	America's Most Feared TV News Magazine
103	A *60 Minutes* Success Story
104	The Dreaded Ambush Interview
106	Just Say No! … When Should You Decline an Interview Request?

109 MANAGING A CRISIS

- 110 Twenty-first Century Crisis Management: A Briefing for Executives
- 120 Suggestions for Your Next Crisis Drill
- 123 Communicating with Employees: Priority One in a Crisis
- 124 No Need to Sacrifice Accuracy for Speed
- 126 Communicating Empathy (the Right Way) during a Crisis
- 129 Your First Line of Defense in a Crisis
- 130 After a Crisis, Do the Following:

133 COMMUNICATING WITH INVESTORS AND THOSE WHO INFLUENCE THEM

- 133 Developing and Selling Your Company's Story
- 136 Ten Earnings Call Mistakes to Avoid
- 138 The Day and Time You Hold Your Earnings Call Matters
- 139 Earnings Calls: A Best-practices Checklist
- 141 How to Present via Teleconference
- 143 Investor and Analyst Road Shows: A Best-practices Checklist
- 145 What's Your Company's Investible Idea?
- 148 Caution: Analyst Interaction Slip-ups
- 150 Tough Earnings Call Questions ... and How to Handle Them
- 153 What to Do When It's Earnings Season and the News Is Bad
- 155 Storytelling: The Secret Weapon in Your Investor Communications
- 157 How One Company Hits Home Runs in Its Analyst Presentations

160 SOCIAL MEDIA

- 160 Social Media Missteps ... and How to Avoid Them
- 163 Yikes! Have You Seen What's on YouTube?

166 SPECIAL SITUATIONS

- 166 The Language of Trust
- 170 How to Introduce a Speaker
- 171 To Read or Not to Read
- 173 Briefing Lessons from Tom Clancy's Jack Ryan
- 175 Mission Possible: Turning Engineers into Effective Communicators
- 178 Note to Women: Forget Gender-specific Communications Advice
- 180 Important News to Communicate? Harness the Power of an Interview
- 182 Lost in Translation: Communicating with Non-native Speakers

	183	Logic 101: Antidote for Muddled Thinking
	186	How Millennials Communicate ... and Why You Need to Know
	188	Dealing with Public Anger: New Approaches to an Old Problem
	193	Communicating Change to Employees
	195	Those Annoying "Uhs," "Ums," "Likes" and "You Knows"
	197	What We Can Learn from Mark Zuckerberg's Two-day Congressional Testimony
	200	Some Bad News about Communicating Good News: It's Tougher than You Think
	203	Impromptu Remarks: Yes, There's a Key to Speaking Extemporaneously
	204	Communication: A Strategic Tool for Successful Project Management
	208	Five, Four, Three, Two, One. You're On!
	209	Listen Up
	210	Ramp Up Your Video Conferencing Skills
	213	Exit Line

215 THE END

218 NOTES

223 PHOTO CREDITS

225 ABOUT THE AUTHOR

ACKNOWLEDGMENTS

During my business career I was fortunate to work for, and with, some talented individuals. They taught me a lot and I'm very appreciative. I want to acknowledge them publicly:

Paul Hesse—the best boss I ever had.

Clyde Hopkins—the smartest person I ever met.

Jim Finegan—a high-energy, creative talent (and a great golfer).

Dan Ammerman—a visionary who asked me to join his firm (twice). Glad I finally did.

Don McMullin—a wise colleague whose humorous lines I've stolen and still use.

"If I went back to college again, I'd concentrate on two areas: learning to write and to speak before an audience. Nothing in life is more important than the ability to communicate effectively."

President Gerald R. Ford

INTRODUCTION

The ability to communicate effectively is frequently ranked the number one key to success by leaders in business, government and the professions. In one survey, executives earning more than $250,000 per year were asked to cite the primary factors in achieving success. First on their list? Communication skills.

One executive who probably would agree with this ranking is someone whose own communication skills were seriously deficient—former BP CEO Tony Hayward. After BP's disastrous oil spill in the Gulf of Mexico in 2010 was finally contained, Hayward acknowledged in a BBC interview, "If I had done a degree at RADA [Royal Academy of Dramatic Art] rather than a degree in geology, I may have done better."

So, do business leaders and aspiring leaders need to enroll at this prestigious school in London? No, but they do need to master a number of critical communication skills:

- Crafting and delivering a top-flight presentation
- Communicating with the news media
- Managing a crisis
- Communicating with investors and those who influence them
- Understanding and using social media
- Communicating in special situations

Unfortunately, far too many business leaders have sub-par communication skills. They communicate using comfortable, but outdated and self-defeating techniques.

Individuals who can communicate clearly, concisely and charismatically—face-to-face, on video, one-on-one, to large groups and small, in formal and informal situations—will be tomorrow's executives. They will get others to listen to, understand, and act on what was said. They will also have lots of job security.

This book will give you an edge in developing your business communication skills. It examines a variety of ideas—some of them unconventional, many of them new or research-based—about what constitutes effective communication. I developed the content from four decades helping business leaders fine tune their spoken communication skills, and from more than ten years teaching Communications for Leaders, a course I created for the Executive MBA Program at the Bauer College of Business at the University of Houston. This university is one of the first (and few) to include a communications element in its EMBA curriculum.

Most business leaders have limited time and short attention spans, but they are quick studies. They want information delivered succinctly. What follows is a quick, practical, yet comprehensive look at the communication situations you will likely face and the communication skills you'll need in your professional life. The book is an easy read, and you can digest the content randomly, sequentially or topically.

Ready to build a successful career? Good. Let's get started.

Ken Haseley
Rocky River, Ohio

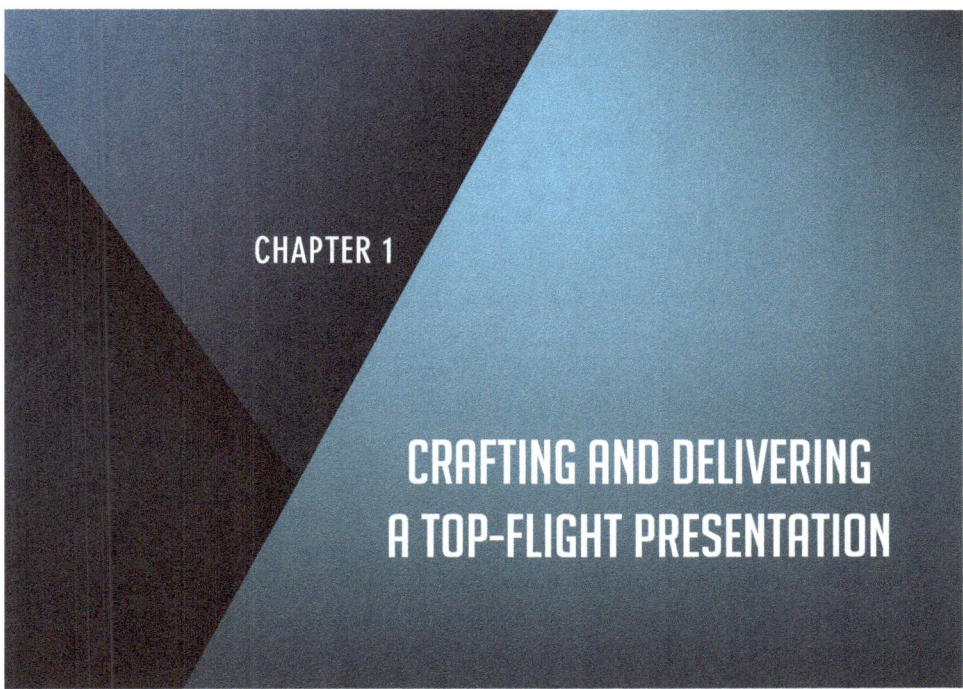

CHAPTER 1

CRAFTING AND DELIVERING A TOP-FLIGHT PRESENTATION

Most business presentations are boring. There, I said it. But chances are you already knew it. On a regular basis, audiences are subjected to poorly prepared and poorly delivered presentations, filled with boring content and mind-numbing PowerPoint visuals. What's more, many of these presentations are ineffective. That they exist is puzzling (and unnecessary). That we tolerate them is even more puzzling.

Business leaders can no longer expect employees and others to hang on every word they utter. Today's audiences are easily distracted, entertainment-hungry, and are likely to multitask during a presentation. What you say has to be more interesting than the listeners' emails and text messages. In addition, audiences are judging you by what they saw on television the night before. In other words, they expect you to perform brilliantly. Welcome to the new world!

WHAT'S YOUR PQ (PRESENTATIONS QUOTIENT)?

Up for a challenge? See if you can ace this ten-question quiz that measures your presentations quotient.

1. After listening to a 10-minute presentation, the average listener has heard, understood, accurately evaluated and retained about _____% of what was said.
   - A. 10
   - B. 25
   - C. 50
   - D. 75

2. People begin to make up their minds about others within _____ of meeting them.
   - A. 10 seconds
   - B. 30 seconds
   - C. 1 minute
   - D. 5 minutes

3. When delivering a presentation to a group of people, you should:
   - A. Let your eyes sweep across the audience from side to side.
   - B. Look at one person long enough to deliver one complete thought, then look to another individual and repeat the process.
   - C. Focus your eyes on people sitting in the back row.
   - D. Avoid looking at faces, but instead look just above the tops of heads.

4. Eye contact is critical in both one-on-one and group communication. What is the optimum length of time to maintain eye contact with an individual?
   - A. 1-2 seconds
   - B. 5-10 seconds
   - C. 30 seconds
   - D. One minute

5. When delivering a presentation, most speakers need to increase their energy level approximately _____%.
   - A. 10
   - B. 25
   - C. 50
   - D. 75

6. In business presentations, it's best to:
   A. Tell a joke to break the ice.
   B. Use humorous stories or anecdotes that relate to your message or to the situation.
   C. Either of the above.
   D. Avoid humor altogether.

7. Visual aids are generally ineffective tools in business presentations.

   True   False

8. When we judge others (including presenters), we look first at two characteristics: how warm or trustworthy they are, and how strong or competent they are. Which of the two characteristics is more important to project first?
   A. Warmth
   B. Strength

9. There is only one part of a presentation guaranteed to get audience attention—the opening. But how much time in that opening do you have to prove you have something valuable or interesting to say?
   A. 5 seconds
   B. 15 seconds
   C. 30 seconds
   D. 1 minute

10. The goal of some presentations is to persuade. Which of the following is an effective tool in the persuasion process?
    A. Analogy
    B. Story
    C. Example
    D. All of the above

ANSWERS:

1. C. In addition, within 48 hours that 50% drops another half to a 25% effectiveness level. By the end of the week, that level goes down to about 10% or less.

2. A. We start to make up our minds about other people within 7 seconds of meeting them. Much of this is non-verbal as we communicate through body language (posture, gestures, facial expression, movement, etc.). Impressions made in the first few seconds are so powerful that it takes another 4 minutes to add 50% more impression—positive or negative—to that communication.

3. B. This is one way to make a personal connection with the audience. It also aids in the presenter's ability to think.

4. B. When you glance at someone for just 1-2 seconds, your eyes are darting, a habit that undermines credibility. Eye contact that exceeds 10 seconds might be interpreted as intimidation or intimacy. When we are fully engaged, we tend to look at someone for 5-10 seconds.

5. C. A high energy level is critical to success in public speaking. Communication is selling, and successful selling involves transferring energy and enthusiasm from speaker to listener.

6. B. The use of humor is one of several ways to help you connect with the audience. Telling jokes, however, is risky. They can offend people, the audience may have already heard them, and they are difficult to deliver well. Leave joke-telling to professional comedians.

7. False. Studies show that retention increases when listeners see as well as hear. In addition, when visuals are used, a speaker's goals are met and consensus occurs more often, and the time required to present a concept can be reduced.

8. A. Research suggests that it is best to project warmth before strength. People who project strength and competence before establishing warmth and trust run the risk of eliciting fear or apprehension. This is why skillful salespeople usually engage in small talk before getting down to business.

9. D. Audiences quickly decide whether they will listen to you. Satisfy them within the first minute or you may lose them.

10. D. Research shows that analogies, stories and examples are among the most powerful tools of influence. Analogies engage an audience—turning passive listeners into active participants or puzzle-solvers. Stories make people stop and listen. (Human beings, regardless of culture, are story-telling creatures.) And examples are a slice of reality.

SCORECARD:

9-10 CORRECT ANSWERS: **Touchdown.** Chances are, you're already an outstanding presenter. If not, you definitely have the potential to become one.

6-8 CORRECT ANSWERS: **Field goal.** Your knowledge of effective presentations is probably greater than that of most people.

4-5 CORRECT ANSWERS: **First down.** Your performance is fair, but wouldn't you prefer to put some points on the board?

0-3 CORRECT ANSWERS: **Fumble.** You risk being benched. Study the presenter's playbook more carefully.

OH NO! I HAVE TO GIVE A SPEECH

Surveys show that what Americans fear most—more than snakes, heights, illness, financial problems, even death—is speaking before groups. About 85 percent of us feel anxious speaking in public. Even the famous aren't immune.

Some of the most successful politicians, entertainers and businesspeople have suffered from stage fright or speech anxiety. Among them: Winston Churchill, Barbara Streisand and Carly Simon. Thomas Jefferson was so lacking in confidence and afraid of speaking in public that even though he was upset with the changes the Continental Congress made to his carefully written Declaration of Independence, he was unable to speak up to defend his work.

Although most of us experience some degree of anxiety before delivering a speech, for some people, public speaking causes great distress. Some individuals make important decisions, such as avoiding certain careers or turning down promotions, because of public-speaking fears.

When you are nervous, your body begins to act as if it were preparing for some strenuous physical activity. Adrenaline is released and your heart beats faster, which causes you to take in more oxygen. That makes you feel more nervous, so your body releases more adrenaline.

The good news is that new research is helping us to better understand speech anxiety and is showing us new ways to control it.

So fearful of public speaking was Thomas Jefferson that even though he opposed changes the Continental Congress made to the Declaration of Independence, he was unable to speak up and defend his work.

WHAT CAUSES SPEECH ANXIETY?

Several factors can contribute to developing glossophobia, the fear of public speaking. Childhood experience is one. Many people can remember a specific moment that contributed to their fear. Perhaps other students laughed during "show and tell" period in elementary school. Or maybe someone was put on the spot in class or in some social situation. (Remember when a teacher called on you to answer a question or go up to the board to solve a math problem? And you choked.) What started out as a minor episode when someone was an impressionable child mushrooms into a situation that causes anxiety attacks.

On a professional level, when people have to speak publicly, they often put pressure on themselves to perform well and not "screw up" in front of a client or supervisor. In addition, many people feel embarrassed because they think others don't share their fears.

For most of us, the primary cause of speech anxiety is inadequate preparation. Your comfort level in presenting rises in proportion to your preparation. Finding the time and assigning the proper priority to preparation are difficult in today's fast-paced world. It's important not to adopt a mindset that says, "No problem, I'll just wing it." Your audience deserves (and expects) better than that, and you owe yourself more.

The number one protection against nervousness is knowing your subject matter cold. Be over-prepared and you'll automatically feel better about your presentation.

Another critical component of preparation is practice. Your confidence level will increase with practice. Often, the first time some speakers hear their presentation is when it's delivered to the audience. That's unfortunate. Without practice, you don't know how long your speech is. You don't know how well organized it is, or whether you can easily say the words in your script or notes. Practice your presentation three times, aloud, on your feet, into a recording device (your smart phone will do).

BEFORE YOUR PRESENTATION

- Get to the venue early. Check out the room. Maybe walk around a bit to release nervous energy. Then relax. If you've prepared and practiced, there should be no need to "cram." Don't tinker with your presentation, making last-minute changes. (President Clinton was known to make changes to his speeches as he walked from the waiting area to the stage. It drove his speechwriters crazy, but he could pull it off. You and I probably can't.) Plan your work, then work your plan.

- When the event you're speaking at is in progress and you're in the room waiting your turn, there are some things you can do to warm up. No one will notice: Breathe slowly and deeply. Keep loose by shrugging your shoulders, moving your hands, fingers, legs and feet slightly, pressing your palms together tightly, and pulling up on the bottom of your chair for a few seconds.
- If you plan to use audiovisuals, test all equipment and know how to use it, including lighting and sound controls, etc. Equipment failure is guaranteed to raise your anxiety level.
- Don't rely on drugs or alcohol to calm your nerves. (Alcohol is a depressant, not a stimulant.) The result may be slowed reaction time. Also, avoid soft drinks (carbonation promotes burping).
- Engage in positive self-talk. (See **Memo to Self: Talk to Self**, p 44.)
- Use positive visualization. Recall a past presentation that was successful. (See **A Lesson from LSU**, p 11.)
- Know exactly what your opening line is going to be. Knowing it will reduce worry about getting started—the most difficult part of a presentation for most speakers.

DURING THE PRESENTATION

- If you're nervous, don't announce it. If you do, the audience will start to worry about you. People who cause worry don't inspire confidence.
- Talk to one person at a time. Literally, look directly into the eyes of one listener at a time, just as you normally do in one-on-one conversations. Contact eyes—not faces or tops of heads—for five to ten seconds. You might think doing this will make you more nervous, but the opposite is actually true.
- Gesture naturally. One effect of gesturing is that it helps release anxiety (that nervous feeling in your stomach), channeling it out in the form of energy.
- Stand up straight. Correct posture makes it easier for you to breathe properly (take deep breaths) which, in turn, makes it easier for you to get your words out naturally.
- If you mispronounce a word, lose your place or train of thought, or realize you forgot to include something, don't draw attention to it by announcing it. Chances are the audience didn't notice. Simply pause, then continue on. For material you omitted, near the end of the presentation, say something like, "One final point worth mentioning is...," then address the missing material.

SOME FINAL POINTS

Achieving a comfort level when speaking or presenting in public is a desirable objective. One of the things audiences will not forgive in a speaker is being uncomfortable. But remember, you don't want to eliminate all nervousness or anxiety. Doing so is likely to result in a flat delivery, devoid of energy and emotion. The goal is to control nervousness and use it to enhance your performance.

If you're serious about conquering your fear of public speaking, develop a game plan for yourself. It could include attending a workshop, getting some coaching or practicing in low-risk situations (e.g., speaking at school, church, charitable or civic functions). You might even want to join your local chapter of Toastmasters International (www.toastmasters.org).

Finally, there are people with severe public speaking anxiety disorders. In such cases, professional help may be needed. And it's an astute, compassionate and enlightened boss who recommends that the individual consult a physician or therapist.

QUESTIONABLE CURES FOR STAGE FRIGHT

Over the years, there's been no shortage of advice on how to cure the fear of public speaking. Some of that advice is just plain bad.

Visualize your audience naked is one of those suggestions. Presumably, the idea is that by seeing the audience without clothes, you reduce some of their "power" and bolster your own confidence. Oh, really? Please! A book that's been around for quite awhile, *"I Can See You Naked,"* thankfully debunks that piece of questionable wisdom.

Second cousin to picturing the audience naked is looking over the tops of their heads. We've been told that if you're nervous, don't make eye contact with the audience. This is great advice—if you want to come across as remote, distant, detached. Most of us make eye contact when we're talking to others. Your brain gets used to this. If all of a sudden, you change that pattern to look out into the audience—at nothing in particular—your brain is puzzled. It's saying, "What's happening? What's wrong?" While it may seem counterintuitive, the best strategy for anxious speakers is to select a few friendly faces and deliver one complete thought to one pair of eyes for about 5-10 seconds. Repeat this with the other proxies you've selected.

Then there's inventor Thomas David Kehoe, who came up with an in-ear device purported to help with public-speaking fears. The device, with a small microphone and earpiece much like those used by news anchors, allows speakers to push a button and hear their voices digitally altered to sound "confident and authoritative." Another button produces a "happy and enthusiastic" voice. No one but the speaker hears the auditory feedback, which is delayed by about one-tenth of a second to trick the brain.

Kind of reminds you of those annoying "seven-second delays" on radio or television, doesn't it? Can you imagine how hearing even a split-second delay might affect the speaker? And what happens if there's a technical glitch? I'm guessing this invention would get a thumbs-down on *Shark Tank*.

Next up: We see it in TV and movie dramas: some character faces a daunting challenge—something he's been dreading. So, to muster the courage to tackle it, he downs a stiff drink. Alcohol—that's the ticket. Only it's not. As we learned in middle school health class, alcohol is a depressant, not a stimulant. Presenting "under the influence" will weaken your performance and de-energize your audience. And you'll pick up on their negative feedback—hardly a confidence builder.

What about memorizing your speech? I once worked with someone who was part of the executive team that spoke at the company's annual analyst presentation. That executive had some pretty solid presentation skills. But one year, to my surprise, he showed up at the rehearsal and delivered his presentation from memory. It was not good. It was delivered haltingly—not fluidly—as he tried to remember what to say. It sounded formal and scripted rather than conversational. The audience was fully aware that he was reciting words—perhaps words that someone else wrote.

When I asked him why he chose that style of delivery, he indicated that many of his direct reports would be in the audience, and he didn't want to fail. I told him that if he stayed with that delivery style, he would fail. My advice to him: Unlearn the presentation in the few days remaining before the real event, and rely on his knowledge of the subject and speak from notes. He took that advice.

Trying to deliver a speech from memory is often a recipe for disaster. First of all, it's nearly impossible to do, and it increases rather than reduces stress. Most likely, you'll stumble at some point—drawing attention to your dilemma. (Most pitches on the TV show *Shark Tank* are memorized; some of the entrepreneurs who choose this route falter badly—resulting in a critical comment from one of the "sharks.") And even if you get through without stumbling, the audience will know you've memorized your remarks. They can hear it. And they equate reading or memorizing something with lack of knowledge. The only part of a presentation that should be memorized is humor. Jokes and other forms of humor must not be read; commit them to memory and deliver them while looking right at the audience.

Joe Burrow, quarterback at LSU, anticipating his championship ring. Players were fitted for their rings prior to the game. There's a lesson in that for anyone who presents.

A LESSON FROM LSU

Louisiana State University quarterback and Heisman Trophy winner Joe Burrow threw five touchdowns and ran for another touchdown in his team's 42-25 win over Clemson in the 2019 National Championship Game. After his fifth touchdown pass, Burrow pointed to his finger as if to say he was ready for his championship ring. Right after the game, when a reporter asked him if he knew his ring size, he replied, "Ten and a half. We already got fitted for 'em."

Getting players fitted for rings ahead of the game was nothing short of brilliant. Think about what that gesture said to the players.

There's a lesson here, courtesy of LSU, for those of us who deliver business presentations: **Before you present, adopt the right mindset.**

Here's what most people are thinking before they present: "Oh no, I have to give a presentation. This is not going to go well. I'm probably going to bomb." Not only does this kind of thinking set you up to fail, it drains energy.

Instead, say to yourself, "You've got something valuable to share. The audience is really going to benefit from it. You're going to nail this presentation." (By the way, speaking to yourself in second person is more effective than doing so in first person.)

In addition, take a page out of just about any sports playbook—visualize a successful performance. You see it all the time: an athlete is standing alone quietly—eyes closed—picturing how a particular action will unfold. Figure skaters use this technique when they listen to their music while picturing how they'll perform every element of their program. Author and motivational speaker Zig Ziglar used to tell the story (legend?) of an American prisoner of war in Vietnam who played an imaginary round of golf in his mind each day during his captivity and found upon his release that his game had improved markedly.

Remember, your brain does not know the difference between a real and an imagined experience. And three imagined experiences are said to be equal to one real one.

Thanks, Joe Burrow, for the reminder.

HOW TO CRAFT A WINNING PRESENTATION

For most people, crafting a business presentation is a difficult, time-consuming, frustrating process. That's understandable. Few of us have been shown how to do it. It's not taught in school. Employers don't provide guidance or instruction; the assumption is that if you've made it to the business world, you should know how to develop a presentation. And unless you have access to a company speechwriter (few people do) or someone in the firm's communications function (few of these professionals have the time, inclination or sometimes even the expertise to help), you're on your own.

Let's simplify the presentation preparation process with a template that can be used to develop just about any presentation. Here it is:

For a lot of people, the process starts with PowerPoint. They begin thinking about and creating the visuals they plan to use. This is the wrong approach. If you're guilty of it, you are putting the cart before the horse. We'll get to PowerPoint shortly. I promise. Here's a better way to craft your presentation:

1. BEGIN WITH A THOROUGH AUDIENCE ANALYSIS

The more you know about the audience, the more likely you are to make correct inferences about how to reach them.

- Who are they?
- Why are they there? (By choice?)
- What is their knowledge level of your topic?
- What is their interest level in your topic?
- What information needs and wants do they have?
- What size is the audience?
- Are there any audience sensitivities you should be aware of?

In 1990, First Lady Barbara Bush was asked to deliver the commencement address at Wellesley College, a private, women's liberal arts college in Massachusetts. When students learned who'd be speaking, many of them objected, and voiced their objection. (If you're wondering why—no, it wasn't because Mrs. Bush was a conservative or a Republican—although that reason seems reasonable. Students objected because Mrs. Bush wasn't a college graduate, and they saw her as someone whose fame came through the achievements of her husband—ambassador to China, head of the CIA, president of the United States.)

The news media picked up on the brewing controversy: Would the school dis-invite Mrs. Bush? Would the students be rude as she spoke? Or maybe even boycott the commencement? None of that happened. On June 1, Mrs. Bush showed up (and brought along Mrs. Gorbachev, who happened to be in the United States at the time.)

Students at Wellesley College objected to the choice of First Lady Barbara Bush as commencement speaker. Mrs. Bush won them over with a single remark.

At one point in her remarks, Mrs. Bush said, "And who knows? Somewhere out in this audience may even be someone who will one day follow in my footsteps and preside over the White House as the president's spouse...I wish him well!" Thunderous applause followed.

Mrs. Bush knew there were sensitivities in the audience, and she won the students over with that line. It was her way of assuring them that America would one day have a female president.

One of the EMBA courses I teach at the University of Houston meets on Monday and Thursday nights, from 5:30 to 9:30. Nearly all of the students in that course are working professionals who have put in a full day of work before class. And for some of the students, English is their second language. Those are audience sensitivities that impact how I conduct those four-hour sessions.

2. KNOW THE FOLLOWING

- What's the venue? (Formal or informal presentation? Panel discussion?)
- Are there other speakers? (If so, what are their topics?)
- What's your allotted time?
- Will there be a Q&A segment?
- What's the room set-up? (If possible, visit the room or get a photo.)

3. DETERMINE THE PURPOSE OF YOUR PRESENTATION

Are you there to inform or educate, demonstrate, inspire, motivate, persuade, entertain? Most presentations combine several of these objectives. Be clear about your purpose; it impacts content.

4. DECIDE ON A CENTRAL MESSAGE

There are two types of objectives when it comes to communications: a production objective ("producing" something—an advertisement, a memo, a speech, a news release, etc.) and a communications objective—the message you want your audience to hear, understand and act on. Focus on the latter. Write your message down in a single sentence. Anything longer than that is clutter. Too many people define success in presenting as simply getting through their presentation (that's a production objective) rather than having their message(s) received and understood (that's a communications objective).

5. GATHER INFORMATION

This is the research phase of crafting. Think about how we buy gifts for people we love. If a holiday, birthday or some other event is approaching, a little voice inside our head reminds us that dad is an outdoorsman, so be on the lookout for something cool he could use while hunting or fishing. Then, when we're thumbing through those Sunday paper ad inserts or walking through the mall and see something cool, we immediately know it's the perfect gift for dad. Putting on our "dad glasses" enables us to look at merchandise from his perspective. When crafting a presentation, put on your "audience glasses" to help you determine what information you need to assemble and share.

6. ORGANIZE THAT INFORMATION INTO AN OUTLINE

Remember back in high school or college how important an outline was when you had to write a term paper? It helped you create order out of chaos. Develop the body of your presentation (the longest, most substantial part) from an outline. Major points or sections of the body become the Roman numerals. Supporting points and detail are the letters and numbers.

    I. Key point
        A. Subpoint
        B. Subpoint
            1. Supporting detail
            2. Supporting detail

    II. Key point
        A. Subpoint
        B. Subpoint

Using this format helps you avoid including information that doesn't fit your purpose and central message, and makes it easier to eliminate information if length or time considerations arise.

Structure your content carefully. For example, should your strongest arguments come first or last?

Research indicates that it usually doesn't matter when you deliver your most substantial fire power. But if you find yourself in a situation where others can interrupt or time becomes an issue, don't save your best arguments for last.

You can communicate your points directly or indirectly, so what's the better approach? Studies show that explicit conclusions or recommendations are the most persuasive. Also, Americans are practical people who tend to favor directness. Don't expect your audience to infer or "read between the lines."

And in situations where there are counter-positions to what you're advocating, should you address or ignore them? Two-sided persuasion (giving both sides) is generally the best approach. Addressing an opposing viewpoint directly is especially effective with an educated audience that is probably aware of those counter arguments. Doing this enhances your credibility and says that you fully understand that there are other points of view.

Ask yourself which, if any, of the content you've assembled is worthy of elaboration through what I call "sparklers": analogies, stories, examples, anecdotes, illustrations, compelling data, memorable lines. Consider using a few. Shakespeare knew the value of sparklers. He sprinkled bawdy humor and sexual inuendo throughout some of his plays to keep audiences engaged—especially audience members who were less educated.

7. DEVELOP A POWERFUL OPENING AND A STRONG CLOSING

For example, do you want a traditional or non-traditional opening? And what inspirational remarks can you close with? Some individuals find it helpful to think about these two parts of the presentation earlier on in the crafting process. Do what works best for you. (See **Presentations That Rock: What Business Leaders Can Learn from Rock Concerts, p.19.**)

8. CONSIDER POWERPOINT

OK, now it's time to think about PowerPoint. Review your content and decide what elements, if any, lend themselves to a visual representation.

In his book, *Who Says Elephants Can't Dance? Inside IBM's Historic Turnaround*, Louis Gerstner, Jr. tells the following story about his early tenure as president of IBM:

"One of the first meetings I asked for was a briefing on the state of the [mainframe computer] business. I remember at least two things about that first meeting with Nick Donofrio, who was then running the System/390 business…

"At that time, the standard format of any important IBM meeting was a presentation using overhead projectors and graphics that IBMers called 'foils' [i.e., overhead transparencies]. Nick was on his second foil when I stepped to the table and, as politely as I could in front of his team, switched off the projector. After a long moment of awkward silence, I simply said, 'Let's just talk about your business'."

For a detailed discussion of PowerPoint, see **Please, Not Another PowerPoint Presentation**, p.33.

9. DETERMINE HOW YOU'LL DELIVER THE PRESENTATION

Do you plan to read verbatim from a prepared text or speak from notes or bullet points? Develop the appropriate script or notes.

LET'S TALK "FRAMING"

… Not the kind you do with a painting or photograph. Or when building a house. And certainly not the criminal kind. No, the kind of framing I'd like to discuss has to do with communication.

Here's an example: In one of our fifty states—Alaska, to be specific—there's an oil reserve that contains about ten billion barrels of recoverable oil. At full production, that reserve could supply one million barrels of oil a day. The reserve is located in an area called the Arctic National Wildlife Refuge (ANWR, for short), and for decades, by law, it was off limits to exploration and drilling. That's framing. Those four words—Arctic National Wildlife Refuge—evoke images of a beautiful, inviting land too pristine to open up to drilling—even though the portion of ANWR where drilling would occur is essentially tundra (that's also framing), containing no trees, no deepwater lakes and no mountains. What's more, in winter, temperatures there drop to thirty degrees below zero. Let's face it: a tourist destination it's not.

Framing has to do with the mental representations created by certain words and phrases. It's similar to connotation. All words have a denotation—a dictionary definition. But some words also carry a connotation—a special meaning an individual or group associates with the word. For example, the phrase, "No comment," has taken on the suggestion of guilt or hiding something.

Sometimes, your goal is to produce a shift in someone's mental representation—how he or she perceives or retains something. Framing can help you do that.

A few other examples: Visit Germany today and you're likely to see and hear Germans refer to the period of their history during some of the 1930s and 1940s as the "period of national socialism." That phrase generates a different (and more acceptable) mental image than that of the phrase, "Nazi period."

Or think about how the Obama administration referred to BP during the Deepwater Horizon oil spill in the Gulf of Mexico. Even though just about everyone knows BP by the name BP, the administration used the name British Petroleum over and over to remind Americans that this was not an American company.

Ask yourself what mental representation is created by this name: Barack Hussein Obama.

> **Successful framing involves several things:**
>
> 1. Targeting your communication to a specific audience. Knowing that audience and what makes it tick is crucial. For example, what values or beliefs does the audience hold? Incorporate those values and beliefs into your message. By the way, here's a list of basic American values:
>
> - Value of the individual
> - Achievement and success
> - Change and progress
> - Equality of opportunity
> - Hard work
> - Optimism
> - Humor
> - Patriotism
> - Efficiency, practicality, pragmatism
> - Rejection of authority
> - Generosity and considerateness
> - Science and secular rationality
> - Material comfort
> - Sociality
>
> 2. Using language that resonates with the audience.
> 3. Keeping your message short—10-25 words, if possible.

Want a few other examples of <u>successful</u> framing? Consider these:

At one time, the U.S. Army faced a serious bout of parental disapproval—parents did not want their young sons or daughters to enlist. (The Middle East is not a safe place after all.) The Army had to reframe parents' mindsets—get them to associate the Army less with war, fighting, injury and death, and more with achievement, self-actualization and personal growth. That's why many of the Army's commercials and ads started talking about, "being all you can be" and featured proud parents.

Or think about the iPhone. This device has a lot of features and functions. When launching it, Apple had to decide how to position it. The company settled on these three things: First, it was a revolutionary phone. Second, it was the internet in your pocket. And third, it was the best iPod ever created. Framing the iPhone this way eliminated potential confusion about the product, and helped consumers develop a clear and accurate understanding of it.

PRESENTATIONS THAT ROCK: WHAT BUSINESS LEADERS CAN LEARN FROM ROCK CONCERTS

Considered by many to be the greatest British band in history, the rock group Queen easily sold out just about any venue they played. In an interview, band members Brian May and Roger Taylor talked about the structure of their concerts:

"We were very aware as entertainers that the shape of the show is vitally important. A lot of people have no concept of this. But you can't just put songs together willy nilly and expect the whole thing to work. You have to have a shape to maximize your impact.

"Basically, blind and deafen them [the audience] in the first ten minutes, and while they're recovering from that, do a few things [songs] that people recognize. Then take it down; do something slow that takes a little more thought and then gradually build to the next climax.

"But basically, the beginning and end of the show is vital, and we were very aware of that."

The shape of a business presentation is no less important than the shape of any concert. And while I'm not suggesting that you "blind and deafen" your audience, I am saying that the "bookends" of a presentation—the opening and closing—are worth special attention.

START WITH A BANG!

There's only one part of any presentation guaranteed to capture audience attention—the opening. But most audiences will give you only about one minute to show you have something interesting or important to say. If you don't grab them at the onset, you could lose them for the rest of your remarks.

There are two approaches to the opening of a presentation—traditional and non-traditional. Regardless of the approach you choose, don't be long-winded. Keep it short—no more than about ten percent of your total presentation length.

In the traditional approach, the speaker usually greets the audience, introduces himself, and identifies the topic of the presentation and the agenda or key points he plans to cover. It's part one of the standard, three-part format of a presentation: "Tell them what you're going to tell them, tell them, and tell them what you told them." This is probably the most frequently used opening technique. And there's nothing intrinsically wrong with it (other than its predictability)—especially if it's delivered powerfully.

One year to the day of George Harrison's death, the memorial *Concert for George* took place at the Royal Albert Hall in London. To open the concert, Eric Clapton simply said the following:

"Hello, welcome. Thank you for coming ... and looking forward to an evening of beautiful music and warm feelings. We're here to celebrate the life and music of George Harrison. We've been rehearsing for about three weeks and I think we might have got somewhere near getting the music right. But we haven't practiced any talking, so I have no idea really what to tell you, other than that we brought a few friends together—mainly people who were involved in his life and the making of his music. And we're going to be entertaining you tonight ... and we've had a great deal of fun and enjoyment and got a lot of grieving that's been dealt with by playing his music. And it's been a very spiritual and soulful experience—getting together, putting this together for you, so I hope it comes out as good as it sounded in rehearsal.

"First of all, there will be an Indian section. The first half will be some music that was composed especially for this by Ravi Shankar. His daughter Anoushka is going to play. Then there will be a little intermission, and then we'll have some Western music. We'll be playing George's songs and we'll be having some guests. I'll let you spot them, and I'll introduce them as they come on.

"And that's it. This is a blessed occasion for me because I can share my love of George with you. And I think most important of it all is that his wife Olivia and his son Dhani can experience and witness how much we loved him through his music tonight. So, thank you for coming again."

That opening, which provided a preview of the program, was powerful in its simplicity. And it was spoken—not read—without the use of any notes.

The opening of your presentation can be just as powerful—and you may not even need any PowerPoint visuals (e.g., agenda slide) or clever lines to make it so. Command the attention of your audience simply with some powerful words...delivered powerfully.

Then there's the non-traditional opening. In this approach, the presenter begins with something unexpected—for example, maybe a story. The audience is intrigued, and for a few moments, wonders where the speaker is headed. Afterwards, the speaker may introduce herself and identify the topic and purpose of the presentation before continuing. It's unconventional—not unlike in the James Bond movie, *Skyfall*, where the opening credits didn't appear until 13 minutes, 11 seconds into the film. Don't be afraid to try something different.

Here's the non-traditional opening of a speech delivered by Chief Justice John Roberts at the Ronald Reagan Presidential Library:

"Mrs. Reagan, distinguished trustees, ladies and gentlemen: It's a terrible thing to ask someone to speak here at the Ronald Reagan Library.

"The best efforts of the most gifted speaker would pale compared to the echoes of the speeches that reverberate in these halls. The trustees have compounded that difficulty by inviting tonight as a speaker, a judge—and to make it worse, a judge in his first public speaking engagement since I was confirmed last September.

"When I was confirmed, I adopted a very strict policy: I was going to accept no outside speaking engagements my first year—for two reasons really. One, I needed to devote all my energies to my responsibilities, and two, it wasn't clear that I had anything to say. So, my policy with respect to speaking invitations has been to just say no. [That line got quite the reaction from the audience. They recognized that Roberts was tipping his hat to Mrs. Reagan, who was in the audience, for the anti-drug program she championed while First Lady, called, "Just Say No to Drugs."]

"I had a great model in that respect to follow from my immediate predecessor, Chief Justice Rehnquist. He had two form responses to speaking invitations prepared. The first one was for invitations for speaking in the coming year. It said, 'Thank you for your kind invitation. I'm afraid I must decline. I'm sure you appreciate my schedule fills up quickly.'

"The next letter was for invitations more than a year out: 'Thank you for your kind invitation. I'm afraid I must decline. I'm sure you appreciate I can't schedule that far in advance.'

"All of this was working out beautifully until a few months ago I found myself seated next to Mrs. Reagan at a dinner—at a house in Washington—a house with which she was much more familiar than I was. Over appetizers, the possibility of speaking at the library came up. I explained my very strict policy. By the time we were finishing the entrée, we were just nailing down the specific date."

Every Queen concert began with a song that immediately brought the audience to its feet. Don't squander your opening on the ordinary or the mundane.

DON'T END WITH A WHIMPER

At the end of his important speech outlining plans to deal with the country's 2007-2009 financial crisis (see **How to (Correctly) Use a TelePrompter**, p. 52), former Treasury Secretary Timothy Geithner simply turned and walked away, causing his audience to wonder, "Is he done? Well, I guess we should leave."

You've likely observed something similar where the presentation ended abruptly, with no clear indication whether it was over.

The closing of your presentation should return to the most important idea or ideas covered in the body of the presentation. The reason for this has to do with what's called the "principle of recency." People tend to remember best what they heard last.

That doesn't necessarily mean that you simply "Tell them what you told them." You can repeat your key messages, but do so differently, creatively, inspirationally. Find a way to get your audience thinking about what they just heard or learned, or what you want them to do.

President Reagan always saved his best line for last (he was an actor after all). Don't give your closing short shrift. End with something memorable.

Ronald Reagan was the first U.S. president to use the "hero in the balcony" technique at the State of the Union Address. Lenny Skutnik (shown here flanked by his wife and Nancy Reagan) was the first "hero" to be so honored.

HERO IN THE BALCONY

At one point in his 1982 State of the Union Address, President Reagan pointed out a guest in the balcony. The man, sitting next to Mrs. Reagan, was Lenny Skutnik, who several days earlier put his life at risk when he dove into the freezing Potomac River to save a survivor from a commercial jet that had crashed.

For a few moments, those in the audience and those watching on television were transfixed as Reagan briefly acknowledged Skutnik's heroic deed. Reagan was the first U.S. president to use this powerful communication technique. (Author and commentator David Gergen calls it the "hero in the balcony.")

President George W. Bush used the technique when he delivered his first address to a joint session of Congress. To illustrate the value of his proposed tax cut plan, he had waiting in the wings a young Hispanic couple and their daughter. Bush introduced them and explained that if his tax cut legislation were enacted, the family would receive $1,600—and would use the money to pay down their credit card debt. He concluded by saying, "The American public has been overcharged, and I'm here on their behalf asking for a refund."

That was a powerful image and soundbite. When you present, one way to increase the likelihood that what you say will resonate with the audience is to move beyond the abstract and conceptual to the concrete. Make your message come alive through analogies, stories and examples. To learn more about these three powerful tools of persuasion, read on.

ANALOGIES: POWERFUL CHANGE AGENTS

Back in 2005, The *Wall Street Journal* ran an op ed encouraging Congress to open up the Arctic National Wildlife Refuge (ANWR) to exploration and drilling to increase America's energy supply. Estimates are that ANWR, located in Alaska, contains ten billion barrels of recoverable oil, but up until 2017, federal law prohibited exploring and drilling there.

The *Journal* used this analogy in its editorial: "Thanks to modern drilling technology, all of this oil and gas can be developed from a sliver of the state: fewer than 2,000 acres, or less than 0.01% of the wildlife refuge's acreage. If Alaska were the size of the front of this newspaper, that 2,000 acre footprint would be a single letter."

Considered the most powerful communication tool of persuasion, an analogy is a comparison of two different things that are alike in some way. Analogies engage an audience. When you hear an analogy, at first you're puzzled or confused. You think, "Hey, wait a minute. That's odd. Why are those two things being compared? They're totally different." But as you begin to think about them, you realize that they have something in common. Your confusion begins to subside, and you feel more comfortable about the comparison.

Analogies turn passive listeners into active puzzle solvers. More importantly, analogies help get an audience to understand something (especially something complex) or come around to the speaker's point of view.

For example, most boat owners know how important it is to protect the bottom of a boat's hull from slime, larvae and other damaging organisms. Applying antifouling paint every few years is the most common way to protect the hull. But how do these paints work?

Most antifouling paints are partially soluble which means that as water passes across the surface of the coating, it reduces the thickness of the paint at a controlled rate—always leaving a fresh biocide (it kills living organisms) at the surface of the paint throughout the boating season. Here's an analogy: the paint coating wears down much like a bar of soap would wear away without losing its effectiveness.

When most people in business communicate, they rely heavily on facts and logic. Their presentations, speeches, media interviews, even their conversations are peppered with statistical information. But people rarely respond to facts and logic alone.

Statistics lack impact largely because they're abstract and lack color. Studies show that people absorb information in proportion to its vividness. And most analogies are vivid. Also, that vividness creates more memory recall than a fact-heavy style of communication does.

Before the United States entered World Wat II, President Roosevelt used this analogy to try to get Congress to provide war supplies to Britain:

"Suppose my neighbor's home catches fire and I have a length of garden hose four or five hundred feet away. If he can take my garden hose and connect it up to his hydrant, I may help him to put out his fire. Now, what if I do? I don't say to him before that operation, 'Neighbor, my garden hose cost me $15. You have to pay me $15 for it.'...I don't want $15. I want my garden hose back after the fire is over.

"If it goes through the fire all right, intact, without any damage to it, he gives it back to me and thanks me very much for the use of it. But suppose it gets smashed up—holes in it—during the fire. We don't have too much formality about it, but I say to him, 'I was glad to lend you that hose. I see I can't use it any more. It's all smashed up.'... He says, 'All right, I will replace it.' Now, if I get a nice garden hose back, I am in pretty good shape."

Let's end with one of my favorite analogies: It comes from the movie, *Flash of Genius*, starring Greg Kinnear. The movie is based on the true story of Dr. Robert Kearns (played by Kinnear) who invented the intermittent windshield wiper. When Ford steals his idea, he takes on the auto giant in court.

In one courtroom scene, a professor testifies on behalf of Ford that Mr. Kearns didn't create anything new. His basic unit consists of a capacitor, a variable resistor and a transistor—all basic building blocks in electronics that can be found in any catalog. "All Mr. Kearns did was to arrange them in a new pattern. It's not the same as inventing something new," says the professor.

Then Kearns, who is representing himself, cross-examines the professor. Kearns is holding a book by Charles Dickens—*A Tale of Two Cities*—and reads the first few words: "It was the best of times. It was the worst of times. It was the age of wisdom. It was the age of foolishness."

Kearns asks the professor if Dickens created the words "it," "was," "the," "best" and "times." The professor responds, "No."

The jury, mesmerized, listens as Kearns says, "Look, I've got a dictionary here. I haven't checked, but I would guess that every word that's in this book can be found in this dictionary. There's probably not a single new word in this book. All Charles Dickens did was to arrange them in a new pattern. But Dickens <u>did</u> create something new by using words, the only tools that were available to him—just as almost all inventors in history have had to use the tools that were available to them. Telephones, space satellites—all were made from parts that already existed—parts that you might buy out of a catalog. Right, professor? No further questions."

No further comment!

STORIES: NOT JUST FOR KIDS ANYMORE

Human beings—regardless of culture—are storytelling creatures. When someone starts to tell a story, people stop and listen. For example, if you were presenting and noticed the audience's attention was waning, you could quickly get the audience to re-engage by saying these words, "You know, a couple of days ago I saw..." Stories are narratives that describe events that unfold over time. They command attention. They are also powerful change agents. Along with analogies and examples, stories are among the most powerful tools of persuasion. If your presentation is designed to change minds, consider including a story.

One reason stories often don't find their way into business presentations is that professionals (especially men) are uncomfortable with emotional content. Another reason is that telling a story requires an additional step in the communication process—wrongly seen as wasting time.

Do the following: Find one of your past business presentations. Read through it. Was there a story in that presentation? If not, what story could you have told to drive home an important point—one that might have been firmly implanted in the audience's long-term memory?

> **Telling your story:**
> - Stories have a place in just about any business communication—speeches, presentations, media interviews, impromptu remarks, even earnings release conference calls.
> - Get over any reluctance to tell stories in a business environment. Remind yourself that businesspeople are also human beings—who have an emotional side as well as an analytical side.
> - The storytelling process begins when you are developing the content of your communication. Identify the story you'll tell. Don't expect it to come to you while you're talking.
> - Select stories that relate to the key messages you're trying to convey.
> - Keep your stories short. Two minutes or less is a good rule of thumb.
> - Be sure your story is audience-appropriate. For example, what resonates with adults may not work with younger audiences.
> - Mix it up. Sometimes deliver the message first, then share your story. Other times, lead with your story, then explain its significance.
> - Delivery is crucial. Don't read the story; tell it—even if you're delivering a speech from a script. If you don't tell the story with passion and energy, don't expect it to have a powerful impact on the audience. You must make them believe that you believe before they can believe what you believe.

Want to hear a good story to learn how to tell a good story? StoryCorps is a nonprofit organization that provides Americans the opportunity to record and share their stories. Since 2003, it has collected and archived thousands of stories. It's one of the largest oral history projects of its kind. Visit www.storycorps.org. StoryCorps stories are also featured every Friday on National Public Radio's *Morning Edition*.

e.g. (EXEMPLI GRATIA)

After analogies and stories, the third most powerful change agent is an example. An example is something that's typical of its group or something worthy of imitation. The power of an example lies in its reality; it's a slice of life. Humans have a strong desire to "predict"—they want to know what's going to happen.

And they use past experiences to project forward. Ideas based on examples are the least vulnerable to refutation.

If you wanted to drive home how important it is for a company to constantly evaluate its business model in light of changing consumer trends and economic conditions, an example similar to this one could help:

Coffee consumption in America had been declining for years when three Seattle entrepreneurs opened the first Starbucks. At that time, the major American coffee brands were embroiled in a price war that led them to use cheaper beans to reduce costs. The result was a significant decline in quality, which led to a decline in coffee consumption.

However, on the West Coast, interest in finer European coffees offering richer, fuller flavors was perking. Starbucks decided to open a store dedicated solely to selling the finest coffee beans and coffee-brewing equipment. At that time, Starbucks coffee was not brewed in-store; consumers bought the beans or grounds and brewed their coffee at home.

It wasn't until some ten years after the company's founding that legendary exec Howard Schultz came along and transformed Starbucks from a coffee retailer to a café business. During a trip to Italy, Schultz saw people stopping to enjoy a cup of coffee throughout the day at cafés. He believed Americans would do likewise. The rest, as they say, is history.

Examples take longer to share than do short statements of fact or brief generalizations, but they're more valuable; they help the listener experience the idea being conveyed. They're also more interesting, easier to understand and more memorable.

EMOTION: THAT ELUSIVE BUT NECESSARY COMPONENT OF A PRESENTATION

Chances are you've seen their commercials. More importantly, you probably remember them. I'm talking about commercials from St. Jude Children's Hospital and the American Society for the Prevention of Cruelty to Animals or ASPCA.

In their TV spots, both organizations are asking for your financial support. St. Jude does it by showing a number of children being treated for life-threatening illnesses. ASPCA shows you the sad faces of dogs and cats that have been abused or abandoned.

It's an unfeeling person who's not moved (or moved to action) by these images that tug at the heartstrings.

Charitable organizations and consumer product companies alike are masters of persuasion. They know what works and what doesn't work when trying to influence. And what works is an appeal to emotion. For people to act, they have to care.

Most people try to persuade with a lot of facts. And facts are not unimportant. They ground the presenter—showing that there's substance to what's being said. But facts, data, evidence, documentation, case studies and the like are just one type of content—analytical.

The other type is emotional—humor, stories, analogies, anecdotes, props, powerful images. Emotional content gives your audience a reason to care.

So, why do so many business presentations lack emotional content? For one thing, Americans are a practical lot—no-nonsense, get-the-job-done people who prefer to get right to the point. No need for embellishment or wasting time. Remember Sergeant Joe Friday's favorite line from that '50s TV show, *Dragnet*? "Just the facts, ma'am." Adding an emotional element adds an additional step in the communication process.

Also, tradition and some company cultures discourage employees from straying from "the way we've always done it"—namely, loading presentations and PowerPoint visuals with lots of analytical content.

For another thing, most people have not been told or have never figured out that analytical content alone is not enough to create a successful presentation.

What does emotional content look like?

In a TED Talk on malaria, Bill Gates pointed out that the million deaths a year caused by malaria greatly underestimate its impact. More than 200 million people at a time suffer from it, which means you can't get the economies in these afflicted areas going.

At one point, he moved toward a small container sitting on a table on stage, opened it, and said, "Now, malaria is of course transmitted by mosquitos. I brought some here so you could experience this. We'll let those roam around the auditorium a little bit… There's no reason only poor people should have the experience.… Those mosquitos are not infected."

The audience laughter was infectious (pardon the pun). Gates' message was memorable.

I'm not advocating that you release mosquitos at your next presentation. Or that you abandon analytical content. Use it but balance it with emotional content—whether in the opening, the body or the conclusion of your presentation.

AIM FOR THE AMYGDALA

The human brain has two memory systems. In one part of the brain, the hippocampus, we store ordinary facts and day-to-day experiences—a lot of them.

For example: the route we take to and from work. That information is important, but not particularly noteworthy.

The other part of the brain, the amygdala, is for emotionally charged information and experiences—for example: the day we were married, the birth of a child, the death of a parent. These experiences are imprinted in the amygdala with an added degree of strength.

Back in 1972, I was teaching high school English and journalism in Ohio. One day in January, my principal called me into his office to tell me that one of my students and her family lost everything in a house fire the night before. No one was injured, but the house was a total loss. He was simply giving me a heads-up.

To my surprise, later in the day, that student showed up for class. I'm guessing her parents wanted her to continue with her normal routine. Before class started, I pulled her aside and said a few words to her. I don't remember those words. What I do remember is her face and the blue winter coat she was wearing (probably one of the few things she was able to save). To this day, I still can smell the smoke in that coat.

That experience is firmly planted in my amygdala.

Now, I'm not so naïve to suggest that there are things in the business world as powerful as the birth of your child. But I am saying that we frequently fail to recognize and talk about some powerful things that happen in business.

Here's one of them: It comes from a video that went viral on the internet. Chris Oslovich, a New Jersey FedEx driver on his normal route, spotted a tall flagpole that had fallen to the ground in a front yard after heavy winds. He stopped, walked onto the property, carefully removed the flag, reverently folded it, and placed it on the owner's front porch. All of this was captured by the home's security camera. Not a word was spoken, but the driver's actions spoke volumes. (I hope FedEx has recognized and rewarded that employee for his patriotic act.)

Ask yourself what story or anecdote in your company might find its way into someone's amygdala—or at least might be stored pretty close to it.

GIVE THOSE STUDENTS AN "A"

I teach a communications course in the University of Houston's Executive MBA program. To provide the students with practice in crafting powerful presentations, I have them form teams and I give each team a scenario. The team's mission is to develop one part of a presentation based on that scenario—for instance: the opening, the closing, a compelling argument or example, etc. One member of the team then delivers that part of the presentation to the class.

One team's presentation was a fictional energy company's "road show" seeking funding from angel investors. The company specialized in recovering oil and gas from fields that were thought to be depleted.

The presenter began by talking about the standard process of exploring for and producing oil and gas—namely, that the reserves that are easiest and cheapest to tap are targeted first. As he spoke, he took a lime, cut it in half and began squeezing out the juice by hand into a glass. Naturally, he could extract only so much liquid.

Then he continued his discussion of oil and gas reserves. As attractive reserves are depleted, and as demand for energy (and its price) rises, there's an incentive to revisit those "depleted" fields or target other less attractive fields. His fictional company had the technology and the expertise to get at those reserves.

He picked up that squeezed lime half, put it into a small, hand-held press, held it over the glass, and squeezed the handles—producing even more juice.

Give that team of students an "A." For several reasons:

First, analogies are among the most powerful tools of persuasion. Their power comes from their ability to engage an audience—in this case, getting it to understand the connection between squeezing a lime and producing oil. Those students chose a solid analogy—one that won't soon be forgotten. In fact, the next time the students in that class see a lime or a juice press, they'll probably think of oil recovery.

Second, props are effective communication tools. They create memorable visual imagery. Unfortunately, props have fallen out of favor with most presenters. And that's a shame. Those students showed how props can be used to engage an audience and effectively convey an idea.

HOW TO INCORPORATE HUMOR

In a word—carefully. Humor can be a valuable addition to a presentation. To keep an audience engaged, TV shows and movies usually include occasional changes in a story's content and tone. (Think of some of the James Bond movies where a humorous line or event is inserted in a powerfully dramatic scene. It's done because audiences find it difficult to sustain one emotion for an extended period of time.) That same technique can be used effectively in a presentation. But in business, humor can be tricky, and it's often misused.

Some presenters settle on a joke—usually to establish a connection with the audience. This is risky for a number of reasons: First, jokes are difficult to deliver—well. Standup comedians spend years in comedy clubs perfecting their craft—learning the importance of timing, pauses, tone, facial expression, etc. Yet, businesspeople think they too can deliver humor, but without that training and practice. They usually fail. Second, jokes are constantly being told and re-told; they're making the rounds, so the audience may have already heard them. And finally, in today's politically correct world, jokes can offend. Telling a joke that bombs—especially in the opening, where the presenter most wants and needs positive feedback from the audience—can damage, if not destroy, a presentation.

Another problem with jokes is that sometimes they have no relationship to the meeting or event, the audience or the presenter's topic. Joel Osteen, a well known pastor, televangelist and author, usually begins his televised sermons with a joke that has no connection to anything he goes on to discuss. It's gratuitous.

If you decide to tell a joke, try it out on a few colleagues who know your audience and who will give you honest feedback on the joke and your delivery.

In contrast to jokes, amusing stories from real life (especially business life) make for a successful change of pace. Some presenters skillfully find and highlight something funny that happened during the meeting, event or presentation.

Two other missteps to avoid:

- Don't announce to the audience that you're about to share something humorous. Let them be the judge. Let the humor speak for itself.

- Never read jokes or any other humor verbatim from notes or a prepared script. All humor and stories must be memorized and delivered while looking at the audience.

One of the most thoughtful commencement addresses I've ever come across also happens to have one of the most humorous openings of these typically tedious speeches. This winner was delivered by University of Oxford Professor Michael Ward at a Hillsdale College (Michigan) commencement ceremony. Here's a portion of the opening:

"Class of 2015, honored guests, faculty and members of the board of trustees of Hillsdale College: I bring cordial greetings from your erstwhile colonial overlords. I bear warmest felicitations from Her Majesty The Queen, Professor Stephen Hawking, James Bond, Sherlock Holmes, and the entire cast of Downton Abbey.

"I think that covers all the important people in England. I, on the other hand, am distinctly unimportant, and so I'm all the more grateful for the invitation to be part of this special day. Thank you for having me. I only hope I can say something worthy of the occasion.

"And I must say this, before I say anything else: Congratulations class of 2015! In the famous words of that great Englishman, Sir Winston Churchill: 'This is not the end. It is even not the beginning of the end. But it is, perhaps, the end of the beginning.'

"Today, you move from the end-of-your-beginning to the start-of-your-Commencement. I come from the Old World and in particular from Oxford, the home of lost causes, where we don't have 'Commencement': we just graduate and diminish and go into the west and remain embittered. So America's status as the home of fresh starts, of the pioneer spirit, of beginnings *leading to* commencements, sounds to me alarmingly positive and energetic.

"Someone once remarked that if you combine British pessimism with American optimism, you get divine realism. Maybe this is why Churchill, with his British father and American mother, is such an Olympian figure, and I'll be returning to Churchill at the end of my talk. But this is not yet the end of my talk; it is not even the beginning of the end. But it is, perhaps, the end of the beginning."

THE TWENTY-MINUTE RULE

When bestselling author and former Reagan speechwriter Peggy Noonan was asked why no speech should last more than twenty minutes, she said, "Because President Reagan said so!"

Often called "the great communicator," Reagan knew that you didn't need a lot of time to deliver important ideas.

Case in point: Abraham Lincoln's Gettysburg Address. It's a mere ten sentences—271 words, and Lincoln delivered it in just over two minutes.

You'll recall that the purpose of the speech was to dedicate the Gettysburg cemetery and eulogize the 50,000 fallen soldiers. What's less known is that eulogists at that time traditionally spoke for hours, and that Lincoln wasn't even the featured speaker. That honor went to Edward Everett, a Massachusetts politician who spoke for more than two hours. The day after the speech, Everett sent Lincoln a note complimenting him for the "eloquent simplicity and appropriateness" of his remarks. "I should be glad, if I could flatter myself that I came as near to the central idea of the occasion, in two hours, as you did in two minutes," said Everett.

Lincoln was so concise that photographers were still setting up their equipment as he finished. That's why there are no photos of him delivering the speech.

As it turns out, research shows that twenty minutes is an ideal amount of time for a presentation. Dr. Maureen Murphy conducted an experiment testing the difference in memory and reaction to a business talk given in one sixty-minute presentation versus the same talk given in twenty-minute segments with short breaks in between. She found that people enjoyed the twenty-minute presentations more and learned more and retained information longer when it was delivered in twenty-minute chunks.

Some presentation tips:
- The average attention span for most adults listening to a presentation is about twenty minutes. (This assumes the speaker has solid presentation skills.) Try to limit your presentation to that length. A twenty-minute speech is about ten, double-spaced pages.
- Beware the "curse of knowledge"—having a lot of information and trying to share it all. Instead, be selective in terms of content. Less is more.
- Did you ever hear anyone say, "I wish that presentation had been a little longer."? Don't go long. Stick to your allotted time. Impose self-discipline. Better yet, use less time than you're given. If the printed agenda shows that you have an hour, take 45 minutes. The audience will love you for it.
- Time your presentation during practice. Many presenters have no idea how long their talk is because they never timed it beforehand.
- If you must present for an extended length of time, be sure to incorporate sufficient breaks. Take multiple short breaks rather than one long break. For example, in a half-day session, plan two, 10-15-minute breaks along with a 5-minute "stretch" or "bio" break.
- Other ways to keep attention during longer presentations include audience activities, exercises or interactions, and using multi-media such as video. Incorporating stories and analogies into your material also helps you get and keep audience attention.

Franklin D. Roosevelt once said this about speechmaking: "Be sincere, be brief, be seated." Good advice.

PLEASE, NOT ANOTHER POWERPOINT PRESENTATION

Visual aids can be a powerful tool to help convey information in a way that's clear, creative and compelling. Today, the most popular presentation-graphics tool is Microsoft's PowerPoint. Nearly everyone uses it. Almost no corporate decision-making takes place without it. The *Wall Street Journal* reported that even second graders are drawn to it. Talk about show and tell.

But despite its widespread use, perhaps no other communications tool in business receives as much ridicule—from the very people who use it or sit through it. Recognize these expressions? "Death by PowerPoint." "We have met the enemy and he is PowerPoint."

The fact is most PowerPoint presentations miss the mark. This amazing tool is simply being misused. Let's talk about how to change that.

The Night Before the Big Meeting Frank Receives a Visit from the PowerPoint Fairy.

PowerPoint—the most popular, but misused, presentation-graphics tool.

But first, a few points in defense of PowerPoint. Research shows that when PowerPoint is used:

- Information retention can increase 50 percent. (The key is seeing <u>and</u> hearing.)
- A speaker's goals are met 30 percent more often.
- Group consensus in meetings occurs 20 percent more often.
- The time required to present a concept can be reduced by 40 percent.

Plus, add a multi-media component (e.g., animation, sound, video), and products and services featured with it are more likely to be perceived as credible, professional or reliable, even if not true.

That's the good news. Here's the flip side, along with some guidance on how to use PowerPoint to enhance your presentation, not detract from it:

One of the easiest ways to lose an audience is to subject it to a barrage of mind-numbing slides. Yet, this is exactly what happens in many presentations. A seemingly endless number of images is projected on a screen, rendering the speaker secondary, second fiddle to those images. In effect, your slides are competing with you for the audience's attention, and if your delivery skills are wanting, guess which choice the audience makes? It's worth remembering that no visual can compete with the power of a human being to make a personal connection with an audience.

PowerPoint works best for information that lends itself to a graphic representation—pie charts, bar graphs, flow diagrams, pictures. But it has turned into a prompt for the presenter—loaded with words. A lot of them. Avoid copy-heavy slides. If you do use words, keep them to a minimum—such as in a headline or a classified ad: No complete sentences. Skip unnecessary words (e.g., "a," "an," "the," etc.). Take a look at the following typical slide:

TYPICAL SLIDE

Learning to Sail

- Familiarize yourself with the unusual vocabulary of sailing (e.g., port, starboard, halyard, sheet, jib, close-hauled, etc.).
- Know what each piece of equipment on the boat does.
- Take lessons from a licensed captain or an experienced sailor.
- Venture out when the wind is no more than 15 knots and the waves are two feet or less.
- Practice turning the boat by tacking and jibing.
- Practice docking the boat – both bow in first and stern in first.

It's deadly! For one thing, the audience will start to read it as the presenter is talking. And most people can read at 600 words per minute (WPM), while the speaker is probably talking at 150-200 WPM. So, the presenter has essentially lost control of the flow of information. He's talking about sailing vocabulary, but the audience has already begun thinking about sailing equipment. The human brain can process only one incoming message at a time; an audience can either read your visuals or listen to you. It cannot do both simultaneously.

Nancy Duarte, who wrote a thoughtful book called, *slide:ology The Art and Science of Creating Great Presentations*, would say that the "Learning to Sail" slide above is not a slide at all. "If a slide contains more than 75 words, it has become a document... True presentations focus on the presenter and the visionary ideas and concepts they want to communicate. The slides reinforce the content visually rather than create distraction, allowing the audience to comfortably focus on both. It takes an investment of time on the part of the presenter to develop and rehearse this type of content, but the results are worth it."

EDIT THAT SLIDE

Go through it and pick out the most important words. In a classified ad, you pay per word, so you find a way to convey your message succinctly and inexpensively. Do likewise when developing your slides.

Learning to Sail

- Familiarize yourself with the unusual vocabulary of sailing (e.g., port, starboard, halyard, sheet, jib, close-hauled, etc.).
- Know what each piece of equipment on the boat does.
- Take lessons from a licensed captain or an experienced sailor.
- Venture out when the wind is no more than 15 knots and the waves are two feet or less.
- Practice turning the boat by tacking and jibing.
- Practice docking the boat – both bow in first and stern in first.

REVISED SLIDE

Add a photo and now you have a slide you can use to guide your audience through a discussion of sailing. Note that complete sentences have been eliminated, words have been reduced from 81 to 14, and the bullets have been removed (do you really need them?).

Another option on that revised "Learning to Sail" slide is using a "build" or "reveal," where you sequentially reveal information on the slide. In other words, each of the six points on the revised slide is added one at a time—allowing you to discuss it without the audience being able to read ahead. (This is similar to what presenters did years ago when they used overhead projectors; they used a sheet of paper to cover up portions of the transparency until they were ready to reveal the information.)

BETTER OPTION

An even better option is to create six individual slides—each with an appropriate photo. Here's one of those slides:

Many presenters cling to the types of slides shown in that first version of the "Learning to Sail" slideshow because they've never realized how ineffective it is. And besides, don't all their colleagues use slides like that? Also, they depend on its detail as the prompt for their remarks. But those visuals are not meant for the presenter; the visuals are meant for the audience. Effective use of PowerPoint requires the presenter to know the material well.

Some other suggestions

- Presenters often cram multiple messages onto one visual (e.g., several pie charts or bar graphs, along with some copy). Limit yourself to one idea per slide.

- Put your company's logo on your first and last slides, but keep it off all others (clutter).

- Be sure your visuals are readable—from the back row. Few of us are graphics experts, but PowerPoint places responsibility for the design elements (e.g., choice of typeface, color, size, proportion, etc.) in our hands. What might look good on your computer screen may not project well on a room's large screen.

- Don't talk to (or worse—read) the screen. Glance down briefly at your notes or laptop, then look at the audience and elaborate on the visual being shown.

- Remember the "B" key. When using PowerPoint, you can "black" the screen by hitting the "B" key. This technique works well at the opening of your presentation, at the end, during Q&A, or whenever you want the audience's full attention. (Keep a visual up on the screen too long, and the audience will repeatedly look at it—to see if it has changed.) To return to PowerPoint, hit the "B" key again. Most remotes have a button that lets you accomplish this without going to your keypad. Hitting the "W" key will give you an annoying white screen; avoid this.

- Effective use of PowerPoint often means that two versions of your visuals may be needed—the one you project during your talk, and a more detailed, hard-copy or electronic version you provide to the audience as a leave-behind. Yes, it's more work, but it's effective communication. (As I said earlier in the book, you want to achieve more than a "production" objective; your goal is to achieve a "communications" objective.)

- Most laser pointers are misused. Presenters end up circling words or images for no particular reason. Use the laser pointer to guide the audience through a flow diagram or to draw attention to a particular element on the visual. Don't play with this feature found on most remotes; use it sparingly. And make sure the little red dot is visible on the screen.

- Don't deliver your presentation in a totally dark room. (Remember what you did when you wanted your kids to fall asleep? You read to them in a darkened room.) Make sure the audience can see you, not some faceless figure.

- Ideally, presentation handouts should be given to the audience after the presentation. You don't want the audience to be reading while you're presenting. However, this is rarely practical, and most audiences want the material up front, especially if your presentation is technical in nature. Give it to them but recognize that you must "perform" at a level where the audience will choose to listen to you rather than read your material. It's doable.

Much of the information just discussed runs counter to what we regularly see during PowerPoint presentations. (The blind are truly leading the blind.) In fact, some companies mandate specific guidelines for PowerPoint use. Those guidelines are usually wrong. So, you're likely to get pushback when you begin to make some changes in how you use PowerPoint. Do your best to stay in your company's good graces, but inch forward with incremental improvements that will help your presentation achieve its communications objective. After all, isn't that what's important?

POWERPOINT'S ROLE IN THE SPACE SHUTTLE DISASTER

In 2003, the Space Shuttle Columbia disintegrated as it re-entered the Earth's atmosphere, killing all seven crew members. Shortly after the disaster, the Columbia Accident Investigation Board studied the accident in detail and concluded that it was caused when the shuttle's left wing was hit by insulating foam that had come loose during launch.

But the board also pointed a finger at another culprit: PowerPoint. Investigators argued that in its briefings, NASA relied too heavily on PowerPoint rather than on traditional written reports. For example, when discussing possible wing damage during a mission, engineers used an incredibly complex PowerPoint slide—loaded with bullet points, sub-points and jargon. "It is easy to understand how a senior manager might read this PowerPoint slide and not realize that it addresses a life-threatening situation," the report stated.

On the next page is the offending slide—delivered in a presentation prior to the Columbia disaster: Note that the final bullet point, buried at the bottom of the slide, in small type and overshadowed by other data, indicates that the foam insulation tested prior to the mission was more than 600 times smaller than the size of a chunk of insulation that could cause damage in actual flight conditions.

> **Review of Test Data Indicates Conservatism for Tile Penetration**
>
> - The existing SOFI on tile test data used to create Crater was reviewed along with STS-87 Southwest Research data
>   - Crater overpredicted penetration of tile coating significantly
>   - Initial penetration to described by normal velocity
>   - Varies with volume/mass of projectile (e.g. 200ft/sec for 3cu. in.)
>   - Significant energy is required for the softer SOFI particle to penetrate the relatively hard tile coating
>   - Test results do show that it is possible at sufficient mass and velocity
>   - Conversely, once tile is penetrated SOFI can cause significant damage
>   - Minor variations in total energy (above penetration level) can cause significant tile damage
>   - Flight condition is significantly outside of test database
>   - Volume of ramp is 1920cu in vs. 3 cu in for test
>
> *BOEING*   2-21-03   6

Columbia space shuttle accident investigators cited loose insulating foam as the cause of the disaster. They also cited PowerPoint. Here's one of the offending slides.

Now, you could argue that PowerPoint wasn't at fault; it was the fault of the engineer who could have (and should have) flagged that final bullet point for the audience. Fair enough. But PowerPoint critics say that inherent in PowerPoint use are some serious flaws. PowerPoint's most vociferous critic, Edward Tufte, a professor emeritus at Yale University, offers these criticisms of PowerPoint:

1. It locks presenters into a linear, slide-by-slide format that discourages free association and creative thinking.
2. It imposes artificially and potentially misleading hierarchies on information.
3. It breaks information and data into fragments, making it more difficult to see logical relationships between different sets of data.
4. It encourages oversimplification by asking presenters to summarize key concepts in as few words as possible (i.e., bullet points, which can lead to gross generalizations, imprecise logic, superficial reasoning, misleading conclusions). It allows speakers to dodge responsibility to tie information together.
5. It encourages "chart junk"—gratuitous graphics.

Regardless of whether you agree with Tufte, what's certain is that companies are wasting huge amounts of time and money on poor PowerPoint presentations. What's more, their messages may not be getting through. The good news is that these PowerPoint pitfalls can be avoided.

OOPS! WHERE'S THE LAST PAGE OF MY SPEECH?

When Florida Senator Marco Rubio gave a major speech on foreign policy at the Brookings Institution, here's what happened: Toward the end of his speech he realized that the last page was missing, prompting him to look toward his staff and ask, "I lost the last page of my speech. Does anybody have it?"

After someone handed him the missing page, he concluded his remarks. But the damage was done, and the speech—which should have ended with a bang—ended with a whimper. And you guessed it, the misstep made it onto YouTube.

The lesson for all of us, of course, is to make sure that all pages of your script or notes are there—before you begin your talk.

Here are some other suggestions:
- Be sure your notes are typewritten (not handwritten)—preferably in at least 16-point type and in a typeface that's easy to read (e.g., Times New Roman).
- Double- or triple-space your copy.
- Have plenty of "white space"—wide margins, including using only the top two-thirds of the page. (This minimizes "head bobbing.")
- Avoid large blocks of copy. Use one- or two-sentence paragraphs so you can quickly find your place.
- Don't begin a thought on one page and conclude it on the next. This hampers fluidity and draws attention to the fact that you're using notes.
- It's okay to insert some prompts as a reminder to deliver certain parts of the presentation in a specific way. For example, you can underline, use a color marker or write the word, EMPHASIZE in the margin.
- Don't staple your pages together. Instead, place them on the lectern in two piles and slide them seamlessly from right to left as you speak. That way you'll always have two full pages of material in front of you.
- And finally, number all pages (in case you drop them)—then make sure they're all there.

PRACTICE MAKES PERFECT

When working with clients on their presentation skills, I usually ask this question at the beginning of the session: "Do you practice your presentation before you deliver it, and if so, what does that practice look like?" Here are the most frequent responses:

- "I usually don't practice because I don't have time."
- "I never practice because I want my presentation to sound spontaneous."
- "I go over what I'm going to say in my head."
- "I practice the presentation while I'm driving."
- "I ask my spouse to listen to it."

If you tend to skip practice or if your practice falls short of what's ideal, you're not alone. You're typical of most presenters. But as our parents, teachers and coaches told us, "Practice makes perfect." Or at least it helps improve performance. Athletes, musicians and other performers certainly know that. Adam Vinatieri, one of the greatest kickers in NFL history, put himself through some pretty demanding practices. He always trained with his helmet on. Team officials even piped in crowd noise during practice. So, make sure practice—proper practice—is part of your preparation for every business presentation you deliver.

HOW DOES PRACTICE WORK?

Whenever we learn a new skill, we're changing how our brain is wired. Scientists describe the brain as "plastic"—in other words, it remains "soft" or changeable rather than "hard" or fixed throughout our lives. When we perform any task, we're activating different portions of our brain. For example, how does a receiver catch a football? Stored in his brain is the memory of the muscle commands needed to catch the ball. He wasn't born with this memory; it was learned over many years of practice.

When we deliver a presentation, the brain is coordinating a very complex set of actions such as motor function (e.g., movement, gestures, etc.), visual and audio processing (e.g., eye contact, voice volume and inflection, etc.) and verbal language skills (e.g., our message—the words we choose, the stories we tell, etc.).

The first time we practice our presentation it's usually poorly delivered—it's not fluid, we forget some of our points, we lack energy, we misspeak, we're anxious, etc. We've all been there. But with additional practice we see dramatic improvement—we nail our points, we look and sound energetic, we're confident.

Practice gets the brain prepared to coordinate all the activities that go into delivering a speech or presentation. During practice we're triggering a pattern of electrical signals through our brain. The goal, through repetition, is to trigger the right patterns. You do this by practicing the right things (e.g., sustained eye contact with the audience, high energy, etc.). If you don't correct your mistakes during practice, you'll be strengthening the wrong brain signals. (If you're a golfer, you know how important it is not just to practice, but to practice the right stance, grip and swing.) In short, if you want to improve your presentation skills, you must practice repeatedly, get feedback on that practice (e.g., through video or a reliable colleague) and practice the correct skills.

HOW TO REWIRE YOUR BRAIN DURING PRACTICE

The best-kept secret to presentation practice is this: three times, aloud, on your feet, into a recording device. Repetition during practice helps your brain eliminate past errors and remember the successful responses. Three practices can accomplish that.

If your presentation is twenty minutes, practice all twenty minutes. Don't stop or skip some parts (because you're unhappy with the practice). Soldier through it, knowing it will improve later. You don't need to do all three practices at one time. You might spread them over several days—shortly before the actual presentation. But don't cram! In other words, doing all three practices or even one of them at 6:00 AM the day of the presentation is a bad idea. (It's no more effective than "pulling an all-nighter" before finals was in college.) Also, be sure the presentation you're practicing is in its final form. There's little or no value in practicing material that will change. Plan your work, then work your plan.

During practice, vocalize. Say the words aloud, not silently. When the opening of a presentation is a self intro, some people skip that part during practice. After all, you know who you are, right? Wrong! You must know exactly what you're planning to say about yourself—how much detail you want to provide. The time to determine that is during practice, not during the main event. Also, don't sub-vocalize during practice—saying some parts of the presentation in hushed tones, almost silently (usually because you're unsure of the material or because you know it well), and others loudly and forcefully.

Most presentations are delivered with the speaker standing. So, practice them that way. It also helps if you can replicate the setting you'll be in. Will you be delivering in a large auditorium or a small conference room? Will the presentation be more formal (e.g., behind a lectern) or informal (standing in front of the audience)? For your prompts, where will you be putting your laptop or notes? Remember, if you'll be using PowerPoint, the screen in the room is meant for the audience, not for you. In situations where you'll be delivering sitting (volume and energy tend to go down), practice while sitting; lean forward to increase your volume.

Video is the best teaching tool ever invented for feedback on presenting. Record, review and critique your practices. Use a smart phone if you don't have access to a stand-alone camera. Some of the things to note during the review include:

- Are there any words, phrases or sentences that should be deleted or changed (perhaps because you stumble over them)?
- Is your eye contact with the audience good or is there too much reliance on notes?
- How's your energy level—both visual (facial expression) and vocal (volume, inflection)?
- What about stance—standing erect? Excessive movement (swaying, pacing)? Good gestures?
- How long is your presentation?

DON'T FORGET ABOUT Q&A

Practicing for Q&A is an activity that's usually ignored or handled superficially by most presenters. But you can, and should, practice for this important segment of most presentations. (See **Q&A: Not as Hard as You May Think**, p. 46.)

Most executives are busy folks, and time is at a premium for them. But they should not expect a stellar performance from themselves if they simply don't have the time or the will to practice. That same harsh truth applies to the rest of us as well.

MEMO TO SELF: TALK TO SELF

Most of us think talking to ourselves is a practice that should be avoided—especially if others are around to observe it. But researchers say "self-talk" is more common than most people think. And it can make a big difference in mood, behavior and performance.

Here's what the research shows:
- Some 95 percent of our emotions are determined by how we talk to ourselves. And most of us do it in a negative way. It's the default setting. Ask someone about his golf game and he'll immediately give you a litany of negatives—sliced the ball, couldn't putt, etc.
- Self-talk is a form of thinking. It's a conversation you're having with yourself—usually to comment on something or to provide advice or reminders.
- Self-talk can be motivational (for encouragement) or instructional (for information).
- How you address yourself matters. Speaking to yourself as another person—using your own name or the pronoun "you"—produces better results than referring to yourself as "I."
- Self-talk should be short, precise and consistent.

Here's how self-talk can help you improve your communication skills. Try these techniques:
- Before delivering a presentation or speech, most people have this mindset: "Oh no, this is not going to go well. I'm nervous and I'm probably going to fail. The audience will not like this." This kind of thinking programs the speaker to fail. A better approach is to say something like this: "You have valuable information to share. Your audience is going to benefit from what you say. You're going to be a hit."
- Most of us know our strengths and weaknesses as communicators. Before you speak, remind yourself of what you need to do to perform better: "You need to speak more loudly. And don't talk to the screen when using PowerPoint."
- After a successful presentation, congratulate yourself: "You nailed that presentation. You had the audience hanging on your every word."
- After a less-than-successful presentation, identify what went wrong and how you plan to improve. Use encouraging words. Don't say, "I really screwed up that presentation." Instead say, "Bill, that was not your best effort. Before your next presentation, you need to practice."

"This is the part of capitalism I hate."

Q&A: NOT AS HARD AS YOU MAY THINK

In a scene from one of those instantly recognizable cartoons from *The New Yorker* magazine, several top executives have just concluded their remarks at the company's annual shareholders' meeting. Now it's time for the shareholders to ask questions. Just as one of the shareholders is about to ask a question, one executive whispers to the other, "This is the part of capitalism I hate."

If the Q&A portion of your presentation is something you hate, take heart; it's not as hard as you may think. Here are some tips to increase your comfort and success:

Q&A is an important element of your presentation. It's two-way communication—the best kind of communication. It provides your audience with an opportunity to participate, and you with an opportunity to get feedback.

Although most audiences eagerly await the opportunity to ask questions, they do have a few gripes about the Q&A segment. One is when the speaker doesn't answer or doesn't adequately answer the question. Another is when answers are too long. And the other gripe is when they can't hear the questions being asked by other audience members. Think how frustrating it is to have to use the answer to figure out the question. All of these problems are preventable, and it's up to the speaker to prevent them.

Not all individuals adequately prepare and practice their presentations. I think it's accurate to say that even fewer people prepare for Q&A. This portion of the presentation usually gets short shrift. But there are several things worth doing:

Anticipate the questions you're most likely to be asked, including the questions you hope no one asks. Make a list, and then answer those questions—perhaps in writing, but more importantly, out loud. Better yet, record your answers on your smart phone and replay them. By vocalizing answers, you are beginning to put the right words into your short-term memory.

As the speaker, you should determine when to field questions. Generally, it's best to do that at the end of the presentation. That way, you prevent interruptions that can derail the presentation. Tell the audience that you're saving time for questions and ask them to hold their questions. An exception could be questions from the top executive or during a technical presentation where immediate clarification is needed.

Sometimes, the toughest part of Q&A is getting people to ask questions. The best approach is simply to follow the example of David Byrne, former lead singer of Talking Heads. In the groundbreaking concert film, *Stop Making Sense*, he turned to the audience at the conclusion of one of the songs and jokingly asked, "Does anybody have any questions?"

Do likewise. Ask if anyone has any questions, then wait 10-15 seconds while looking and smiling confidently at several audience members. Don't gather your notes or close your laptop during this time; these actions may signal that you're eager to leave or that you really don't want questions.

If there are no questions, pose one yourself by saying, "One of the questions I'm frequently asked is..." (Choose a question related to one of your key messages.) Then answer your own question. Next, ask if there are any other questions. Again, wait a few seconds. If there's no response, don't appear uncomfortable or disappointed. No questions could be an indication that your presentation was a success. Thank the audience or make some other closing remark.

Another option to jump start questions is by "planting" a question or two. Ask a colleague or someone else in the audience you know to help kickstart the Q&A segment. The only time this approach might be a bit awkward is if the first questioner is the moderator or facilitator for the event; the audience may see the question as perfunctory.

If you were using PowerPoint in your presentation, don't leave your last slide up on the screen during Q&A. It will be a distraction. Hit the "B" key to black the screen.

With larger audiences or in large rooms where there are no microphones for the questioners, you may need to repeat the question, so everyone knows what question you're about to answer. You don't have to repeat the question verbatim (never do so with one containing negative words); rephrase it, being sure to keep its essential meaning.

For each question, listen…think…then respond—in that order. If necessary, take 5-10 seconds before responding. The silence will seem like an eternity to you, but to the audience you will appear thoughtful. This is a better strategy than "buying yourself time" by prefacing the answer with, "That's a very good question…" That phrase is an overused cliché, and if you don't use it uniformly, some questioners might wonder what was wrong with their question.

When answering a question, look at the person who asked it. However, if your response is lengthy, make eye contact with others in the audience as well in order to keep their attention.

Don't bluff. Many people feel pressured to answer every question. If you don't know the answer, say so, and perhaps indicate that you will find out. Ask the questioner for contact information.

One reason some people fear Q&A is that they feel control shifts from them to the audience. Not necessarily. Audience questions can actually be used as a springboard to your agenda if you use the bridging technique (see **Q = A+1**, p. 78).

FIRST IMPRESSIONS DO MATTER

President Ronald Reagan and Soviet General Secretary Mikhail Gorbachev met for the first time in 1985 at a chateau in Geneva to hold talks on international diplomatic relations and the arms race. Edmond Morris, who would go on to write *Dutch: A Memoir of Ronald Reagan*, described the scene when the two leaders first met:

"And I see it now in memory and slow motion—it was supremely dramatic. This great, gleaming, black Zil comes whispering around the corner—on the gravel—crunches to a halt. Down the stairs comes this great, gliding, blue-suited, unbelievably self-confident and calm President—without a coat on, in the freezing air. Out of the big, black Russian limousine comes this awkward, short, rather dumpy, heavily overcoated, heavily scarfed, hatted Communist leader—who fondled his scarf and fondled his coat, and approached this great benign presence. And they met at the foot of the stairs; Reagan towered over Gorbachev. Gorbachev looked up at Reagan's face—looked at him very intently. Reagan smiled down at him—gently choreographed him up the stairs."

USSR Foreign Minister Sergei Tatasenko added this observation: "Gorbachev's in standard Politburo hat, standard Politburo overcoat. It reminds me of the KGB agent from bad American films. So I said to myself, 'We have lost this photo opportunity; we have lost this first round.'"

What impression do you create when you walk up to the lectern or to the front of the room to speak or present? Do you come up timidly, sheepishly, cautiously? Confidently? What's your facial expression—fear? Excitement? Before you even say anything, the audience has already sized you up. Impressions made in the first few seconds (primarily visual) are so powerful that it takes several minutes to add fifty percent more information.

When Barack Obama ran for president in 2008, the public would frequently see TV coverage of a fit, trim, highly energetic candidate bounding onto a stage at some campaign event. The contrast to his opponent John McCain was pronounced.

Actor Sean Connery reportedly spent hours perfecting his use of body movement. In one interview, he explained, "The body is our first impression, and it's what makes people respond or not respond."

Your "performance" at a meeting, speech or presentation begins before you speak. Perform appropriately.

SMILE!

Few things can do more to facilitate effective communication than a smile. It reveals your inner state and propels your message with energy and emotional force. Smiles are such an important part of communication that we see them far more clearly than any other expression. We can pick up a smile at 120 yards—the length of an American football field.

We tend to trust a smiling face implicitly. George Rotter, Ph.D., a psychology professor emeritus at Montclair University in New Jersey, cut out yearbook photos of college students and then asked people to rate the individuals pictured for trustworthiness. In almost every instance, people chose the students with smiling faces as the most honest.

When delivering a speech or presentation, "program" your audience with a smile. Make sure the first thing they see is a winning smile. Most of the audience will respond in kind (it's called "mirroring"), which in turn, will generate additional energy and enthusiasm in you. Likewise, in most TV media interviews, smile early and often. Doing so will keep the audience and the reporter engaged and eager to hear what you have to say.

Just remember, phony smiles don't work, and there are clues to insincerity. We tend to hold a simulated expression longer than a real one. If we look carefully, a phony smile may have the slightly fixed expression that a child's face gets when setting a smile for a photograph. Also, we use different muscles for felt and fake expressions, and we are apt to blink more when we're lying.

ANOTHER REASON TO GESTURE

Using appropriate gestures can help you relax and appear more comfortable when speaking in public. That's a given. But gesturing while you speak can also improve your brain's recall ability.

Have you ever found yourself gesturing intensely, trying to find an elusive word and suddenly had it pop into your head? Why this happens is unclear, but Donna Frick Horbury, a professor of psychology at Appalachian State University in North Carolina, conducted a study which found that preventing subjects from gesturing in tip-of-the-tongue situations reduced their chances of recalling what they wanted to say.

Gestures can help in presenting, but keep these guidelines in mind
- Use your hands to make natural gestures, just as you do in normal conversation, only make them broader. Small gestures make you appear tentative and uncertain when you're in front of a group.
- Avoid the front "fig leaf"—arms lowered and hands clasped in front. Men, more than women, typically assume this weak stance. (Presumably, they are protecting what's important!) It gives the impression that you lack confidence and certainty. Instead, keep your hands at your side; in a matter of moments, you'll begin to gesture. Then there's the reverse "fig leaf." This is a similar stance, but your hands are clasped behind you. It too is weak—unless you are in law enforcement or the military, where it sends out a strong message.
- Arms crossed over the chest: It's defensive; you look like you're protecting yourself from the audience. This stance is also frequently interpreted as dislike.
- What about hands in the pocket? (Usually men.) It can make you look comfortable and relaxed, and it's especially appropriate in informal situations. But don't keep your hands in your pocket for long periods of time; doing so restricts gesturing. Also, be sure to avoid rattling coins, keys or other items your hands might find to play with.
- Avoid pointing your finger directly at members of the audience. This gesture is intimidating and to some people quite threatening. It makes no difference that you intended to single someone out for friendly purposes; the effect of this particular gesture is always negative.

Remember that televised image of an angry President Clinton shaking his pointed finger as he said, "But I want to say one thing to the American people. I want you to listen to me. I'm going to say this again. I did not have sexual relations with that woman—Miss Lewinsky."

- Avoid closing your laptop or gathering your notes or other belongings as you near the end of your presentation. Also, avoid looking at your watch. These gestures may signal that you are eager to leave. (In a 1992 town-hall style presidential debate, an audience member asked President George H.W. Bush a question about the national debt. During the question, Bush took a quick look at his watch, which made him seem as though he didn't care or have time to listen to the concerns of average Americans. The gesture was captured on camera and got a lot of repeat air time; Bush went on to lose the election to Bill Clinton.)

- One of the most important benefits of gesturing is that it can take all that anxiety that may be inside you and release it in the form of energy.

Here are a few other visual no no's
- Failing to make (sustained) eye contact with the audience.
- Excessive reliance on notes or "talking to the screen."
- Looking up at the ceiling (as if seeking divine intervention).
- Business poker face. (Research shows that the human face is capable of making more than 7,000 different facial expressions. Use some of them.)
- Excessive movement (e.g., pacing, swaying, shifting). Try watching a Chris Rock stand-up comedy performance; his constant pacing will exhaust you. Some movement is fine—but move and then "plant" (i.e., stay there awhile) before moving again.
- Playing with or touching hair, fingers, tie, pen, jewelry, etc. or other distracting habits.
- Inappropriate clothing or accessories which "say more than what you say."

Curious about your own gestures and body language? Record a presentation you deliver, preferably during practice, and then critique it. Better yet, during that critique, occasionally mute the audio, which will enable you to focus solely on the visual aspect of your delivery. You may be surprised by what you see.

HOW TO (CORRECTLY) USE A TELEPROMPTER

During the financial crisis of 2007-2009, the U.S. faced some serious problems: Banks were failing. Credit was tight. Unemployment was soaring. The stock market was plummeting. 401(k)s were tanking. Americans were worried. So, President Obama directed Treasury Secretary Timothy Geithner to come up with a plan to rescue the country from this crisis.

When it was time to communicate that plan, Geithner faced a VIP audience, cameras and the press. Markets were expecting something big. He came to the lectern, flanked by two TelePrompters. He looked nervous and started his speech but wasn't very good at delivering it. His head turned from one TelePrompter to the other, and he gave the entire speech with his head going back and forth—like a tennis ball.

His speech was a disaster—partly because it lacked specifics, but also because his performance did not inspire confidence. By the end of the day he spoke, the stock market dropped almost 400 points.

TelePrompter use is not widespread in the business world. Some executives use it occasionally at key events. Nonetheless, it's a tool worth knowing how to use.

Some background: A TelePrompter is that textbook-sized pane of glass on a stand some speakers use when delivering prepared remarks. Typically, two are used—located a few feet apart, in front of and on either side of a lectern. The speaker's remarks are scrolled from a laptop computer onto the glass screens.

A TelePrompter is a powerful tool, but its use does pose some challenges for the speaker—all of which can be overcome. Creating rapport with the audience is a primary objective for any speaker, and reading from a script can make that job difficult. Also, reading tends to narrow a speaker's vocal range, creating a "sameness" in sound or even a monotone. As energy drops, the speaker can sound wooden or monotonous. What's more, audiences sometimes see script readers as less authoritative. On the other hand, reading from a prepared script tells the audience that you cared enough about them to prepare.

If you use a TelePrompter, keep the following in mind:

- Be sure to read the script aloud several times to get familiar with the material.
- Take ownership of the script. Make it your own. Some scripts are written by someone other than the speaker, and the writer may not have captured the speaker's voice (i.e., style). So it's okay to modify the script. Don't be afraid to change words and phrasing. Also, there's a difference between the written and spoken word. It's especially important to use a conversational tone. Otherwise, the delivery will draw attention to the fact that the speaker is reading.

- Don't allow the TelePrompter operator to set the pace. It's up to the operator to follow the speaker (e.g., slow down, speed up or pause in response to the speaker's delivery). In other words, the speaker should be in the "driver's seat."
- It's okay to improvise slightly. Don't feel compelled to deliver the material exactly as written. Give yourself permission to use a different word or phrase occasionally. Also, going "off script" once or twice (e.g., to tell a story, etc.) helps create the perception that much of the speech was delivered "extemporaneously."
- Eye contact with the audience is critical. It's no different from delivering a speech using a hard-copy script. You must maximize eye contact with the audience (85%) and minimize looking at the glass screens (15%). Select some proxies in the audience and look at them (both directly and through the glass screens). A big mistake some people make is thinking they simply can read the material as it scrolls on the screens.
- Most TelePrompters today allow for some "stage directions"—i.e., different fonts, colors, symbols, notes. (This is similar to putting visual reminders or instructions on a printed page.)

Want to see someone who knows how to use a TelePrompter? Watch your local or national news anchors. These folks are using TelePrompters, and they're good at it.

THE PRESENTATION GENIUS OF STEVE JOBS

Steve Jobs presided over an amazing company—Apple. Equally amazing was Jobs' skill as a presenter. His product introductions for Apple were legendary. People attended them as much to see Jobs perform, as to see the new products. Here are just a few observations about what made him such a great communicator:

He understood the importance of practice.

Great communication doesn't happen by accident. It's the product of hard work. As Adam Lashinsky, author of "The Decade of Steve," said, "A key Jobs business tool is his mastery of the message. He rehearses over and over every line he and others utter in public about Apple." Watch any of the product introductions delivered by Jobs and you'll see someone who likely invested not just hours, but days of practice time—often at the venue where he'd be speaking.

Audiences attended Apple product launches in part to see the "insanely great" presentation skills of Steve Jobs.

He could sustain audience attention.

The average attention span of most adults during a business presentation is about twenty minutes. Jobs could (and frequently did) hold audience attention for well over an hour, in part because of the way he talked about Apple products.

He used figurative language, including analogies.

According to research, analogies are among the most powerful tools of persuasion. And Jobs used lots of them. When introducing the iPod in 2001, he said, "iPod is the size of a deck of cards," While he spoke, a rotating photo of a familiar box of Bicycle-brand playing cards was projected onscreen.

Four years later, he described the iPod Nano this way: "And yet all of this weighs one and a half ounces—42 grams. That is less than eight quarters in your pocket."

Jobs knew the value of repetition.

He used certain words and phrases repeatedly to reinforce key ideas. In his 2007 iPhone launch presentation, he used the phrase "reinvent the phone" five times. Another example of repetition and reinforcement: "And it's the highest-resolution screen we've ever shipped. It's 160 pixels per inch—highest we've ever shipped."

He used "language of the living room."

Whether it was because of his age (Jobs was a baby boomer), his casual style and free-spirit personality, the industry he worked in, his target audience or none of these, Jobs was plain-spoken and avoided "corporate speak." Case in point: "What we want to do is make a leapfrog product that is way smarter than any mobile device has ever been, and way smarter to use."

He entertained.

One of my favorite Steve Jobs moments: He pulled an iPod out of his pocket and talked about it briefly. Then, pointing to the small, coin pocket on his signature jeans, he said, "Ever wonder what this pocket's for? I've always wondered that. Well, now we know…" and pulled out an iPod Nano.

In the iPhone launch, he called a colleague, played a message from Al Gore and called Starbucks and jokingly ordered 4,000 lattes to go.

To tease the audience, he showed a photo of an iPod, made to look like it had an old rotary phone dial on it.

Jobs knew how to use Keynote (Apple's version of PowerPoint).

Never did you see him "talking to the screen" reading a lot of words. Instead, he'd be looking at the audience while photos or a few key words reinforcing his message appeared on the screen. Also, not once did he ever use those often-unnecessary agenda slides that begin most presentations.

He moved seamlessly from idea to idea.

In other words, he used transitions. In most presentations, the speaker moves along in a jerky, clumsy manner: "And now I want to talk about…" or "My next slide shows…" Here's how Jobs moved from talking about how many songs the iPod could hold to discussing battery life: "Now, it doesn't matter how many songs you have with you if your battery is dead, right? So, we have built in an extraordinary battery in the iPod."

If you're wondering whether Steve Jobs ever messed up when presenting like the rest of us mere mortals do, the answer is yes.

At a Macworld convention in Boston, Jobs announced a partnership between Apple and Microsoft. During the announcement, Bill Gates' face appeared on a huge screen via satellite downlink. Gates' image dwarfed Jobs who was standing at a lectern. Afterwards, Jobs said, "That was my worst and stupidest staging event ever. It was bad because it made me look small, and Apple look small, and as if everything was in Bill's hands."

A misstep? Sure, but one that's overshadowed by many amazing presentations that are the envy of presenters everywhere. Want to see Steve Jobs in action? Most of his product launch presentations (e.g., iPod, iPod Nano, iPhone, iPad) are on YouTube. Check them out.

TO DEVELOP EXECUTIVE PRESENCE, OBSERVE AND LEARN FROM THE BEST

Some presenters have it. Most do not. "It" is an executive presence—a certain something that captures an audience's attention, sustains it and leaves a lasting impression. It also helps the speaker achieve that all-important communications objective—getting the audience to listen to, understand and act on what was said.

How do you develop executive presence and join the ranks of top-tier communicators? If you observe these talented individuals carefully, here's what you'll see:

High energy

Your "business poker face"—that unemotional, inexpressive persona that may serve you well during an intense negotiation—prevents you from connecting with your audience. Just as people naturally gravitate to individuals with outgoing personalities, they are inclined to listen to ideas presented with energy and conviction. Communicating is selling, and successful selling involves transferring energy and enthusiasm from speaker to listener. To help sell your message, increase your normal energy level 50 percent when presenting.

Everyday language

Great communicators sound conversational. They speak plainly, avoid jargon, and use simple words, contractions and uncomplicated sentence structure. This kind of language—let's call it "language of the living room"—resonates with people who are fed up with "corporate speak" and words and phrasing that sound like they came from speechwriters.

Minimal reliance on notes

Although it often appears that skillful presenters are "winging it," this is rarely the case. To paraphrase from a Rod Stewart song, "Their ad-libbed lines are well rehearsed." The paradox of successful public speaking is making prepared remarks seem spontaneous. Strive to look at your notes no more than 15 percent of the time while presenting. Fluid delivery comes from knowing your material cold. And that means practice—preferably three times, aloud, on your feet, into a video recording device.

During a questioning segment between Texas Senator John Cornyn and Judge Amy Coney Barrett, the supreme court nominee was asked to reveal the notes she might be using to answer detailed and specific legal questions. "You know most of us have multiple notebooks and books and other things like that in front of us. Can you hold up what you've been referring to in answering our questions?" Cornyn asked Barrett. Judge Barrett held up a blank notepad and smiled. "Is there anything on that?" Cornyn asked. Barrett responded: "Just a letterhead that says United States Senate."

Storytelling ability

Human beings—regardless of culture—are storytelling creatures. Presenters who tell stories are making an important leap from the abstract to the concrete. Remember Ronald Reagan's "hero in the balcony" technique where the President would tell a brief story about a real person sitting in the balcony at the State of the Union Address? Who among us wasn't fully engaged (and often moved) during that portion of the speech?

Sustained eye contact

Most business situations call for "involvement." And one of the best ways to show it is through eye contact. When we're excited and fully engaged, we tend to look at someone for about 5-10 seconds. Great presenters have mastered this skill and deliver one complete thought to one pair of eyes. In large-group situations, they focus on several individuals who serve as proxies for the entire audience.

Limited use of PowerPoint

Although PowerPoint is ubiquitous in the business world, top-level executives use it sparingly. They know that no visual can compete with the ability of a human being to make a personal connection with the audience. Other than using the occasional pie chart, bar graph, diagram or photo, powerful speakers rely on themselves rather than on projected images to reach an audience.

Q&A savvy

Most speakers dread the Q&A portion of a presentation. Accomplished presenters don't. They prepare by anticipating the questions they'll likely get, and by asking themselves, "What questions do I hope no one asks?" Then they prepare answers. If the audience is silent, they jump start the Q&A segment by planting a question or two with a colleague, or by saying something like, "One question I'm asked most frequently is …"

The ability to deliver an effective presentation is an essential skill. Business deals, employee support and professional reputations can be damaged or lost by sub-par communication. Yet most business presentations are poorly crafted and delivered. Since most of us acquire our platform skills through observational learning, it's critical that we observe and learn from the right people—those talented few who can get up before a crowd and dazzle them.

PLAN B: WHAT TO DO WHEN THINGS GO WRONG

Your speech...your business presentation: it's a performance—or at least it should be. Successful presentations combine thoughtful content with a powerful, perhaps even entertaining, delivery. It's the same combination you usually see in theatrical or musical performances. And just as in plays or concerts, things can, and do, go wrong.

During a concert some years back, Peter Frampton (a rock musician who once played with the bands Humble Pie and Ringo Star & His All-Star Band) stepped to the edge of the stage for a solo. As he moved backwards, he tripped over a stage monitor. Laughing at himself, he finished playing the solo flat on his back. He never missed a note, got up and finished the song to roaring applause.

As he began the next song, he paused briefly, went to the mic and told the audience to hold on a minute. Then he lay down on his back again and played the opening of the song. The crowd loved it.

A less embarrassing moment came for blues rock guitarist and singer Joe Bonamassa at his Royal Albert Hall concert. During his final song, he moved just a bit too far from the mic and a few seconds of lyrics could barely be heard. When he realized his mistake, he quickly moved back to the mic.

All actors and musicians experience problems during a performance. So might you. Knowing how to recover and "go on with the show" is critical.

Today's audiences are tough, demanding. They will not tolerate a speaker who is unprepared, uncomfortable, not committed and not interesting. At the same time, they can be very forgiving. Occasional stumbles such as losing your train of thought or mispronouncing a word is quickly forgotten. Audiences don't expect perfection. In fact, when you stumble, they're secretly cheering you on to success—much like spectators might do at a speed skating race when their favorite skater falters briefly by not fully completing a stride.

Let's look at some of the most common business presentation glitches:

Say you forget to make an important point, and a few minutes later you realize the mistake. Most speakers announce the flub and add the omitted information. But why draw attention to the misstep? Simply add the information—perhaps prefacing it with something such as, "Another thing to keep in mind..." or "One other important point..." Most likely, the audience will not know the information is out of sequence.

On the other hand, if you realize you misspoke, and the error is significant, tell the audience you want to correct something you said. Make the correction as soon as you realize the mistake or do so at the end of the presentation. Be straightforward but deliver the correction with the same confidence used in the rest of your presentation. No sheepish demeanor.

Struggling to remember your next point or thinking how you want to express that point? Simply pause. Pauses are among the most powerful tools a speaker can use. They give the audience a chance to catch their breath and give presenters a chance to reboot. If the point or words still elude you after a few seconds of silence, move on to another point or choose an alternate word or expression. A lot of speakers put unnecessary pressure on themselves to use the exact words they used during practice or use the exact words found in the script. But there are multiple ways to express an idea; give yourself permission to change vocabulary.

Not surprisingly, the most frequently occurring problems presenters face are—you guessed it—technical in nature: laptop computers, PowerPoint, imbedded video, LCD projectors, sound, the remote device…the list is endless. Because presentations today rely so heavily on technology, savvy presenters leave nothing to chance. They anticipate and identify potential problems and take preventive measures. Here are a few questions to jumpstart your thinking about some of those problems:

- Will you need a microphone? If so, is a wireless mic available (so you can move around) or will you need to use a mic fixed to the lectern?
- Is the room's lighting adjustable, or will you and your PowerPoint visuals be hamstrung by too bright or too dark of a room?
- Will you be able to place your laptop computer on a lectern or table so you can easily access it and use it as your prompt for the PowerPoint visuals? Or will you have to use the room's large screen behind you for that purpose?
- Will you use a remote for your PowerPoint visuals? If so, do you know how to use it? Or will someone else control your slides (not recommended)?
- How reliable is the room's internet connection?
- Have you tested your PowerPoint presentation (including imbedded audio and video) on the equipment in the room you'll be using?
- Are your PC or Mac connectors compatible with the projection equipment in the room you'll be using?
- Will you have access to a technician? If so, will he or she be immediately available if needed?

You get the idea. Think through all the possible touchpoints where technology can fail or make presenting less than ideal. Doing so can prevent a lot of problems. But if one surfaces, have Plan B ready:

- Acknowledge the problem directly with the audience. Tell them you're trying to fix it or ask if anyone in the audience can help. Most audiences will give you a ten-minute grace period; after that, they will get restless.

- If someone else is troubleshooting the problem, use the time for a short break or have something specific set aside to discuss that relates to your topic. It's similar to the appendix in a book. Q&A is another possible option.
- If the technical problem cannot be resolved in a timely fashion, move forward with your presentation—either by delivering it without visuals or after handing out hard copies of your visuals. (For some presenters, visuals are such an important part of the presentation that they opt for this level of preparation.)

Sometimes presentations can be derailed...by skeptical or angry audiences or by bosses with a willingness to interrupt. In these situations, or if you notice audience attention waning, you may need to modify your game plan...on the spot. For example: shorten the presentation by eliminating some content or reducing its detail, jettison your PowerPoint visuals, switch from one-way communication to an exchange of information with the audience, decrease analytical content (e.g., facts, numbers, etc.) and increase emotional content (e.g., stories, anecdotes, etc.), begin Q&A earlier than planned.

One final thought: Any of the problems just discussed can create yet another problem—panic, and all of its related components: rise in blood pressure and heart rate, sweating, strained breathing, difficulty concentrating, etc. At the first sign of heightened nervousness: pause, take several deep breaths (in through the nose and out through the mouth) to re-program your breathing, and soldier on with the belief that your presentation may well turn out to be one of your finest.

WHY THE DECK IS STACKED AGAINST YOU

Think back to our earliest ancestors—Neanderthals. (No, not the ones who occasionally appear in TV commercials.)

One of the things we know about them is that they had smaller, undeveloped brains. Scientists use the terms, "first," "primitive," "reptile" or "crocodile" brain. This brain was not designed for reasoning; its reasoning power was quite limited. Instead, it focused on survival. It enabled these ancestors to deal effectively with threats. For instance, if a dangerous animal approached, this primitive brain triggered an immediate "fight or flight" response. To be sure, this brain served our ancestors well.

Today, our brains are larger and more developed. In the neocortex, for example, reside the amazing skills of language, logic and creativity. But modern humans still have vestiges of that primitive brain. Incoming information is being

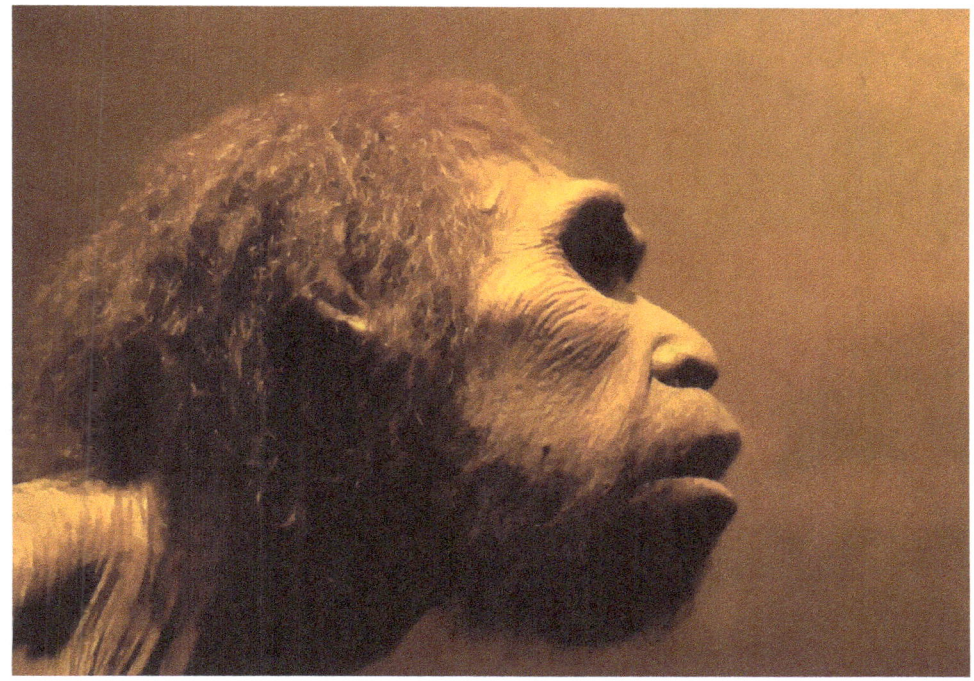

The "fight or flight" response so helpful to our earliest ancestors is alive and well—ready to help audiences tune in or tune out to your presentation.

received and processed or screened in that primitive brain before moving on to other parts of the brain.

Now, most of us don't encounter threatening animals very often, if at all. But that primitive brain is ready to protect us from modern-day threats—such as boring presentations. Think about the mindset of most people when they have to sit through a business presentation: "Boy, I'm really busy; I wish I didn't have to go to this thing." "Not another presentation!" "I bet this is going to be boring." "I already know this stuff."

Which brings us to why the deck is stacked against every presenter. Your audience comes predisposed to fear or resist your presentation. They've been burned in the past. Their primitive brains are ready to trigger the fight or flight response. "Flight" could mean not coming, leaving early, tuning out, multi-tasking. You don't want that. You want "fight"—meaning, the audience is fully engaged—ready and eager to listen. You engage your audience by using many of the techniques discussed in this book.

CHAPTER 2

COMMUNICATING WITH THE NEWS MEDIA

The ability to communicate effectively with the news media is an essential skill for certain individuals in just about any organization. Today, five different media interactions are most likely to occur: the standard informational interview, the "remote" or satellite interview, a press briefing, a news conference and the feared "ambush" interview. In some ways, talking to a reporter is a "game"—but it's the reporter's game, played by their rules, on their territory. Reporters play that game daily, so they're good at it. The rest of us must learn the "rules of the road" in order to succeed.

THE NEWS MEDIA TODAY

You've heard the complaints: The news media are biased. They're liberal and are in the tank for Democrats. Talk radio is overwhelmingly conservative. The news is fake.

I'll let others sort all this out. What I will say is this: The news media have changed, and those changes have implications for any individual or organization that interacts with reporters. Here's my take on some of the changes and what they mean for your media relations efforts:

The news business has been transformed from one tied to public service to one linked to profit and entertainment.

Back in the 1960s, CBS head William Paley told his journalists, "You guys cover the news; I've got Jack Benny to make money for me." Today, news is big business, and it can make big profits. For instance, news is an important profit center for local stations. One thing this means is that what's considered newsworthy and how a story is covered have changed. For example, a company event or issue that might have been ignored by the news media in the past may now get the limelight or even be treated as a crisis. In short, expect more media inquiries about subjects you might consider marginally newsworthy or not newsworthy at all.

America's infatuation with celebrity has had a profound impact on journalism.

Today, much television news is delivered as theatre, often with journalists serving as celebrities (think: Anderson Cooper). High-end graphics, music, quick edits and unusual camera angles are commonplace. Some call this the "tabloidization" of the news. You may not like it, but it's no reason to shut reporters out. Remember, they'll write their stories—with or without your help. In most cases, better to cooperate.

Soundbites have shrunk.

When John F. Kennedy ran for president in 1960, he could expect 45 seconds of what he said aired on the evening news. Now, presidential candidates typically get fewer than ten seconds. Today, both broadcast and print reporters alike prefer 6-12-second answers to their questions. Want proof? Turn on your car radio or listen to a TV news broadcast and time the length of just about any quote. It's important that you answer questions with word economy to avoid being interrupted or edited.

The emergence of citizen journalism.

Today, everyone is a potential reporter. Anyone armed with a smart phone can instantly use social media to pass along news, photos and video. You see it every day—the name of some individual who provided video or a photo appears on screen or in print. Remember the US Airways plane that landed on the Hudson River? News of that event was first reported via Twitter by an average Joe (actually, Janis Krums) with a Twitter account who happened to be nearby on a ferry.

Being discreet in what you say around others has taken on added importance with the emergence of social media.

Expect more contact with junior-level and female journalists.

Changes in traditional and new media outlets, and economic pressures on news organizations mean less experienced reporters make it to the big leagues earlier. Use of freelancers is also growing so you'll need to be more patient and do more "hand-holding." For example, don't assume the reporter (even a beat reporter—someone who covers a particular topic) has a solid grasp of the topic or will admit to anything less. Instead, assess whether the journalist fully understands what you're saying. If you detect problems in comprehension, backtrack and explain the subject a different way. (Be careful not to be condescending.) Other helpful strategies include encouraging the reporter to call you for follow-up questions, or if the story is highly technical or complex, volunteering to review it for accuracy.

Also, keep in mind that female journalists now outnumber their male counterparts. In the presence of a female reporter, some men tend to be knowingly or unknowingly deferential. Avoid this tendency.

Be prepared to respond to media inquiries more quickly.

Thanks to cable TV and the internet, today's news cycle is 24 hours. And TV makes frequent use of "cut-ins" (interrupting programming for breaking news) and "crawls" (running information across the screen). The public expects and gets instant news. Likewise, they expect an instant response from you. In a crisis, you typically have about 15 minutes to respond to the news media. Speed wins.

Don't underestimate the value of newspapers.

Newspaper readership may be declining, but print reporters still do much of the original reporting. Local newspapers set the news agenda in most cities. Many of the items on TV and radio are lifted right out of newspapers. Get to know the print reporters who cover your organization and cultivate a positive business relationship with them.

CORPORATE MEDIA RELATIONS—THEN AND NOW

It's not unusual to hear managers and even some executives occasionally express frustration with their company's media relations policy requiring them to obtain approval before talking to reporters. These individuals find it ironic that their company invests time and money for them to get media training, but then puts restrictions on their ability to use what they learned. And if their corporate headquarters is in a different time zone, obtaining timely approval (especially in a crisis) is often difficult, if not impossible.

Let me weigh in on this issue and propose a possible approach to present-day corporate media relations.

First, some history:

In the not-so-distant past, most organizations had one individual who served as media spokesperson—usually someone in the communications or PR function. Reporters often knew who that person was, and accepted him or her as the face and voice of the organization.

That approach seemed to work well. And it did so at a time when a speedy response from the company was less important. Before the 24-hour news cycle, reporters might have had hours before they had to file their stories. Companies had lots of time to get their messages approved by lawyers and others in management.

But then things changed:

- Reporters wanted to talk to someone other than the "PR flack." They wanted direct access to the "content expert"—the person closest to the issue or problem.

- Media training took off in the '70s. It provided these new spokespersons with the confidence and competence needed to represent their organizations.

- Media outlets expanded in number, and technology necessitated a much faster response from the interviewee.

These and other developments led many companies to ask non-communication professionals to interact with the news media—but not without developing and enforcing strict approval procedures. Which brings us back to those frustrations voiced by the managers and executives mentioned above. If your organization is looking for that balance between spokesperson freedom and corporate oversight, perhaps these suggestions will help:

- Establish media relations guidelines and communicate them to all employees. Some things to address include:

  Which individuals are authorized to speak to reporters?

  When and how should corporate be notified of a media inquiry?

  Under what circumstances, if any, should a designated spokesperson who cannot reach someone for corporate approval in a timely fashion talk to the media?

  What is the company's position on employee use of social media?

  What about interacting with citizen journalists?

  How should errors in reporting be handled?

- Ambush or unexpected media inquiries are particularly tricky. Be sure that employees who are not authorized to speak to the media know what to say when politely declining media requests. To keep them from saying, "I was told not to talk to reporters," give them more appropriate suggested responses. For example, "I'm not the company's designated spokesperson, so it would be inappropriate for me to do the interview. Let me get you to the right person."
- Provide media training, including refresher training, to those individuals who will represent your organization to the news media. Don't forget about front-line employees. For example, show them how to interact with the news media until a designated spokesperson arrives.
- Distinguish between routine, easily handled media inquiries and those that are critically important or high risk. For example, a local media inquiry about your company's contribution to a local charity probably doesn't warrant corporate involvement or approval. An inquiry from CNN or the *Wall Street Journal* about a serious local matter probably does.
- Providing spokespersons with templates containing suggested talking points for likely scenarios is a good strategy. But don't presume you can anticipate every development. Provide macro rather than micro guidance.
- Utilize technology (phone, email, text) to enable your spokespersons to reach corporate contacts anywhere and anytime, but don't assume they will always succeed. Remember Murphy's Law.
- In a crisis, where speed wins, have your spokespersons contact corporate for guidance before interacting with the news media. Some organizations allow spokespersons to talk without getting guidance, and to make corporate notifications later—depending on time constraints, the issue and the position of the spokesperson.
- Consider identifying and partnering with local PR firms or communications consultants that can provide immediate assistance to your field spokespersons.

Every day, corporations entrust their field management with important decision-making authority—decisions about equipment, personnel and the like. Delegation is a logical, well accepted practice in business. Don't be afraid to extend it to media relations.

WHO SPEAKS FOR YOUR INDUSTRY?

As one of your company's marketing professionals, you get a call from a trade press reporter who follows your industry. He's doing a market update and would like your perspective on current and future market conditions.

You see no benefit in talking to him, only quite a few risks: Perhaps he'll ask some questions you'd rather not answer. For example, "Why are prices and volumes falling?" Maybe you'll unknowingly reveal sensitive company or industry information. Talking to him might also be against company policy. What if you're misquoted? Besides, you really don't have time. You're even slightly resentful (if not envious) of someone whose "raw material"—your knowledge—is obtained for free.

Declining such an interview request is common practice. It may also be a mistake. Here are some reasons to reconsider the next time you're called:

Serving as an industry spokesperson affords you and your company a visibility which often is seen as leadership. People like doing business with industry leaders, and speaking for your industry is one way to demonstrate leadership. Seeing or hearing your views expressed publicly, customers gain reassurance that their purchasing decision was correct. Former customers may reevaluate their decision to go elsewhere. And prospects may decide to take a closer look at you.

A company I once worked for, one of the world's largest producers of several key commodity chemicals, purposely invested management time and effort to establish and cultivate relationships with the trade press. Consequently, that company is considered one of the most knowledgeable and accessible sources of market information about those chemicals. If a reporter wants an in-depth look at that segment of the chemical industry, chances are he or she will contact that firm.

Talking to the trade press and other business reporters is a way to shape the discussion of key issues within your industry. "Be willing to talk" is a cardinal rule of media relations in any crisis situation. It's not bad advice for those with marketing responsibilities either. Reporters will write their stories with or without your help. If you're not willing to talk, don't be surprised to see an analysis that misses the mark, or to be disappointed to find the views only of a competitor, a consultant or someone marginally involved in your industry represented in the story.

A business manager I know once complained to me that the market updates in his industry's leading trade publication always seemed to have a particular slant. As it turned out, no one representing any of the manufacturers was willing to talk, so the reporter regularly called a distributor, whose market analysis understandably reflected his particular perspective. When the business manager finally agreed to be interviewed, the publication's market updates began to contain insights only a manufacturer could provide.

Bill Gates' accessibility to the media (he even agreed to a *Playboy* interview in order to promote his ideas) was one way Microsoft was able to influence the discussion of computer software.

Few businesspeople who talk to reporters consider an interview a two-way street. Most are passive rather than active participants—and simply respond to questions, never thinking to ask a few of their own. Yet interviews are often as much an opportunity to obtain information as they are to provide it. Reporters who closely follow an industry regularly talk to various sources: manufacturers, distributors, customers, consultants, regulators, legislators. As a result, they uncover a wealth of information, not all of which is reported. Contrary to popular belief, most reporters will gladly share some of that wealth, but only if asked.

One of the most effective industry spokesmen I know is a vice president who never lets an interview end without asking a few probing questions of his own: "Is my assessment of the market shared by others you've talked to?" If not, "In what ways do their views differ?" "Has anyone in the industry mentioned any plans to expand or consolidate?"

Convinced that talking to the media can be worthwhile?

Here are some guidelines to help you succeed:

- Put yourself in direct contact with reporters. Accepted procedure in some companies is for media inquiries to be handled only by someone in public relations. No PR person, no matter how skilled, knows your industry as well as you do. Rely on the PR department for guidance, including providing background information on the reporter and the publication or news outlet, but not as the only source of information. Do the interview yourself.

- Rarely are trade-press interviews confrontational, but they can be challenging—especially if you lack confidence and competence in dealing with the media. Consider attending a media training workshop that gives you on-camera practice in a small-group setting.

- Bring your own agenda to the interview—a few key points you feel should be addressed. If the reporter doesn't raise those points, inject them into the discussion. For example, use the interview to explain why a price increase was necessary, to alert customers to changing supply conditions, or to educate or mobilize your industry regarding a specific regulatory or legislative development.

Conrad Hilton (of Hilton Hotels) once did a TV interview that ended with the interviewer asking Hilton if he had anything else to say to viewers. Hilton responded, "Yes…place the shower curtain <u>inside</u> the tub." What important message do you want to convey to your audience?

- Consider not only what you say, but also how you say it. A dull, uninspired recitation of facts is unlikely to engage a reporter's interest. Make use of analogies, stories, examples, compelling data, quotable lines.

- Recognize that you have options and exercise some control during the interview. Don't decline an interview because you're concerned about one or two possible questions. If there are some issues you cannot or will not discuss, say so. If your time is limited, establish a time limit for the interview. If it's not appropriate to do an "on-the-record" interview (i.e., everything you say can be attributed to you or your company), consider these alternatives: a "backgrounder" (you can be quoted directly, but neither you nor your company is identified) or an "off-the-record" interview (you are not quoted or identified in any way).

- Be selective in accepting interview requests. Evaluate each news outlet in terms of its importance, credibility and reach. And rather than wait to be contacted, let those on your "A" list know you're accessible. If necessary, ask your PR department or outside PR firm to help facilitate that link. Then keep in touch—just as you would with a customer or prospect. Have lunch with the reporter. Seek her out at a trade show. And be alert to assignment changes at the publication or other outlet.

Establishing a dialogue with reporters who cover your industry is an investment—one that can deliver results at lower cost and with greater credibility than advertising and other forms of sales promotion. Media-savvy managers recognize this and use the media as an integral part of their marketing communications strategy.

DUE DILIGENCE AND THE NEWS MEDIA

Back in the 1980s, I met with some communications professionals at a well known, high-tech firm in Dallas and learned that the company had a full-time position focused solely on media research. The individual who held the position spent her time monitoring what was being said about the company in the news media. Before the company would agree to do a media interview, she would review how the news outlet, and particularly how the reporter, had covered the company or similar companies in the past.

Today, that kind of position is a luxury and a rarity—even in the largest of corporations. But it does serve to remind us that doing some due diligence before a media interview is a good idea.

Often, it's someone in the communications function—someone who may know the reporter, is familiar with the reporter's style, or does some research on the reporter—who provides the interviewee with some valuable background information before an interview takes place. In smaller organizations, the person being interviewed or an outside consulting firm may have to handle this responsibility.

Regardless of who does the due diligence, there are several questions worth answering:

SHOULD I DO THE INTERVIEW?

Many factors go into deciding whether to do an interview, but often the news outlet itself—whether broadcast or print—is a prime consideration. For some companies, *Fox News*, *MSNBC*, *The New York Times* and *Washington Post* are persona non grata. Ditto for those counterculture, free-of-charge, weekly tabloids found in some major cities.

Before deciding whether or not to participate, evaluate each news outlet in terms of its importance (to your company and your communications objective), credibility and reputation, and reach (circulation or viewership).

WHAT ABOUT THE REPORTER?

Expect reporters to do their homework before interviewing you. You should also do some homework of your own. But keep in mind that there are times when it's neither possible nor appropriate to do any research on the reporter. For example, if you get a call or visit from a reporter during a crisis situation, there's probably no reason or way to quickly learn anything about the reporter's background. So the following advice deals with situations where the reporter's background matters:

- Go to the news outlet's website to read the reporter's bio. Key in on educational background, experience, awards won, and most importantly, what position the reporter currently holds. For example, is he or she a general assignment reporter? An investigative or consumer reporter? A beat (specialty) reporter—if so, what beat? However, recognize that these websites are carefully crafted; you're not likely to find anything unflattering.

- Generalizations are dangerous, but there's a bit of activist in every reporter. What they advocate depends on their background and personal circumstances. Journalists are people after all, and it's tough not to bring their personal views into their professional life. So...

- Checking social media is crucial. Facebook, Twitter, LinkedIn and other social media platforms are mirrors to reporters' souls and forums for venting. If a reporter has a potentially damaging agenda, most likely it will be reflected in one of their profiles. And if you're active on social media, especially on sites like LinkedIn or industry forums or blogs, pose a question about others' experiences with the reporter.
- Do a Google search on the reporter. Look for whether the reporter has been involved in any reporting-related disputes, including litigation. Has the reporter "reinvented" himself—e.g., stepped into a different position from one in the past?
- Review some of the stories the reporter has done. What's the reporter's general approach, style or tone? (Larry King had a reputation for asking "softball" questions. Bill O'Reilly interrupted constantly.) I once prepared a client to face Lesley Stahl for a *60 Minutes* interview. Her story was environment-related, so I showed several similar stories she had done in the past to provide an example of Stahl's style. It was quite predictable—similar kinds of questions, similar facial expressions and other body language, similar reactions to interviewees' responses.
- Have a pre-interview discussion with the reporter. You can learn a lot about the reporter's knowledge (or lack of knowledge) of the subject. That can be helpful during the interview. It's also an opportunity to provide some "teasers"—bits of compelling information the reporter may ask you to elaborate on during the interview. Caution: Consider this pre-interview discussion to be on the record; the reporter certainly sees it that way.

Perhaps the best advice comes from a motto used by the Boy Scouts: "Be prepared."

THE EARLY BIRD CATCHES THE WORM (OR HOW TO BENEFIT FROM A CHANGE IN LOCAL TV NEWS)

An interesting development has emerged in many TV markets (especially major ones) throughout the country: Local news programming now starts at 4:00 a.m. That's right, 4:00 in the morning!

In the past, early morning local news shows typically started at 6:00 (Eastern time), followed by national programs such as *The Today Show* and *Good Morning America* at 7:00 a.m. Not any longer. Today, your local TV media is at work long before sunrise. That can mean opportunity for you.

WHY 4:00?

Pre-dawn TV news programs exist for a number of reasons. One is the longer commutes American workers face. People in cities such as Atlanta, New York, Houston and Washington, DC have to hit the road a lot earlier, which means their morning routine—getting up, getting dressed, eating and watching the news—also starts earlier.

Moreover, in order to find new audiences, television executives are courting people who work non-traditional hours—shift workers, nurses, law enforcement personnel, high-tech workers, contract workers, etc.—and those who work from home. In the past, these people were not considered an important demographic.

Also, TV stations must "keep up with the Joneses." If your competitor is on at 4:00, you better be too.

THEIR CHALLENGE IS YOUR OPPORTUNITY

Stations that air these early morning shows face a major challenge. They must now fill 5-6 hours per day (i.e., early morning, along with traditional late morning, afternoon, early evening and late-evening news programming). That's easy to do when there's breaking news—some event or issue that calls for sustained coverage. Stations can also rerun some of the news content that aired the previous day—especially late in that day.

But news is perishable, and stations want something new, something different, something fresh. That's where you come in.

Producers of these early morning programs are hungry for content. They're looking for good story ideas or for guests who are articulate and interesting. If you've got one of those stories or can provide someone who's telegenic, there may not be a better time to get visibility for your company or organization.

SOME TIPS

- **Get over your fear, distrust or dislike of the news media.** View them as an ally or partner rather than as an adversary. Also, don't be reluctant to contact the media. The fact is people in the news business want your tips and story suggestions.
- **The best way to know what kind of content these early morning news shows want is by watching them.** Study the program. Learn the format. For example, you might discover that once a week a local business is profiled. Or contact the station or check its website to see if there's a theme they plan on exploring. (One Cleveland-area station decided to explore the theme, "Changing Gears," and looked at companies that were changing their business model.)

- **Think visually.** Television is a visual medium. Everything revolves around pictures. Stories that have poor or no visuals rarely make the cut. If you can offer a compelling visual—especially one the station can use as a "teaser" (a brief clip shown throughout the day to attract viewers)—you increase the chances that your story idea will be selected.

Which of the following stories do you think has a better chance of making it on camera? Company A decides to make a $50,000 contribution to a local charity, so it decides to have its chairman present a $50,000 check to the head of the charity (think: "grip and grin" photo). Company B decides to donate the same amount to the same charity, but instead has 100 of its employees, each with a $500 company check (or better yet $500 in cash), show up in the charity's lobby or parking lot.

- **Don't pitch trivia.** Companies that expect the news media to be interested in mundane developments such as certain anniversaries or milestones will not be taken seriously and will quickly wear out their welcome. The more you want exposure for your idea, the more it must stand out. One reason some proposals for news show segments are rejected is that there is no identifiable story pattern or drama. The simplest way to describe the structure of a story is: situation, complication, and resolution. All stories follow this pattern. If your organization doesn't have any communications professionals (many of whom are former reporters and know their way around a newsroom), consider using a PR firm for help in identifying (and even pitching) your story ideas.

- **To pitch your idea for an early morning show segment, contact the show's producer.** He or she is the person who has ultimate responsibility for the program's content and for assigning reporters to stories. Typically, the show's producer is identified on the station's website. Some stations also accept story ideas through the "Contact Us" link on their website.

HOW TO MEET THE PRESS

In a word, success with the news media is about control. It's about making happen what you want to happen, rather than hoping it will happen by itself. Put another way, success with the media is about making sure there are two agendas in every interview—the reporter's and yours. Reporters assume control (they're control freaks); you must take and keep control.

Confidence is another component of success. If you're overly nervous or afraid, you're probably not going to do very well. Approaching the assignment confidently and competently is critical. That's why media training came into vogue in the 1970s—and remains one of the best ways to learn how to succeed with the news media. If there's a chance you'll be representing your company to the news media, get some training. Make sure it includes on-camera practice in a small-group or one-on-one setting. In the meantime, here's a brief tutorial on dealing with the news media:

SOME ABSOLUTES

Have a reason for being interviewed

Ask yourself why you plan to talk to the reporter. In addition, ask yourself why the reporter wants to interview you. No interview should ever occur until you know the purpose behind the interaction.

Be prepared

Recognize that the reporter will likely have done plenty of homework. You too need to be prepared. If you participate in the interview unprepared, it's unlikely that you'll achieve your communications objective (i.e., delivering your message). Assign a high priority to preparation.

Have an agenda

Never go into an interview in reactive mode (simply responding to questions). Have some key points (two or three is a good number) that you'll inject into the conversation. How will you do that? One way is when the reporter's questions track with your agenda; simply respond. However, don't assume that will happen. Reporters live in the negative world—What went wrong? Who's at fault? They see the glass half empty. You must see it half full. That's where the bridging technique can help. (See **Q = A+1**, p. 78.)

You cannot win a fight with the media

Maybe you've heard the expression, "Don't pick a fight with anyone who buys ink by the barrel." Before talking to a reporter, ask yourself what your thoughts are about the news media. Some people harbor negative thoughts. And they become combative during the interview, or their demeanor shows antipathy toward the reporter. There's nothing to be gained by you or your company with such an attitude. So do some introspection. Think of it this way: If there's an accident or fatality at your plant, and you're asked to meet with reporters, adopt this mindset—tell yourself you're glad the reporters are there; you welcome this opportunity to tell the public what happened. Don't knowingly or unknowingly come across as confrontational.

Don't lie or bluff

Most people want to be helpful to reporters. So they sometimes guess when they don't know the answer to a question. Avoid the temptation to do this. Tell the reporter you don't know, or that you don't know but will find out. And always tell the truth.

OTHER POINTS TO KEEP IN MIND

Interruptions

Reporters interrupt for a lot of reasons: Your answers are too long. They don't plan to use what you're saying. They have quite a few more questions to ask. They're rude! It's not uncommon for a reporter to interrupt before you've completed your thought. Don't let this happen; you have the right to finish what you're saying. If you are interrupted, continue talking. This happens all the time in normal, day-to-day conversation: two people talk at once; one of them wins out—the more assertive individual. Another strategy is to politely tell the reporter you'd like to finish your answer before moving on to the next question.

Listen—Think—Respond (in that order)

Talking to a reporter can be stressful. So it's understandable that some people respond quickly to a reporter's question (we speed up when we're stressed). However, blurting something out can produce wrong information or poor word choice. Instead, slow the process down. Listen to the question, then think about how to respond. Don't be afraid to take 5-8 seconds. The silence will feel uncomfortable, but here's the good news: thoughtful people pause before answering, so what seems awkward to you actually plays well to the audience. There's a business concept to be avoided, expressed by the phrase, Ready—Fire—Aim. Avoid this as well when talking to reporters.

Use word economy

Both print and broadcast journalists alike prefer answers to their questions to be about 6-12 seconds long. Of course, not all questions can be answered so briefly, so take the amount of time needed. But keep in mind that if you are long-winded (30 seconds is long-winded to a reporter), you run the risk of being edited. The news outlet will find the short soundbite that fits the available space. Long answers also bother TV viewers who are using their remote-control devices to change channels between 36 and 107 times per hour (men and younger people do this more than women and older people do).

Make your messages resonate

As important as it is to go to every interview with an agenda (i.e., your messages) and work that agenda into the interview, sometimes that's just not enough. Some messages are boring. Some are abstract, conceptual—in other words, hard to understand. So ask yourself what messages are worth elaborating on. Here are some tools to do that:

- Analogies
- Stories
- Anecdotes
- Illustrations
- Examples
- Quotable lines

Developing a message with those tools takes up interview time and lengthens the news or feature article, so choose carefully. Determine what message is worthy of additional detail.

MEDIA MISTAKES TO AVOID

Every media interview entails a degree of risk. Here are the most common and damaging mistakes made by those who talk to reporters: (Several are discussed in more detail in this section of the book.)

Personal opinions

Avoid giving them, unless your opinion is in sync with your company's position. The public doesn't care about your opinion; it cares about what your company thinks. Some possible responses to a personal opinion question: "I'm not here to discuss my personal opinion..." or, "My personal opinion is not what's important..."

Speculation

Don't engage in it. "What if...?" questions are dangerous. Talk only about what you know is certain.

Third-party discussions

Don't speak on behalf of someone other than your own organization. For example, if a reporter wants to know why you think one of your suppliers missed a deadline, encourage the reporter to contact that supplier (even if you know the reason for the missed deadline).

Blind source

A reporter may preface a question with, "I've talked to someone who told me..." But how do you know if the reporter actually did talk to someone, or if so, is accurately representing what she was told. Don't respond to comments from unnamed sources—people, news reports, documents, etc. you haven't seen. Instead, say something like the following: "I don't know whom you talked to, but you were given some wrong information. Here's the correct information..." "I haven't seen the news report you're referring to, so I'm not in a position to respond until I can read that report myself."

"No comment"

This terse, two-word phrase is loaded with connotation—all of it negative. It implies evasion or guilt. Explain to the reporter why you won't comment (e.g., lack of knowledge, pending or possible litigation, proprietary technology, etc.).

Off-the-record

It's a complicated concept (discussed elsewhere in this book), but it's best to consider that anything you say in the presence of a reporter will be used.

Repeating negatives

When responding to a question, it's easy to repeat some of the reporter's words in your answer. If some of those words are highly emotional and negative, you're reinforcing them. Here's an example:

Question: "Is this the darkest day in your company's history?"
Wrong answer: "No, I wouldn't say this is the darkest day in our company's history."
Next question: "What would you say was the darkest day in your company's history?"
Better answer to the original question: "What happened today was a very unusual and unfortunate accident…"

Not repeating negatives requires real concentration. You've got to recognize the negative, edit it out of your response, and replace it with something less volatile.

Filling silence

Mike Wallace (legendary *60 Minutes* correspondent) was the master of this technique. At some point during an interview (usually with someone accused of wrongdoing), Wallace would simply stare at the individual and remain silent. Silence is uncomfortable and the interviewee, not knowing what to say or do, would usually start to squirm…and talk. For Wallace: mission accomplished! What the interviewee needed to do was simply remain silent, but confident, or ask Wallace if he had any other questions.

In other interview situations, the reporter may simply pause in order to think of another question. In that case, fill the silence with a new or previous key point.

Losing composure

This runs the gamut from getting emotional or crying to touching a reporter or grabbing the camera or microphone. Any of these actions will get you a lot of air time. Note: In a crisis, such as an accident involving injury or loss of life, it's okay to express the appropriate emotion, but avoid crying; it does not inspire confidence.

Q = A+1

One of the most important communication tools you can use in media interviews and in the Q&A segment of any speech or presentation is a technique known as "bridging."

Think about the equation, Q = A+1. "Q" represents the question. When someone asks you a question, you should answer or address it. That's the "A." Some clarification: "Addressing" could relate to situations where you don't know the answer or where it would be inappropriate to answer (e.g., proprietary information, pending or possible litigation, etc.).

For instance, let's say someone asks you how much you paid for your home. You could reveal the price (answer) or you might say that you prefer not to provide that number (address).

Another option is to address the question by responding that you prefer not to reveal the price, but rather than stopping there, add the following (+1): "What I can say is that homes in the area where I live range between $___ and $___" (if you're comfortable providing a range).

To get to the "1," all you need are some transition words ("+"). Here are a few:

- What I do know is…
- What's more important is…
- What concerns me even more…
- The most important thing…
- That's one view; mine is…
- Let me reemphasize…
- One final point…
- What's important for people to know…
- For example…
- Here's an even tougher question…
- From my perspective…
- Something I'm even more familiar with…
- Another way to say that is…

Bridging provides two major benefits: First, it enables you to use any question as a springboard to your agenda or message (+1). Remember, your "+1" need not relate to the "Q." (Your "A" must relate to the "Q.") Second, it enables you to try to change the direction of the questioning. For example, if you get a question or questions that are irrelevant, negative, etc., respond, but then bridge to another point. The questioner may follow your lead to the topic you introduced. (Reporters are especially good listeners and may pick up on a good piece of new information.)

Use the bridging technique sparingly. Don't bridge with every question. You'll come across as "programmed" or too "controlling." And if the questions are tracking with your agenda, you don't need to bridge at all, unless you want to reinforce a certain message that's already been discussed.

Also, keep in mind what bridging is not. It is not a technique we frequently see politicians use on the evening or Sunday morning talk shows. They get a question, fail to answer or address it, but go directly to their agenda. And their credibility with the audience plummets.

Bill Belichick—not the most media-friendly coach in the NFL.

Bill Belichick, coach of the New England Patriots, frequently skips the "A." Here he is at a weekly pre-game press conference, several days before his team would play the San Diego Chargers. It happened right after he and his team were penalized for "Spygate." (Spygate was an incident during the NFL's 2007 season, when the Patriots were disciplined by the league for videotaping New York Jets' defensive coaches' signals during a game.)

Reporter's question: "Do you care to comment on people suggesting that this has happened in the past?"

Belichick: "All my focus is on the San Diego Chargers. Just working to get ready for that team."

Reporter's question: "You want to address the fans?"

Belichick:	"We're moving on to San Diego. That's what I'm addressing."
Reporter's question:	"Are you able to pay a half-million dollars in installments, or do you have to pay it up front?"
Belichick:	"Just thinking about the Chargers."

I like to think about what I would have offered Coach Belichick as a possible response to a question on Spygate. He would have ignored my advice, but here it is: "We made a bad call. If we could have a do-over, we wouldn't record any signals. Now our focus is on the San Diego Chargers." And to any follow-up question on Spygate, the response would be: "I've already said everything I want to about that matter. Now, our focus is on the Chargers."

Mastering the bridging technique takes some practice. Most of us are used to responding to a question, and then stopping. Bridging involves recognizing that you can occasionally add another point before taking the next question. Write the equation, $Q = A+1$ on the notes you're using during an interview, press briefing or presentation, as a reminder to use this powerful tool.

TO SUCCEED WITH A REPORTER, THINK LIKE A REPORTER

Interacting with the news media can take many forms: a broadcast interview—TV or radio, live or recorded. An interview with a print reporter. A press briefing or news conference. Or you can issue a news release. Regardless of what vehicle or approach you use, you'll always be confronted by this question: "What do I say?"

To answer that question, it helps if you know a thing or two about how reporters do their jobs—more specifically, how they write. Examine any news story and you'll see that it follows a predictable pattern or formula. Most reporters learn that formula in their journalism class or through on-the-job training.

Here are the key elements of that formula:

The 5Ws and 1H

When you talk to a reporter, expect to be asked one or more of the following questions: Who? What? When? Where? Why? How? Reporters consider these to be among the most important tools in their tool kit. So, when developing your message, be sure to address as many of those questions as are appropriate or applicable to the topic. Doing so can help reduce the number of questions or follow-up questions you'll get.

The inverted pyramid

Every reporter is familiar with the inverted pyramid. It's taught on the first day of class in Journalism 101. Picture an upside-down triangle, with the broad base at the top and the small tip at the bottom. The base represents the most important information; the tip represents the least important. If you provide information in most-important to least-important sequence, you're making it easier for reporters to write their stories. In a way, you're gaining some control over the reporting process.

Substantive messages

Reporters are trained to be (or are born) skeptical or cynical, so they are likely to challenge or ignore statements that lack substance. Consider these statements: "People are our most important resource." "Our firm is very concerned about the environment." "Safety is our number one priority." These are not substantive statements. They're glittering generalities, platitudes, clichés. Now consider this statement: "Our company puts a high priority on safety. This plant has gone five years without a lost-time accident, and we've been recognized by the U.S. Occupational Safety and Health Administration as one of the safest industrial sites in America." That's meaningful and powerful.

Brevity

Limit the amount of information you share. Providing too much detail is counterproductive—not only for the audience who'll struggle to remember what you said, but also for the reporter who must ferret out the core. I once came across a news release that was the entire transcript of a presentation made by several company executives, rather than a summary of their key points. Any guess where that news release ended up when it reached some editor? Try "circular file" (aka wastebasket). Responses to reporters also need to be brief—6-12 seconds if possible. Master the skill of word economy.

Memorable quotes

Reporters want good quotes. In fact, they need good quotes—to use in headlines, pull-outs in the story, photo captions, etc. The day after five Dallas police officers were shot and killed, the Dallas police chief said this about his officers at his news conference: "We don't feel support most days. Let's not make this most days." Good quotes are gold to a reporter. Serve up a few in your next media interview.

Reporters have significant control over the reporting process. One example of that is the power of editing—it's totally in their hands. But if you have a powerful message and you package it in a way reporters prefer, chances are it will appear in what they print or broadcast.

THE POWER OF A GOOD QUOTE

A successful interaction with a reporter involves knowing something about how reporters do their jobs. For example, reporters like you to provide information in the proper order—most important information first.

Reporters also want short responses. Avoid long-winded answers to their questions. Focus on the essentials. Provide detail, if asked.

Reporters are always looking for good quotes—to use in the headline, to use as direct or indirect quotes in the story, to use in bold type as pull-out quotes, or to use as captions for photos. Good quotes are among the most powerful and versatile tools in journalism.

Here are some memorable quotes you've probably heard:

> "Never in the field of human conflict was so much owed by so many to so few."
> *Winston Churchill*
>
> "Mr. Gorbachev, tear down this wall."
> *Ronald Reagan*
>
> "That's one small step for man, one giant leap for mankind."
> *Neil Armstrong*
>
> "Ask not what your country can do for you, ask what you can do for your country."
> *John F. Kennedy*

You may be thinking, "But I can't come up with lines like those." Think again. Good quotes are not beyond your reach. All that's required is a little effort. Here are some tools that can help you craft your own memorable quotes. You may recognize a few of these devices from high school English class:

Repetition: Repeating words at the beginning, in the middle or at the end of a series. "… and that government of the people, by the people, for the people shall not perish from the earth." (Lincoln)

Rhyming words: "If it doesn't fit, you must acquit." (Johnny Cochran)

Metaphor: A type of analogy. It describes a subject by comparing it to some unrelated object. "All the world's a stage, and all the men and women merely players." (Shakespeare)

Alliteration: The repetition of a particular sound in the stressed syllables of a series of words or phrases. "Nattering nabobs of negativism." (Vice President Spiro T. Agnew)

Simile: A figure of speech that compares two different things, usually by using the words "like" or "as." "I float like a butterfly and sting like a bee." (Muhammad Ali)

Allusions: References to familiar songs, scripture, literature, movies, TV shows, politics, etc. "Go ahead, make my day." (Harry Callahan, aka Clint Eastwood)

Catchy, clever, unusual words or phrases: "Her ad-libbed lines were well rehearsed." (Rod Stewart)

Unusual sentence structure or word order: "From such adventures spring stories, if not wisdom." (Unknown)

Here are some actual quotes found in various news and feature stories. Which are the winners? Which are the losers?

1. "We're going to stick to our knitting and make the best products. And we think if we do that, we've got a very, very good business ahead of us." (Apple CEO Tim Cook, quoted in *Fortune* magazine)

2. "There are times when you must put force at the service of peace." (Former U.N. Secretary-General Kofi Annan, quoted on NPR)

3. "Changing culture is not a sprint. It's a marathon. It's very, very hard to affect culture." (Former Yahoo CEO Carol Bartz, quoted in *Fortune* magazine)

4. "Today anyone armed with a hundred-dollar digital camera and a connection to the internet is a potential Spielberg or Riefenstahl." (Authors Deirdre Collings and Rafal Rohozinski, quoted in *Harvard Business Review*)

5. "The China we see now is an exclamation point followed by a question mark." (Sidney Rittenburg, quoted on NPR)

Numbers 1 and 3 are weak. They contain clichés—worn out expressions that have lost their power over time. The other three quotes are superb—thought-provoking and memorable. They don't sound contrived or too clever, or like they were written by someone in PR. They're genuine.

You don't need to be an English major to come up with a great line. All that's needed is a little creativity. And a desire to captivate the media by giving them something they'll print or broadcast.

HOW TO ANSWER THE QUESTION, "WHAT IF ... ?"

Janet Reno, America's first female attorney general (1993-2001), was one tough lawyer. Among the challenges she faced during her time at the Department of Justice were the siege of the Branch Davidian compound in Waco, Texas, and the fight over the custody and immigration status of a young Cuban boy, Elian Gonzalez.

Reno was also tough on reporters who asked hypothetical questions. For example, consider these two questions and her responses:

Reporter: "The Treasury Department's report on the Waco tragedy reports that federal agents, its own agents, violated standing orders, and then lied about their conduct. When the Justice Department report comes out next week, if it is found and reported that some of your own people did the same thing, will they be penalized—will they be punished?"
Reno: "I never deal in 'what ifs'."

Reporter: "What if there were a circumstance where an overnight stay at the White House for political donors constituted violation of federal law. Would the Justice Department investigate it?"
Reno: "You know, I don't do 'what ifs'."

Reno's standard reply to hypothetical questions, "I don't do 'what ifs'," frustrated reporters, some of whom tried to defend their hypotheticals and press for a response. No matter. Reno would simply repeat, "I don't do 'what ifs'."

I like Reno's media savvy, but can't recommend that you use the former Attorney General's terse reply if you're asked a hypothetical question. Reno's position and temperament allowed her to use the line. You need to soften your response. More about that later.

But first, what are hypothetical questions and why are they dangerous?

Hypothetical questions are about something imaginary rather than something real. They often begin with, "What if..." and are then followed by a layered set of circumstances that are all fiction. For example, let's say you're a manager at a nuclear power plant and you do an interview with a reporter preparing a story on plant security. The conversation goes as follows:

Reporter: "What if a terrorist were able to gain entry to your facility?"
You: "That couldn't happen because we have tight security."
Reporter: "What if your security failed?"
You: "We have a back-up plan in case that happens."
Reporter: "What if that back-up plan failed?"
You: "That's never happened."

Reporter: "What if there were a first time?"
You: ?

By speculating or answering that first hypothetical question, you set in motion a series of questions that weaken your responses. And you provide quotable material for the reporter.

Hypothetical questions are asked out of interest, as the answers will have no effect on the situation. Another danger, according to research led by Duke University, is that hypothetical questions, depending on how they are worded—positively or negatively—can influence our answers and even our actions. "Hypothetical questions are essentially wolves in sheep's clothing," says Gavan Fitzsimons, professor of marketing and psychology at Duke's Fuqua School of Business.

So, how should you respond to a reporter's hypothetical question? Don't play the "What if" game. You cannot win. Instead, limit your responses to what is known. For example, if there's an accident at your facility, someone is injured, and a reporter asks, "What if that person dies?", your response should not be to express remorse for a possible fatality or talk about what you'd do for the deceased's family. Instead, say, "What we know is that Bill is in the hospital, he's in good hands and we're pulling for him."

How about the earlier question, "What if a terrorist were able to gain entry to your facility?" Here's the recommended response: "That hasn't happened, and we take every precaution to keep the facility and the community secure." If the reporter persists by asking, "But couldn't it happen?", repeat your initial answer.

Oh, by the way, there's one kind of "What if" question I like: The icebreaker kind—popular for parties, work events and dating. Want to get people to connect? To brainstorm? Have them play a "What if" game with questions such as, "What if you were stuck on a deserted island; what three things would you bring?"

HOW TO AVOID AN OFF-THE-RECORD PROBLEM

Shortly after their son Newt Gingrich became Speaker of the House of Representatives in 1995, Mr. and Mrs. Gingrich agreed to appear on CBS's *Eye to Eye* with Connie Chung. During the interview, Chung asked Mrs. Gingrich what her son had told her about President Clinton. Mrs. Gingrich said, "Nothing. And I can't tell you what he said about Hillary."

Chung leaned forward and quietly replied, "You can't? Why don't you just whisper it to me—just between you and me." The response from Mrs. Gingrich: "She's a b----."

After the interview, Chung explained to viewers that "Mrs. Gingrich was sitting before three cameras, with lights and a microphone on. It was clear that what she said would be broadcast." A low blow, but perhaps there are no inappropriate questions, only inappropriate answers.

Off-the-record comments to reporters remain one of the most frequent mistakes made by those who interact with the news media. Many people believe that if they preface or follow a comment made to a reporter with the statement, "This is off the record," the information won't be used. Not necessarily.

Some ground rules: There are several different ways to talk to a reporter:

On the record.

Anything you say can be quoted directly or indirectly and attributed to you or your company by name. Remember this "default" assumption: unless you have already established otherwise, you are always on the record.

Here are some other types of interviews. Keep in mind that you can move in and out of them during the same conversation:

Off the record.

You're giving the reporter information he can't use in the story. For example, say you've agreed to be interviewed, but a day or two before the interview, you learn of a significant company development that will be announced after the interview takes place. To prevent the reporter from writing something that will make him appear foolish or out of touch, you reveal the information, but do so off the record. He cannot use the information until after you make it public, but he takes the embargoed information into account when writing his piece.

Off the record does not apply retroactively, so be sure to establish that you are speaking off the record and get the reporter's agreement before you reveal sensitive information.

Not for attribution.

The reporter can directly quote the information, but can't ascribe it to you or your company by name. If you're concerned about being identified, be sure to negotiate with the reporter the exact wording of the attribution—e.g., "a knowledgeable source," "a Wall Street analyst," "an industry observer," etc.

Background.

The reporter can use the information but not quote it, and the attribution must remain general—e.g., "according to a company official, . ."

Deep background.

The reporter can use the information but not quote it, and may not attribute it to anyone. In other words, she must say it on her own.

Caveat Orator: Speaking to a reporter on any basis other than on the record is risky. You may run the risk that he or she may inadvertently or intentionally reveal something sensitive. If you go off the record, here are several safeguards to keep in mind:

Know the reporter.

If you don't know the reporter and haven't developed a close working relationship, you are more likely to get burned.

Know the medium.

A news outlet with an ongoing interest in your organization is less likely to violate a confidence. Still, the best policy is never to say anything you wouldn't want repeated.

Assume every camera and microphone are on and are attached to a recorder somewhere.

Although the interview or program may not have started, the equipment could be on. Likewise for after the interview.

Don't make off-the-record comments before the interview starts.

Instead, break the ice with the reporter by chatting about safe subjects (e.g., weather, sports, etc.). Better yet, share an interesting (and important) piece of information about your topic; the reporter may bring it up during the interview—handing you an opportunity to discuss it.

Let's end with a classic off-the-record comment: During a radio microphone test in 1984, President Reagan jokingly said, "My fellow Americans, I am pleased to tell you I just signed legislation which outlaws Russia forever. The bombing begins in five minutes."

"THERE ARE NO GUARANTEES." OUCH!

One of the trickiest questions you might get from a reporter (or during the Q&A portion of a business presentation) is whether you can provide a guarantee: "Can you guarantee that you'll never have another explosion at your plant?" "Can you guarantee that this merger will not result in any layoffs?"

Your instinct with such questions may be to respond by saying something like, "No, I can't guarantee that." Or, "There are no guarantees in life." Understandable responses—and usually true statements, but damaging quotes. Avoid them.

Here's a better way to handle the "guarantee" trap: Resist the temptation to acknowledge the obvious—namely, that you can't give a guarantee. That's usually what most people begin with. But then they go on to elaborate: "What I can guarantee is that our company takes safety very seriously, and we're going to do everything we can to prevent this kind of thing from ever happening again."

By responding this way, you still answer the question, but you don't deliver the potentially damaging prefatory statement. If the reporter tries a second time ("But I asked you if you're prepared to provide a guarantee..."), simply repeat your response.

And if by chance you can provide a guarantee, go for it.

THE PERILS OF A PERSONAL OPINION

When Chick-fil-A CEO Dan Cathy publicly stated he disapproved of gay marriage, most likely he never anticipated the firestorm his opinion would create. But create one it did.

Here are some lessons to be learned when an authority figure shares a personal opinion publicly:

First, some background: Chick-fil-A is a fast food restaurant specializing in chicken sandwiches. It operates some 2,400 restaurants in the United States. The company was founded by Truett Cathy, Dan Cathy's father; his strongly held Christian beliefs permeate the company's culture. For example, Chick-fil-A's outlets are closed on Sunday.

Cathy made several public statements opposing same-sex marriage. In one interview with a Christian news organization, he said, "I think we are inviting God's judgment on our nation when we shake our fist at Him and say, 'We know better than you as to what constitutes a marriage.' I pray God's mercy on our generation that has such a prideful, arrogant attitude to think we have the audacity to define what marriage is about."

Once Cathy's comments were widely reported, the following happened:

- Students at several colleges and universities wanted the company's restaurants banned from their campuses.
- Gay-rights groups called for protests and boycotts. (Gay couples staged a "kiss-in" at some outlets.)
- Mayors of Chicago, Boston and San Francisco said Chick-fil-A was not welcome in their cities.
- The Jim Henson Company (think: Muppets) ended its licensing agreement with Chick-fil-A.

It remains to be seen what the long-term effect Cathy's statement of personal opinion will have on the company's reputation. But Chick-fil-A seems to have learned a lesson about the perils of sharing a personal opinion. The company eventually released a statement saying, "Going forward, our intention is to leave the policy debate over same-sex marriage to the government and political arenas."

Consider the following before sharing a personal opinion during an interview:

- In general, the public does not care about your personal opinion. They care about what you say because of whom you represent.
- You cannot publicly separate yourself from your organization. Even if you say you are not speaking for your organization, the public (including the news media) will not make this distinction.
- When someone expresses a view not held by his or her organization, that's conflict. And conflict is newsworthy.
- If your opinion is in sync with that of your organization, there may be no problem in sharing it—depending on what the issue is. (Cathy's problem was that he addressed a sensitive, controversial issue he should have avoided.)
- A good response to a reporter who asks for your personal opinion is to say, "I'm not here to discuss my personal opinion." Or, "My personal opinion is not important." Then go on to share your organization's views.

The best advice is this: Remember that you are not speaking for yourself; you are representing your company. Avoid offering a personal opinion.

"NO COMMENT!"

As part of a news investigation of employee misconduct within the Tarrant County (Texas) District Attorney's Office, WFAA-TV in Dallas-Fort Worth observed chief investigator Don Moore during work hours over the course of ten days. On each of those days, the station's undercover cameras photographed Moore engaging in a predictable pattern of either leaving work early to head to a bar or arriving to work in the morning late—sometimes an hour or two late. And when he left work to go to a bar, he would always be in his county-owned Lincoln. Even on days when Moore didn't go to work, he would show up at the bar to join coworkers for a cocktail. On the tenth day, investigative reporter Brett Shipp decided to ask Moore a few questions as Moore got out of his car:

Shipp: "I'm Brett Shipp with Channel 8 News. May I ask you a few questions?"
Moore: "No comment."
Shipp: "Did you cut out of work a little early today?"
Moore: "No comment."
Shipp: "How many hours a day do you work, sir?"
Moore: "No comment."
Shipp: "Is this a county-owned vehicle you're driving?"

Moore: "No comment."

Moore then got back into his car and drove off.

Regardless of whether Moore had engaged in professional misconduct, most viewers of the broadcast probably concluded that he had. The phrase, "No comment," implies that you are either guilty or hiding something.

So, what should Mr. Moore have done when ambushed? He had several options: One would have been to speak to the reporter—right then and there. However, for this strategy to be successful, Moore would have had to know exactly what to say (and it's doubtful he knew he was the subject of an investigative story) and say it in a confident manner.

A second option would have been to tell the reporter that he'd like to set up a meeting to talk.

Another option would have been to indicate that his organization's policy is that all media inquiries have to go through the appropriate channel at the district attorney's office.

Moore did one thing right: Rather than go into the bar, he got back into his car and drove off. Not a good visual, but preferable to going into the bar (the reporter would have followed him).

MASTERING THE REMOTE ... INTERVIEW

Watch television news today—network or cable, national or local, newscast or news magazine—and chances are you'll see someone participating in a remote or satellite interview, where the interviewer and interviewee are in different locations. There are a number of reasons for this trend, which is likely to continue.

For one thing, Americans consider the electronic media their preferred source of news. Not surprisingly, the number of electronic news sources continues to grow. Today's business executive, for example, has many more opportunities to appear on camera than did his counterpart of yesterday. Just consider the proliferation of business and financial programs on CNBC or Bloomberg—all with an insatiable need for spokespersons.

Also, advances in technology have made microwave and satellite feeds more accessible, reliable and affordable.

In today's highly mobile society, remote interviews allow reporters to link up with experts, no matter where they are—experts who bring greater credibility, importance and immediacy to the broadcast.

Any media interview involves a certain degree of risk and should be approached with caution. However, remote interviews present participants with a unique set of challenges. Here are some of those challenges and how to deal with them:

AN UNNATURAL SITUATION

Doing a remote interview may involve going to a TV studio or some other location. If it's the former, the studio is probably empty and "cold." It's just you and most likely one or two other people, such as the camera operator.

Most importantly, the reporter interviewing you isn't there, so there's no human being to relate to—no face-to-face interaction. All of this is likely to keep you from relaxing or warming up—a difficult thing to do even if a reporter were there. In the absence of someone to play off of, it's really tough.

Suggestions:
- Consider taking a colleague with you in order to make the environment more comfortable.
- If the opportunity presents itself, explore the option of doing the interview from your office or home—a comfortable, familiar, relaxed setting. If that's not possible, get to the studio early so you can get acclimated to the setting.
- During the interview, you must make a special effort to increase your energy (both visual and vocal) and to communicate with feeling.
- Smile (if appropriate)—early and often. Be sure the first thing viewers see is a visage that says, "I'm comfortable and I'm happy to be here."

HEAD AND SHOULDERS

That's the camera shot that will be used—how you'll appear on TV, throughout the entire interview.

Suggestions:
- Sit still. Don't make any unusual movements.
- Natural gestures are fine, but keep in mind that the audience may not see your hands. So you must use your facial expression and voice (inflection) to communicate energy, enthusiasm and confidence.
- Remain seated at the end of the interview. Don't bolt out of the chair. You may still be on air, and you don't want the audience to think you're eager to leave. Don't get up until you're told.
- Don't remove your microphone or earpiece; let the technician do that.

WHERE TO LOOK

The rule of thumb for most media interviews is to look at the interviewer and ignore the camera. For remote interviews, however, the problem with this advice is that the interviewer is elsewhere.

Suggestions:
- In a remote interview, you must master the technique of looking at the camera. It becomes the surrogate reporter.
- Resist the temptation to look at a human face—the camera operator or anyone else in the room.
- If there's a monitor in the room (on which the interviewer appears), don't look at it—even if it's close to or attached to the camera. The presence of a monitor usually does more harm than good. Instead, look at the camera and try to visualize the reporter.
- Be careful of TelePrompters, which are usually attached to the camera. If one is there and hasn't been turned off, you may be able to see yourself in the reflected glass—a real distraction. Ask the technician to turn it off.
- During the interview, consider yourself always "on." In other words, maintain proper eye contact and demeanor (including facial expression) even when the interviewer or another guest is talking. (There may be interest in seeing your reaction to something, or there may simply be a miscue.)

THE EARPIECE OR IFB

It's uncomfortable and can create problems (e.g., fall out, malfunction, etc.). Have you ever noticed how many interviewees are bothered by the earpiece during a remote interview?

Suggestions:
- Be sure to have the technician test the volume level before the interview begins. If it's too loud or soft, say so.
- To minimize the chances of having it fall out of your ear, have the technician tape the wire to the back of your collar or dress—leaving a bit of slack on the wire for you to move your head.
- If you frequently participate in remote interviews, consider purchasing your own earpiece. Customized earpieces are developed by using a mold taken from your ear. They fit better and are less obtrusive—almost invisible. Go to a shop that sells hearing aids to get one.

- If excessive noise is coming from your earpiece, take it out of your ear. Then tell the interviewer what happened, but finish making your point. Likewise, if you lose audio, continue to talk. Such a development can be a blessing in disguise—giving you an opportunity to bridge to a point you'd like to make. For example, say something like this: "Bill, we seem to have lost our audio, but an important point to mention about the issue we've been discussing is…"

SOME ADVICE FOR EMAIL INTERVIEWS

When most of us think of a news media interview, we usually have in mind someone talking to a reporter in person, by phone or in a TV "remote" where reporter and interviewee are in different locations. But another way to interact with the news media is through an email or text message interview.

Although email interviews are still the exception, they are becoming more common. For the reporter, they offer several advantages:

- These interviews make it easier for reporters to handle the greater number of stories they're being assigned per day or per week. Workloads for journalists have increased.
- Email interviews save time—eliminating telephone tag between reporter and interviewee.
- They can increase a reporter's success rate in getting people to cooperate on a story. Individuals who might be reluctant to talk to a reporter often feel more comfortable communicating via email.
- Email interviews are also useful for interviewing people in different time zones, or people who struggle speaking English but can write it more easily.

On the downside:

- The reporter can't be certain who's actually responding. The information could have been crafted by a PR professional and reviewed or revised by layers of management, including a lawyer.
- It's difficult for the reporter to ask follow-up questions.
- The reporter can't see or hear the interviewee, so a lot of nuances can be missed.

For the interviewee, a major advantage of participating in an email interview is that it allows you time to develop thoughtful, precise responses. No need to worry about saying something spontaneous you'll regret later.

Here's some advice to consider if you're queried by a reporter via email:

- Respond to questions succinctly. Remember the admonition that if I ask you what time it is, don't build me a watch. Long, written answers are just as susceptible to editing by reporters as are long-winded vocal responses. And you might not like what the reporter decides to use or not use.
- When most of us write, we tend toward the formal. Avoid this. Respond in a conversational style—contractions, short sentences, incomplete sentences, etc. Write the way you talk. In other words, write for the ear, not for the page.
- Don't approach the interview in a "reactive" mode—i.e., simply responding to the questions asked. Have some key points and find a way to include them in an answer or two. For example, after a question, respond, but then add a point of your own.
- Find a way to include some powerful soundbites the reporter can't resist—analogies, stories, examples, anecdotes, quotable lines, etc.
- Don't feel you must answer every question. If you don't know the answer (and cannot obtain it), say so. Ditto for inappropriate questions or questions seeking confidential or proprietary information. Politely explain why you cannot respond.
- Honor the reporter's deadline. Respond promptly; don't place the query aside or sit on it too long.

Email interviews can be a win-win for reporter and interviewee alike. Some people like them because there's a written record of what was said. True enough. If you've not yet had an email query from a reporter, chances are you may get one.

PRESS BRIEFINGS AND NEWS CONFERENCES

The terms, press briefing and news conference are often used interchangeably. And while there are some similarities between them, these are two different tools used to communicate with the news media.

PRESS BRIEFING

In general, press briefings tend to be somewhat impromptu and informal. They also tend to be brief (hence the name, "briefing"). Here's how they work:

Let's say something happens (e.g., an explosion and fire at your facility). Reporters (a few or many), who may hear about it on the police radios they frequently monitor, show up at your facility—usually very quickly. They're in your parking lot, your lobby, outside your plant gate. You decide to talk to them right where they are. Or perhaps you escort them to a conference room or direct them to a specific location (e.g., a hotel or even a nearby field) if access to your facility is not possible. You approach them authoritatively, and then do the following:

1. **Introduce yourself.** Reporters want to know your name and the organization you represent. Although there are some exceptions, it's generally not a good idea to volunteer your title. For example, if you're an attorney, and you share that fact, a lot of the questions you get will be legal in nature. If asked your title or role in the company, however, give it. Spelling your name also makes sense.

2. **Set some ground rules.** Tell the reporters how you plan to conduct the briefing. For example, "I have very little information to share at this time, but I am here to tell you what we do know. Then I'll take some questions." Setting ground rules is psychological; it's designed to show reporters that you, not they, will control the briefing.

3. **Share your information.** Be sure to express empathy when appropriate. Use notes or read a prepared statement.

4. **Q&A.** It's optional... because early on in a crisis, you may have very little information, so it makes little or no sense to take questions. Or you may decide to take questions at your follow-up press briefing. However, keep in mind that reporters are used to asking questions, and one way for an organization to appear cooperative and forthcoming is by taking questions. In short, it's your call.

5. **End and exit.** One form of control you have in a press briefing is deciding when to end it. Do so politely, but authoritatively. Once you've made the decision to leave, don't hang around and resume taking questions; you'll appear weak.

NEWS CONFERENCE

News conferences tend to be longer and more formal. For a news conference, you contact the news media and invite them to a specific location at a specific time. Obviously, there should be an important reason for the conference (e.g., major announcement, important update, etc.). Set up the room (e.g., seating, lectern, PowerPoint, sound projection, refreshments, etc.) as appropriate. Suggested format:

1. **Welcoming remarks.**
2. **Introductions.** Be sure to introduce yourself and any others who will be speaking. Do it at the outset; you don't want reporters wondering who some of the individuals are.
3. **Agenda.** Identify the sequence you'll follow. For example, with an accident, tell reporters you plan to start with a brief review of what initially happened. Then, you'll bring them up to speed on where things stand now. And afterwards, you'll take questions.
4. **Share your information.** (Remember empathy.)
5. **Q&A** (mandatory). News conferences must include a Q&A segment. Don't invite reporters to your event, and then not let them ask questions.
6. **Concluding remarks.** Usually a quick recap of the key message(s).
7. **Ending.** Thank the reporters and adjourn.
8. **Post-conference interview(s).** This is at your discretion; some reporters may request a brief interview with someone who spoke at the news conference.

PEYTON MANNING: SUPERSTAR ~~QUARTERBACK~~ COMMUNICATOR

If you're an Indianapolis Colts fan, you may remember when Peyton Manning announced his departure from the team. It was at a news conference conducted jointly by Manning and Colts owner Jim Irsay, and it's a great example of how to, and how not to, conduct a news conference.

Manning's portion of the conference was impressive:

He prepared.
He scripted his remarks and stayed on script.

He was concise.
His prepared remarks lasted a mere two and a half minutes.

His message was solid.
Football fans know that circumstances surrounding Manning's departure after fourteen seasons could have tempted the quarterback to make some tough, unpleasant comments. But true to form, he was dignified and classy. He talked mainly about the Colts support staff and his behind-the-scenes memories. He ended with a thank you to Colts fans everywhere.

He showed emotion.

Losing composure in a news conference is something to be avoided. And Manning choked up a bit and he struggled to keep his composure throughout his prepared remarks. But it was perfectly understandable and appropriate. (I'm betting some people watching him got choked up as well.)

Peyton Manning's impressive performance at his Colts departure news conference prompted one sports columnist to write, "The video of his performance should be required viewing for every professional athlete in every sport."

Perhaps Christine Brennan, sports columnist for *USA Today*, said it best: "The video of his performance should be required viewing for every professional athlete in every sport."

Then there was Jim Irsay's portion of the news conference. It was painful to watch:

He seemed unprepared.

It appeared that he either didn't have or didn't use notes. Even the most gifted speaker can benefit from having and using a road map.

He was long-winded.

His remarks were more than six minutes. The audience probably tuned him out after several minutes.

He rambled.

His comments, though gracious and heartfelt, lost their power because they were unorganized and repetitive.

His delivery was poor.

He spoke in a near monotone. So just about everything he said sounded the same. Nothing stood out. And I counted more than a hundred "uhs" and "ums." These "non-words," which destroy fluid delivery, usually disappear when the speaker takes time to practice.

Press briefings and news conferences are two ways to communicate with the news media. Conducting them is not always easy, but they are skills businesspeople (and athletes) are well advised to have.

Oh, by the way: A few weeks after the news conference, Peyton Manning called a number of newspaper reporters in Indianapolis to thank them for the work they did during his years with the Colts. According to one of the reporters, "That's the first time I've ever received a good-bye call from a Colts player in my journalism career. Classy move." Agreed!

HOW TO HANDLE ERRORS IN REPORTING

Errors in news reporting are all too common occurrences—especially in today's highly competitive news business where being first, rather than being accurate, with a story can give a news outlet a distinct advantage.

ABC News chief national correspondent Matt Gutman made a false statement on air following the death of basketball great Kobe Bryant. Gutman inaccurately reported that Bryant and all four of his daughters were on board the helicopter that crashed into the California hills. Bryant and his 13-year-old daughter were killed, but his other three children were not on board the aircraft.

So, what's the best way to handle reporter errors?

First, determine how serious the mistake is. Some errors simply warrant no action at all. If your title is plant manager but you were identified as a site manager in a story, that's probably no big deal. Some mistakes can be frustrating and may even upset your management, but there's no real damage done.

What's more, keep in mind that if you ask for, and get, a correction, the error may be repeated along with the correction. Take a careful, objective look at what happened, and ask yourself if it's a "go to the mat" situation.

In most cases the best approach is to contact the reporter directly and point out the mistake. Your objective is to get the reporter to correct his notes and to prevent future or follow-up stories from repeating the error. Don't run to the editor first; that's like going to someone's boss before trying to resolve a problem directly with the co-worker who caused it. Bad protocol.

If the error is serious, you might want to request a correction, but understand that it probably won't get the same placement and visibility as the original story. Don't try to dictate how the correction should be handled. Tell the reporter why the mistake is damaging.

Within minutes of his telephone interview on *Larry King Live*, former Senator George Mitchell called back to correct factual misstatements being made about Major League Baseball's steroid problem by another guest on the program. The polite but assertive correction was broadcast live. Amazing, but don't expect that kind of treatment.

In situations such as errors in high-profile stories, or mistakes in a series of stories (including mistakes of omission or balance), consider writing a letter to the editor or its broadcast equivalent. Reputable news organizations welcome this feedback.

In rare instances, you might even want to place an ad if there's a dispute about what was said in an interview or if the concerns you raise with the news outlet are ignored.

What about threatening to pull, or actually pulling, your existing advertising as leverage in a dispute? Or refusing future interview requests with a particular reporter or news outlet? Although it's understandable why these actions are tempting, there are better ways to deal with problems with the media. Consider meeting with the reporter or with the editor or news director and sharing your concerns, or contacting the ombudsman if one's available.

Successful media relations is about establishing and cultivating a good working relationship with the reporters who follow your organization. It's an ongoing effort that may occasionally involve working out differences of opinion, but it's an effort worth making.

WHAT TO DO WHEN THE CEO CAN'T CUT IT

Before the Deepwater Horizon accident in 2010, the largest oil spill in the United States came from the Exxon Valdez tanker operating in Prince William Sound in Alaska in 1989. In both disasters, the CEO of each company demonstrated some pretty poor—make that very poor—media communication skills.

Tony Hayward, then CEO of BP, at first downplayed the environmental impact of the spill—providing extremely low and inaccurate estimates of the amount of oil being released into the Gulf of Mexico. What's more, he was often combative with reporters covering the incident. And who could forget that infamous quote? "There's no one who wants this thing over more than I do. You know, I'd like my life back." Ouch!

Twenty-one years earlier, Lawrence Rawl, CEO of Exxon, was even less skillful. He did not comment publicly about the accident for six days—sending out several lower-ranking executives to deal with the press. When he finally appeared on CBS for an interview, his performance was disastrous. Among other things, he looked and sounded angry, his answers were long and convoluted, he seemed to pick a fight with the news media, and he came across as decidedly defensive and unapologetic. That interview still stands as one of the best examples of what not to do in an interview.

Although there clearly are times when it's inappropriate for the CEO to serve as a spokesperson—such as when a reporter simply requests an interview with that individual or when the issue or event doesn't call for an "executive response"—top executives today must be willing and prepared to put themselves in direct contact with the news media. Gone are the days when they can pass that responsibility on to a subordinate or the PR spokesperson.

All of this raises the question, "What do you do—especially in a crisis—when your top executive has sub-par media communication skills?" Here's some advice:

Invest in media training.

The time to learn how to participate in an interview or conduct a press briefing is not during the real thing. Learn how the "game" is played beforehand. And make sure the training includes practice interviews that are recorded and critiqued.

Keep your skills sharp through refresher training.

Media skills can atrophy if you don't use them regularly. A good refresher training schedule is every twelve to eighteen months.

Find your comfort level.

In a press briefing or news conference, decide whether you prefer to speak using bullet points or read from a prepared text. Either approach is appropriate.

Avoid "going live."

Live interviews can be tough. Just because the reporter wants to interview you live, doesn't mean you have to agree. Politely indicate that you prefer to do a recorded interview.

Don't try to do it all.

The CEO's communications role in a crisis is usually to give the "30,000-foot view." Express the appropriate sentiment about what happened but leave the details to someone else.

Become a critic.

Every time you do an interview (especially a broadcast interview), critique your performance. Note what you did well and where there was room for improvement. Also, watch TV news and assess the media skills of executives and others you see.

Issue a prepared statement.

Although a written statement (e.g., a press release) lacks the power and transparency of an in-person interview, until you've honed your media skills, communicate your message through the written rather than the spoken word.

Having stellar media communication skills is a necessity, not a luxury, for today's CEOs.

AMERICA'S MOST FEARED TV NEWS MAGAZINE

It's been said that the four most feared words in corporate America are, "*Sixty Minutes* is here." Indeed, a call or visit from *60 Minutes* usually triggers a "No comment" response from anyone in that program's crosshairs. But that could be a mistake. A common misconception about how investigative reporters operate is that if the topic is negative and you don't cooperate, perhaps the reporter won't have enough information to write the story. The internet and a reporter's perseverance make that a faulty assumption. All that approach will do is limit your opportunity to get your side of the story told.

And *60 Minutes* can help you tell that story to millions of viewers. The show consistently ranks among the top programs in the Nielsen ratings. If you've ever wondered why people agree to go on certain cable news talk shows where the hosts are always tough, sometimes theatrical and usually abrasive, the answer is usually viewership. When someone can tell you that more people are going to watch you on a particular show, that's a very powerful incentive to appear. *60 Minutes* can make that claim.

Here's a look at how to participate in a *60 Minutes* interview (or any other investigative report)—and succeed:

DO YOUR DUE DILIGENCE

Before talking or agreeing to talk to any reporter, be sure to ask a few questions: What is the story about? What subjects will be covered? Caution: Investigative reporters are unlikely to share too much information. They may emphasize one element of the story, while leaving out other aspects, so as not to frighten you off. You may have to "read between the lines" to get a true sense of what the story is really about.

Who will do the interview? Reporters have different styles, and you may decide to accept or decline the interview depending on who the reporter is. There are plenty of *60 Minutes* pieces you can review online to get a good feel for a particular reporter's style.

What are some of the questions that will be asked? Explain to the reporter that you want to be sure you have the most up-to-date information to share. What is the reporter's deadline? In short, know as much about the program, the story and the reporter as the reporter knows about you.

KNOW WHAT YOU CAN AND CAN'T CONTROL

First of all, you can decide whether to participate. Believe it or not, some people feel they have no choice but to talk when approached by a reporter. Think about family members who talk to reporters immediately after some tragic event. Many of them probably never realized that they could politely decline. You can also decide who will speak, and usually where the interview will take place.

Media-savvy interviewees sometimes record their interviews with reporters in order to have an indisputable record of what was said during the interview. One company, Metabolife International, did just that when it anticipated a hostile report from ABC's *20/20*, and posted the complete 70-minute interview with its president on a special website—<u>before</u> ABC's story aired.

Never turn down an interview request because you're afraid of a few questions. You don't need to answer every question; in fact, prior to the interview, you can indicate that there are some questions or topic areas you can't or won't address.

What can't you control? You have no say about who the reporter will be. Notable exceptions are certain public figures. For example, the President and some celebrities probably have the clout to specify whom they want to talk to. Or a story may be so desirable that *60 Minutes* may agree to the choice of reporter specified by the interviewee.

Don't ask for an unedited interview; that request won't be honored. And finally, don't expect to get a chance to review the story before it's aired or printed. There are times when you can politely offer to review the piece for accuracy (trade press reporters are especially open to this), but most reporters are unlikely to oblige you—mainly because of control and deadline issues.

PREPARE AND PRACTICE

As retired basketball coach Bobby Knight said, "More important than the will to win is the will to prepare to win." A successful interview with *60 Minutes* or any investigative reporter starts with preparation. Know exactly why you're going on the program. Have your objectives clearly in mind. Develop an agenda consisting of several key message points. The time you spend talking to the reporter will be much longer than the time you actually appear on TV. That means editing will occur. During this process, the producer and reporter are watching and listening to every second of footage—looking for a few seconds of something different, powerful, damaging. So, make your answers memorable by using stories, anecdotes, analogies, examples and quotable lines. These add texture, dimension and color to your message.

Anticipate the questions you'll be asked, along with the questions you hope won't be asked. Write them down, then answer them aloud.

And don't forget media training. It takes some of the mystery out of the newsgathering process, and it gets you and your message focused. Even if you have had some media training in the past, an encounter with *60 Minutes* is the big leagues, so consider a refresher. A half or full day of practice will provide the confidence and competence needed for a successful encounter.

Prior to the on-camera interview, *60 Minutes* may ask you to participate in a "backgrounder." It's an unrecorded discussion that may or may not involve the reporter, designed to gather information—from your perspective—about the story. Take advantage of this opportunity but treat it as an interview because that's what it is. Be careful of what you say. Don't let your guard down.

A call or visit from *60 Minutes* doesn't have to cause panic—if you know the rules of the road...and can follow them.

A *60 MINUTES* SUCCESS STORY

Looking for an example of a company that went toe-to-toe with *60 Minutes*...and won? There may be no better case study than the Adolph Coors Company (now Molson Coors Brewing Company).

Famous for its "Rocky Mountain spring water" system of brewing, Coors is something of a legend in the beer industry. But throughout the 1970s and early '80s, the company's reputation was in trouble, in part because of conflicts with organized labor.

In 1976, a contract dispute between management and one of the local unions erupted. After more than a year of negotiations, union officials called for a strike. When management announced plans to replace striking workers and called an election to decertify the local union (employees ultimately voted in favor of decertifying the union), AFL-CIO officials declared a nationwide boycott of Coors beer. Labor leaders also protested Coors' hiring and promotion practices—alleging the company discriminated against women and ethnic minorities.

Enter *60 Minutes*. Program executives at CBS were well aware of union accusations of unfair employment practices at Coors and wanted to investigate the multi-year battle between the brewery and organized labor. So, in 1982, CBS producer Allan Maraynes and reporter Mike Wallace contacted Coors about plans for a *60 Minutes* report about the company.

Coors was understandably concerned. Many corporations see *60 Minutes* as anti-big business, and the firm's corporate communications director wasn't sure how Coors officials would respond to the pressure of an on-camera grilling. Also, Coors had traditionally avoided the public spotlight, and company Chairman Bill Coors and company President Joe Coors were afraid of airing the company's "dirty laundry" on national television.

Coors knew that *60 Minutes* was determined to do the story, and that a "no comment" defense would mean organized labor's side of the story would go uncontested. So, in a move uncharacteristic for the firm, Coors decided to go on the offensive. It adopted an open-door policy with CBS and provided the network with access to about a dozen non-union employees at its Golden, Colorado brewery. These employees, interviewed as a group in the plant's break room, came across on TV as honest, hard-working and pro-company. They effectively shot down the union's allegations of discrimination. The broadcast left viewers with the impression that the union represented only a small portion of Coors' otherwise satisfied workforce.

In short, Coors hit a home run! What started out to be a story "explaining that a fascist state exists at Coors" (producer Maraynes' words) turned out to be a story of a company that deserved high marks for its treatment of employees.

THE DREADED AMBUSH INTERVIEW

The ambush. You see it regularly on TV news. An investigative reporter with a microphone and a camera operator is chasing someone on foot. The reporter wants a comment, but all she gets is, "No comment!" as her target hurries into a building and slams the door.

Ambush interviews, made famous by CBS's Mike Wallace, are sprung on the unsuspecting by some reporters, whether local or national, broadcast or print. These interviews (or interview attempts) make for especially good TV. But ambush interviews don't just happen to lawbreakers or those who may have done something questionable. You could be ambushed at the scene of a crisis, before or after a city council or school board meeting, or by phone while you're in your office.

The time to figure out what to do is not during the ambush. You need to have given some thought to your options beforehand.

One mistake some people make is that they fail to recognize situations where they may be approached by a reporter. Reporters regularly attend city council, school board and other public meetings. If you're a school board member or an executive whose company is involved in some high-profile, perhaps controversial, project, and you're at a public meeting, don't be surprised if a reporter seeks you out. If you're the right person to speak, know what you're going to say. If you're not the appropriate spokesperson, know how to politely defer or decline.

In situations where you are unexpectedly approached by the media, don't show any discomfort or panic. Don't walk or run away. Don't say you're on your way to a meeting or other commitment (unless that's true). Introduce yourself to the reporter; shake her hand and get her name and news outlet—just as you would in any normal business situation. Be affable, personable. Then, ask how you can help—in other words, why she's there, what she's interested in.

You now have a decision to make, and you must make it quickly. Should you talk? Doing an interview without being prepared is a bad idea. But in a crisis situation, where a quick response is critical, and where you're authorized to speak and you have a good command of what happened, you might decide to do the interview. One approach to consider is buying yourself a little bit of time. For example, tell the reporter you want to check to get the latest information and that you'll be back in a few minutes to talk.

Your other choice is to defer or decline. Possible responses include indicating that you're not the appropriate person to comment, but you can direct the reporter to the individual who is. Or, you might agree to speak at another time. Once you've conveyed your decision, stay with your strategy. Don't begin answering a few questions (probably softballs), which can turn into a full interview. Reporters are persistent; they'll try to wear you down.

Some other things to keep in mind:
- Don't lie or fudge the truth. A reporter will likely catch you—and that lie will become part of the story.
- If reporters are crowding you and placing their microphones too close, step back slightly or politely ask them to step back to give you room.
- Remove the words, "No comment" from your vocabulary.
- Once you've deferred or declined, try to get the reporter to be the one to turn and walk. (Being seen on video walking away can be damaging.) Unfortunately, reporters rarely do this, so you may have to do it—confidently and unrushed.

JUST SAY NO! ... WHEN SHOULD YOU DECLINE AN INTERVIEW REQUEST?

In an interview in *Sports Illustrated*, former Dallas Cowboys quarterback Troy Aikman expressed regret for not having responded publicly to an allegation made about him years earlier by sports columnist, author and TV personality Skip Bayless. The allegation, which appeared in a 1996 book authored by Bayless, dealt with Aikman's sexual preference.

Said Aikman, "I am probably more upset because I probably should have responded to it at the time it was going on. The advice to me was, 'Hey, just don't address it. It's not worth it. It doesn't make any sense. It's ridiculous. All it's going to do is have people continue to talk about his book.' So I didn't. But I probably should have responded differently and maybe that would have changed things."

Aikman's comment makes you wonder about the wisdom of not responding (especially through the traditional news media) to something that's negative and is getting or may get widespread media coverage.

Cooperating with the news media makes sense—for a lot of reasons. But there are times when it makes sense to pass on a media interview request.

For instance, if you get an unexpected call or visit from a reporter, and you're unprepared, it's best to decline (or postpone), unless you can buy yourself some time—say, 15-20 minutes—to come up with some key points.

Success with the media is about having an agenda of your own and getting your agenda across in the interview. If your organization has someone who serves as a media gatekeeper (typically someone in communications or public relations), encourage the reporter to follow proper protocol and provide him or her with that person's name and number. (Be sure to alert that colleague immediately.) Another option, once you know the reporter's purpose, is to take a few minutes to organize your thoughts, or tell the reporter you'll call back in a few minutes. All of these strategies gain you some valuable "think time."

If you're not authorized to speak or you don't have the subject matter expertise, redirect the reporter. Journalists like the fact that some people will talk to them simply because a reporter calls or approaches them. Don't cave. Say something like, "I don't have the information you're looking for; let me see if there's someone else in our company who can help you."

In a crisis, such as a serious accident, the media are among the first on the scene. And they want information—fast. Probably within 15 minutes. Forward-thinking organizations know this and have prepared their first responders to meet the press. But as important as it is to provide information quickly, if you have other pressing matters—such as ensuring safety or protecting assets—you may need to attend to those matters first. In such a situation, let reporters know that you know they're there, and that you intend to meet their needs as well.

Talking to the media is not for novices. If you haven't yet developed your media interview skills, either through training or experience, you may want to pass. Ideally, someone else in your organization can handle these duties until you get up to speed.

Sometimes, reporters just need someone—anyone—to speak on behalf of some issue. For example, if a reporter is doing a story on teenage drug abuse, he or she may want to get some perspective from a high school counselor or principal. The particular school that's called may not have a drug abuse problem, but that doesn't matter to the reporter who needs information, including a quote or two. If you don't want your organization associated with a particular issue, politely tell the reporter you prefer not to weigh in on it. Do not—repeat, do not—decline the interview by telling the reporter the principal is in a meeting and is unavailable. (Even if that's true, what will you do if the reporter says, "How about tomorrow?") Level with the reporter and keep future lines of communication open—perhaps by encouraging the reporter to feel free to call you on other stories.

A few other things to consider:
- Is the issue at hand serious or frivolous? Some of what's being offered as "news" today is filler. News outlets need material to fill the page or broadcast. It's possible that viewers or readers may see the story for what it is—empty calories, and not take it seriously. Not responding is the media strategy equivalent of the statement, "I'm not going to dignify that comment with a response." Carefully and objectively assess the situation you find yourself in. Remove emotion from your decision. Avoid a knee-jerk reaction.

- What's the credibility of the source of the information, the reporter or the news outlet? If it's suspect, the best approach may be to keep silent.

- What's the likely "shelf-life" of the story? You've heard the expression that some stories have "legs"—meaning, they'll be around awhile. If your assessment is that your story doesn't have legs, you may want to ignore it.

- Are you really involved in the issue, and if so, what's your level of involvement? Sometimes, reporters just need someone—anyone—to speak on behalf of some issue. So, a reporter calls your company. If you're not involved in that issue, politely decline.

Finally, if you're convinced you'll be treated unfairly, don't feel you must participate. Some companies or organizations are reluctant or refuse to appear on *60 Minutes*, Fox, MSNBC or similar programs or news outlets. They don't think they'll get a fair shake.

A successful encounter with the news media involves control—and that may sometimes mean exercising the freedom not to speak. Declining a media interview request may result in a story that includes a comment that you declined to participate. But that might be preferable to what might happen if you do participate.

CHAPTER 3

MANAGING A CRISIS

Despite an organization's best efforts, accidents happen and difficult issues arise. If they are handled well, the organization can demonstrate that it is responsible, caring and competent. If they are mishandled, the organization may be perceived as inept, callous or arrogant.

Crises have become a fact of life in business and make headlines on a daily basis. The issue is not <u>if</u> your organization will face a crisis, but rather <u>what</u> the nature of the crisis will be and <u>when</u> it will occur.

Communication is one very important element of effective crisis management. The need to communicate to a variety of internal and external audiences is critical. And mishandling this aspect and the resulting negative perceptions left with the public can be far more damaging to an organization's reputation—even its ability to do business—than the crisis itself.

TWENTY-FIRST CENTURY CRISIS MANAGEMENT: A BRIEFING FOR EXECUTIVES

In the United States, the discipline of crisis management is generally thought to have started with one particular event—the Tylenol poisonings. Here's what happened: Over a three-day period in 1982, seven people were found dead in the Chicago area. Cause of death was eventually linked to cyanide in Extra-Strength Tylenol capsules. Johnson & Johnson (J&J), which still owns the brand, handled that crisis so well that many people feel the company "wrote the book" on effective crisis management.

In terms of its response to the crisis, the company was clearly ahead of its time:

- Rather than going into denial, it understood and acknowledged that it had a problem.

- It acted quickly in the public interest by issuing an immediate recall—despite FDA and FBI recommendations not to do that. (The Food & Drug Administration worried that public confidence in over-the-counter medicines would be lost; the FBI thought it would signal that a terrorist could bring a corporation to its knees.)

- It communicated: James Burke, J&J's CEO, appeared on TV's *Donahue* and *60 Minutes* to answer questions about the crisis (a gutsy decision back in 1982). Some 2,500 media inquiries were answered in the weeks following the tragedy. More than 500,000 mailgrams were sent to doctors and hospitals (email did not yet exist), and some 15,000 retailers and distributors were notified.

Crisis management has evolved over the years. For one thing, it has become an important part of executive development. For another, much has been learned about why crises occur, and what can be done to manage them more effectively—before, during and after their occurrence. Here are some of the changes every executive should know about:

TODAY'S CRISES ARE DIFFERENT

No longer are most of them the result of sudden events such as fires or explosions. Instead, crises develop over time. Smoldering crises such as employment discrimination, sexual harassment and financial mismanagement are consistently accounting for around 70 percent of all organizational crises. Nearly all of them are caused by people inside the organization—management rather than employees. The good news is that most people-caused crises send out early-warning signals and can be prevented—if those signals are spotted and acted on.

Remember the 1986 Space Shuttle Challenger that broke apart 73 seconds into its flight, killing all seven crew members? A Presidential commission report cited faulty O-ring design as the cause. However, well before the launch, there were those who had doubts about the design. But they were prevented from being heard. A series of memos never made it to the top. One of those memos predicted disaster if the launch occurred when the outside temperature was too cold.

Before Enron Corporation imploded, a financial analyst, an outside auditor and two Enron insiders alerted management to problems within the company—nearly three years before its collapse.

Create a corporate culture that encourages employees to spot and report the early-warning signs of a possible crisis, and then reward them when they do. Public companies should consider reacquainting shareholders (especially employee shareholders) with one very important role of the audit committee of the board of directors—investigating reports of illegal or unethical activity within the corporation.

As your company regularly conducts its "SWOT" analysis (i.e., assessing its strengths, weaknesses, opportunities and threats), be sure your threat assessment takes into account more than competitors and product obsolescence. Identify a wide range of potential problems—especially human problems such as fraud, insider trading and workplace violence. Look beyond problems you've experienced in the past or crises that are endemic to your industry.

A CRISIS IS NOT A SPECTATOR SPORT

The emergence of crisis management as a specialized discipline with specially trained practitioners has led some executives to scale back their involvement in managing a crisis. Regardless of whether a firm has a crisis management team (it should), a written crisis plan (it must) or uses the services of an outside crisis management consultant (it may want to), the top executive must take an active and visible leadership role throughout the crisis. How this individual reacts not only can determine tenure on the job, it can affect reputation long after the crisis has passed.

THE CEO NOW HAS MEDIA RELATIONS RESPONSIBILITIES

In a major crisis, the CEO (or the chairman or president) must be visible and speak for the corporation. He or she should give the broadest view of the situation and express the overriding sentiment. More detailed information is usually best provided by a PR spokesperson or someone with specific expertise.

During the Valdez oil spill crisis in 1989, Exxon Chairman Lawrence Rawl initially failed to do this. He didn't comment for six days but instead sent out several lower-ranking executives to deal with the press. Ford Chairman William Clay Ford, Jr. did just the opposite ten years later, after several employees were killed or injured during an explosion at one of the company's plants in Michigan. Ford went to the site, sought out reporters, and said, "It's awful. Everybody who works at Ford is an extended member of the Ford family. This has got to be the worst day of my life."

What about the practice of using someone from a trade association as your media spokesperson? There are times when it makes sense for an industry or like-minded companies to speak with one voice. But too often, CEOs who defer to outside spokespersons do so simply to avoid having to speak to the press themselves. When a company is the focal point of a crisis—when a firm's reputation is on the line—the CEO should place himself in direct contact with reporters.

NEGLECT CAN LEAD TO LITIGATION

Decades ago, chemical companies that had accidents with off-site impact invariably would be sued. But when they began to send insurance adjusters out into the community immediately after an accident to resolve problems—replacing broken windows, paying for visits to doctors, etc.—there was a dramatic decrease in litigation. Most people sue not because of what initially happened to them, but because they feel ignored, mistreated or marginalized afterwards. How you treat victims or their families can impact your legal exposure and reputation.

TRUST IN CORPORATE AMERICA HAS ERODED

Business executives are among the least-trusted professionals in America. This distrust makes it more difficult for you to get to that all-important recovery stage of a crisis. At one time, corporations under siege could draw upon the reservoir of good will they built up through jobs they created or contributions they made to charities, education or the arts. You can no longer buy the public's trust or support. In today's climate, even the victim in a crisis sometimes becomes the villain.

You earn trust by telling the truth, telling it all, and telling it quickly. One of the most dramatic changes in corporate communications has been the shift from refusing to comment, to commenting only if asked, to initiating comment. Forward-thinking organizations know the value of being the first to release their bad news, define an issue, or properly position themselves when locked in controversy.

You communicate trust by putting a human face on your organization. Issuing a press release is preferable to saying nothing, but having a real person talking on camera means you are willing to be judged for trustworthiness. You enhance trust by expressing empathy, acknowledging mistakes and accepting responsibility.

ANATOMY OF A CRISIS

Crises pass through predictable stages. The key to effective crisis management lies in taking prompt, appropriate action throughout the crisis.

Identification:
- A critical stage—often mismanaged.
- You must recognize and accurately assess the situation. Avoid denial.
- Gather information. Separate facts from speculation.
- Project forward. How might the current situation evolve or escalate?

Containment:
- The goal is to keep the event or issue from spiraling out of control.
- Focus on operations. Execute your emergency response plan fully and use all necessary resources to control the problem.
- Exercising sound judgment can result in less expansive news media coverage (e.g., local vs. national or international coverage, one-day vs. ongoing story, page-twenty vs. page-one placement, etc.).

Communication:
- Another critical stage that is often mishandled. Problems in crisis recovery frequently result from poor, untimely or no communication.
- In a crisis, many companies scale back communication at a time when more is needed. Communicate as quickly as possible and as frequently as is appropriate.
- Coordinate your external and internal communications.

Correction:
- Explain what you are doing (or are planning to do) to investigate the problem, and if possible, identify what corrective measures will be taken to prevent the problem from recurring.

Recovery:
- Starts at the beginning of the crisis—when you properly identify your event or issue as a crisis.
- Your goal is to have as short a recovery period as possible.
- If you "break even" after a crisis by keeping your organization's credibility and reputation intact, you have succeeded.

CRISIS MANAGEMENT PLAN

Every organization—whether large or small, public or private—should have a crisis management plan. These plans can be implemented at the macro (corporate) as well as the micro (location) level. In other words, corporate and its plants or locations should each have a crisis management plan.

In the past, these plans were quite lengthy and complex—sometimes running to hundreds of pages. They included such things as lists of every possible crisis the organization might face, and detailed flow diagrams showing specific steps or actions to take depending on what was happening. Typically, they made their way into a three-ring binder…and sat on a shelf…unread…gathering dust. User friendly they were not.

Today's crisis management plans are different. They are shorter and less complex. They resemble roadmaps, checklists or reference tools—focusing more on the mechanics than on the content of a crisis. In part, this is because we now realize that it is neither possible nor advisable to try to predict every crisis that could occur, or pre-plan every action in response to it. Also, the three-ring binder has disappeared; plans now exist in electronic form.

Crisis management calls for the application of sound, analytical business thinking. The goal is to prepare people to know how to deal with adversity, and then have them apply those skills to the challenge at hand. A good crisis management plan helps make that task easier. Here are some suggestions on the kinds of information that should be included in today's crisis management plans:

1. **Introduction:** This appears at the beginning of the plan and addresses the organization's philosophy or approach to doing business. As such, it typically includes a statement of beliefs and values on matters such as health, safety, the environment, the quality of its products or services, social responsibility, etc. It also articulates the organization's approach to handling a crisis. The statement is usually signed by the top executive in order to underscore its importance. Keep it to a page or less in length.

2. **Crisis Management Team.** In a crisis, trained people with assigned responsibilities will carry the day. Although there are different ways to staff a crisis management team, a best-practices structure usually contains the following positions:

Team Leader:
- Decides whether to activate the team
- Determines what staff functions should provide support
- Leads the team and seeks input from its members

- Has final decision-making authority
- Is usually not the organization's top executive
- Rarely serves as primary media spokesperson

A best-practices crisis management team structure. In a crisis, trained people with assigned responsibilities will carry the day.

Assistant Team Leader:
- "Shadows" the team leader and serves as his or her "right hand"
- Assumes leadership role if the team leader is absent or fatigued

Incident Secretary:
- Should be able to reach all team members at all times
- Keeps a log of all major developments, activities and decisions during the crisis

Communications:
- Ensures prompt, accurate communication with external and internal audiences (e.g., media, customers, elected officials, employees, etc.)
- Drafts a variety of communications (including press releases, talking points, standby response statements, Q&A, etc.)
- May serve as the primary spokesperson to the media
- Monitors all media coverage

Crisis Center Head:
- Champions crisis management planning; conducts audits and training exercises
- Ensures that the crisis management center (including alternate sites) is properly equipped
- Typically reports to the CEO or COO
- Spearheads post-mortem initiatives such as evaluations, policy or procedure changes, etc.

Functional Representatives:

Depending on the crisis, representatives from various functions, such as the following, may need to assist the team. These individuals will be called upon and may "come and go" as appropriate:

- Manufacturing
- Engineering
- Health, Safety, Environment
- Security
- Research & Development
- Sales/Marketing
- Legal
- Human Resources
- Public/Government Affairs
- Investor Relations
- Information Technology
- Executive Office

Develop a team that works for your organization. Have alternates for each position. Identify the roles and responsibilities for each position. Your team member list should include such information as: position, name, title, address, phone numbers (office, home, mobile), email address. This list must be scrupulously updated.

3. **Crisis Forecasting.** Consider including a list of the kinds of crises that typically can occur. According to crisis management expert Ian Mitroff, research indicates that crises fall into general categories or groups. Smart crisis management involves preparing for at least one crisis in each group because crises within the group share strong similarities. For example:

Economic:	Labor issues, such as strikes Significant decline in a company's stock price Decline in sales and earnings
Informational:	Lost or stolen sensitive information Computer hacking False information
Physical:	Loss of key facilities Equipment breakdowns

Human Resource: Loss of key executives
Sexual harassment
Racial discrimination

Reputational: Rumors
Tampering with corporate logos

Psychopathic Acts: Product tampering
Kidnapping
Hostage taking
Terrorism
Workplace violence

Natural Disasters: Earthquake
Fire
Flood
Hurricane

4. **Policies and Procedures.** Among the most important parts of any crisis management plan are the policies and procedures an organization establishes that must be followed during a crisis. These are the do's and don'ts. For example:

- Only authorized spokespersons who have been properly trained will be permitted to speak on behalf of the organization.
- The names of employees who are injured or killed in an accident are not to be released until relatives have been notified <u>and</u> permission from family members has been obtained.
- The company will not speculate on the cause of any accident or event.

Policy statements need not be long and complicated. They simply provide guidance to those in the organization on a variety of issues. Identify these policies and procedures in a separate section of the plan or list them under an appropriate subject-related section.

Some organizations ask each function to develop a one-page summary outlining how that function might assist during a crisis. For example, the legal function might identify such things as internal resources (e.g., which attorneys and support staff can provide assistance), external resources (e.g., outside law firms with expertise in a particular field), a checklist of key legal considerations (e.g., client privilege), etc.

5. **Communications.** Communication is a critical element of effective crisis management. Mishandling the communication aspects of a crisis or issue, and the resulting negative perception left with the public, ultimately can be far more damaging to an organization's reputation—even to its ability to do

business—than the crisis or issue itself. In this section of the plan, include the following:

- Compile a checklist of the various external and internal audiences you may need to contact during a crisis. Be sure to go beyond the obvious (e.g., employees, news media, etc.) and include such audiences as government officials (national, state, local), contacts at neighboring facilities, customers, key opinion leaders, nearby residents, etc.). The idea here is to think ahead so as not to have errors of omission. Include contact information.

- Develop a separate media contact list of the primary media outlets in your area. Remember, in addition to responding to reporters, you may need to initiate contact (e.g., to correct inaccurate information, etc.). Know who they are and how to reach them.

- Consider creating a series of fact sheets: what your organization does, its products or services, bios of key executives, backgrounders on specific facilities (e.g., history, activities, number of employees, etc.). Typically, this info is available on the company's website.

- Create a news release template (or series of templates). These are designed to help you quickly write a news release.

- Identify possible locations where you can brief the news media or conduct a news conference. Have both on-site and off-site (e.g., hotel conference rooms, schools, churches, municipal facilities, etc.) locations identified. Make a list of the equipment that needs to be available (e.g., adequate phone lines, electrical outlets, wi-fi, etc.).

- Outside resources: Identify the outside consultants or organizations you may need to call on for help. These include: PR firms, media trainers, crisis management experts, ad agencies, social media specialists. Have contact information, including 24-hour access.

- Website: Have a process in place that will quickly enable you to post late-breaking information on your website. (Reporters today use websites as a major source of information—as do others.) You may even want to have a special website ready to launch, if need be. (For example, a company may direct people to a special website for information on product recalls, etc.)

- Identify the technology you'll use to deliver timely information to key audiences (e.g. text messages, social media, etc.).

6. **Human Services Response.** People who have suffered serious injury (whether physical or psychological) or the death of a loved one frequently need help. They have a variety of emotional and other needs. For example, they may have the need to talk to someone about how they are feeling. Or they may

need help in getting to the location where their loved one is hospitalized.

In the past, companies made grief counselors available to provide help. Grief counselors are clinically trained professionals, but they are unknown outsiders, and many people are uncomfortable sharing their feelings with a stranger. Financial services firm Cantor Fitzgerald lost 658 employees on 9/11, but when the firm made grief counselors available to the families of those who died and to surviving colleagues, it found that many of them preferred not to talk to those professionals.

Today, forward-thinking organizations are prepared to provide different kinds of assistance to people impacted by a crisis. Human services response is a comprehensive, supportive approach to providing for those various needs. The assistance is provided by employees within the company (sometimes called care and compassion teams). That's not to say outside grief counselors will no longer have a role, but human services response goes beyond simply providing emotional support.

7. **Crisis Management Center.** Within an hour after two bombs exploded at the Boston Marathon in 2013, the Boston Police Department set up a command post in the ballroom of the Westin Copley Place Hotel. During that first hour, the number of people stationed in that center expanded from 12 to 100. Ultimately, some 1,000 local, state and federal authorities, including the mayor and governor, were based there.

According to the Boston Police Commissioner, law enforcement quickly realized that they needed a place near the bombing site where a large number of investigators could collaborate, bring in computers, review video and process the evidence (e.g., bomb parts, etc.) that was cascading in. Media briefings were also conducted from the hotel.

Preparing for a crisis involves many things. One of them is having a place where a crisis management team or members of an incident command structure can meet and work. Every organization (indeed, every location of every organization) should identify an on-site space where its team can meet. In the past, some companies installed sophisticated emergency operations centers (sometimes called "war rooms"). These were dedicated rooms, used only during crises, and were equipped with the latest technology, including teleconferencing capabilities (e.g., enabling headquarters to communicate visually with other company locations), electronic "white boards," multiple television monitors (to monitor news coverage), etc.

These dedicated rooms required quite an investment and some companies still have them. But today it's more common for a company to designate a conference room that can quickly be transformed into a temporary crisis management center. These rooms generally work fine, as long as they are adequately sized, configured and equipped.

In one crisis drill I observed, the client used a conference room that was far too small for the assembled team. Chairs and table space were at a premium, and at times the room got very noisy as people held phone and face-to-face conversations, including when the team leader or other team members were briefing the entire team. Electrical outlets were in short supply and some people had to rely on battery power for their computers. Even coffee and other refreshments had to be placed outside the room; this increased the chances that when people briefly left the room, they might miss something important.

As the situation in Boston illustrates, it's critical to have access to an alternate off-site crisis center location. This is especially important when events such as fires, explosions and hostage situations prevent you from using your own facility as a command center. A good strategy is to scope out possible alternate locations. Hotels, schools, churches, community centers and similar facilities are usually good candidates. Visit these facilities, arrange for their use in a crisis, and add them to your list of possible venues.

Regardless of where your crisis center is, develop a checklist of the equipment and supplies that will be needed. Think big (e.g., internet access, printers, copy machines, phone lines, etc.) and small (e.g., note pads, flip charts, etc.).

A new approach in crisis management has crisis management teams in a virtual crisis management center. This allows team members to assemble in minutes because they are able to gather via the internet—a major advantage when responders are in far-flung locations that may not allow them to gather for hours or days. If your organization uses such a web-based system, your plan should provide detailed information on how the meeting process works, along with step-by-step instructions on how to access the online crisis management center. If your company has not considered such an approach, now might be the time to explore this technology and test it during one of your drills.

SUGGESTIONS FOR YOUR NEXT CRISIS DRILL

Simulations are still the best way to learn to deal with the unexpected. So, whether your organization is planning its first drill or regularly conducts drills, and whether those drills are table-top, live action or hybrid (limited to some departments or locations), there are some best practices for this valuable tool.

Develop your drill scenario wisely.

Most companies conduct drills to improve the way they handle emergencies they've faced in the past. A better strategy is to also consider crisis scenarios outside your company or industry. In developing them, rely on your employees who know the organization best. Ask them to don their "villain" hats and come up with unconventional, abnormal attacks on company products, services and systems. Better yet, bring in outsiders who tend to have very different perspectives on your company and its vulnerabilities. Finally, don't limit your drills to events or incidents; test your company's ability to manage issues as well.

Have your scenario start with an event, but then have it escalate with a related or unrelated issue. For example, let's say the drill scenario for a consumer products company begins at a track and field clinic for youngsters. Children and adults at the event who drink a fruit juice drink made and donated by that company begin to get ill. Later in the drill, protesters who are concerned about the high-sugar content of those fruit drinks show up at the company's headquarters to announce a boycott and to draw media attention to their cause. Now the company's crisis managers must deal not only with a possible product contamination situation, but also with the broader issue of the nutritional value of its fruit juice drinks.

Involve top executives.

Key top executives—CEO, president, CFO, COO, etc.—often don't participate in crisis drills, despite the fact that they are likely to be key participants in managing any real crisis. Such drills tend to produce unrealistic results. Fortunately, the highly visible poor performances of some executives in real crisis situations has caused many executives to invest time in their company's crisis drills. Be sure your executives take an active role in your drill. They should not be mere observers or part-time participants.

Incorporate a communications element.

Some organizations do a fine job of containing and correcting an emergency but fail to communicate their actions. Don't limit the focus of your drill to operations. Also test your organization's ability to communicate with a variety of audiences.

Interactions with the news media: Test your spokespersons' ability to handle many different kinds of media requests—broadcast, print, on-camera, phone interviews, press briefings, news conferences. Conduct some ambush interviews. For example, on the day of the drill, have a "reporter" show up at the CEO's home to interview him. Try to get security guards and other employees not authorized to speak to reporters to do just that. Record these interactions and critique them during the post-drill review. Create simulated news stories (with sensational headlines and intentional errors) to test the company's ability to respond appropriately.

Phone calls: In a crisis, companies are often inundated with phone calls—from upset or angry family members, reporters, customers, government leaders, neighboring facilities, nearby residents and the public in general. A drill is an opportunity to test your organization's ability to handle the volume and variety of calls you'll get. Deluge your company with calls, and note the number of voice mails reached, unreturned calls and poorly handled calls.

Social media: Social media (e.g., Facebook, Twitter, YouTube, LinkedIn, etc.) has become an important element in crisis management, so forward-thinking organizations are incorporating it into their crisis drills.

It's fairly well known that organizations now operate in an environment where a single antagonist can target an organization and pose serious threats. The organization can be caught off guard by blogs, tweets and text messages. What's less known and understood is how social media can be used by an organization during a crisis. Social media provides a low-cost platform to communicate—rapidly and simultaneously. It also offers an opportunity to learn from instant information. Use your drill to test your company's acumen in using social media to manage a crisis.

Take a lesson from chess.

During a crisis, most crisis team members focus on what's currently happening. That's understandable. But a smarter strategy is to "project forward." Try to anticipate how the crisis will evolve. What could it be like in a day, a week or a month? During your drill, condition your team to do what chess players do—think several moves ahead. Have the drill facilitator ask the team or a few team members to brainstorm about possible future developments.

Conduct a post-drill critique.

Your drill is not over when it's over. Immediately after the drill, do a comprehensive evaluation. Use the following approach: First, have the facilitator ask each crisis team member to share his or her observations: What went right? What went wrong? (If a function has multiple members on the team, have one person speak for the function.) Next, have the team leader share his or her observations. The facilitator speaks last. A key objective of the critique is to identify strengths and weaknesses—in policies, plans and people.

Although conducting a crisis drill requires time and effort, organizations willing to make that investment will perform more confidently and competently during a real crisis.

COMMUNICATING WITH EMPLOYEES: PRIORITY ONE IN A CRISIS

It's happened to us all...at the airport gate or maybe even on the plane: There's a delay. You're waiting for an update—expecting to get some word of when the flight will leave. But no one provides any information. Or else long periods elapse between updates. You're frustrated. But your frustration stems more from the lack of communication than it does from the flight delay.

Forward-thinking organizations know that communicating—and doing so effectively—is important in the best of times. In the worst of times it's absolutely critical. And a company may have no more important audience to communicate with than its employees. Yet, ask employees to characterize their firm's effectiveness at internal communications during a crisis and many will probably respond with a line from the movie, *Cool Hand Luke*: "What we have here is a failure to communicate."

What constitutes effective employee communications during a crisis?

1. **Make communications a high priority.** Today's employees are intelligent and sophisticated. They have a keen interest in all matters affecting their company. After all, they may be investing their future in the firm. They want substantive information. In its absence, the rumor mill will shift into overdrive. What's more, employees are amazingly capable of handling bad news. (Remember one of the first rules of effective supervision or management? Provide subordinates with feedback. Even negative feedback is preferable to no feedback.) Also, in a crisis, your employees can help you disseminate accurate information to a variety of external audiences, including customers and the community—but only if you keep them informed.

2. **Increase the frequency of your communications.** In a crisis, developments occur rapidly. As a result, employees want and need more frequent updates. Yet, many organizations maintain their normal patterns of communication or may even scale back because management is preoccupied with the crisis. Employees have come to expect timely information from the news media. They expect nothing less from their employer.

3. **Be able to reach all your employees—quickly.** Today, a company's employees are rarely found in just one location. They are traveling, working from home, on vacation or spread around the country or world. Be sure you have systems in place (email, voice mail, texting, intranet, etc.) to reach them. In some crises, being able to reach retirees may be important.

4. **Address employees' concerns—real or perceived.** Regardless of the issue or situation you're dealing with, remember that employees ultimately want to know how it affects them personally. Your focus or perspective may not be

theirs, so be sure to consider the issue's implications for employees, and address them in your communications. For example, when a firm's bond rating is lowered, communications from management typically focus on reassuring investors and analysts. But employees too need reassuring—that their company is still financially sound, that their jobs are secure, etc.

5. **Coordinate your internal and external communications.** Make sure employees don't first learn of important developments through the news media. Employees, not the media, are your first communications priority, so be sure to coordinate the timing of your outreach to employees and the general public. A good practice to follow is to release information to your general employee population approximately 15 minutes before doing so externally.

6. **Use employees' preferred sources of information.** Most employees prefer to get critical information from their immediate supervisors, senior executives and small-group meetings—in that order.

7. **Be sure your communications are two-way.** The best kind of communication is two-way. Be sure information flows in both directions—to your employees and from them. Soliciting input from employees enables you to learn what they are thinking so you can address their concerns. It also lets you know whether your messages are being heard and understood.

8. **Tap the expertise of employee communication specialists.** If your firm has communication professionals, be sure to tap their expertise when developing employee communication strategies and tactics. Allow these experts to write and/or review the communications you plan to issue. Their input can be as valuable as that provided by your legal department. If you don't have professional communicators on staff, seek help from a PR firm—especially one with expertise in employee communications.

NO NEED TO SACRIFICE ACCURACY FOR SPEED

Pilot Flying J, America's biggest diesel fuel retailer, was under investigation in 2013 for claims that it cheated customers out of rebates on bulk fuel purchases. FBI and IRS agents showed up at the company's headquarters looking for evidence of rebate fraud that allegedly took place for more than five years.

On the day of the raid, Jimmy Haslam, company CEO (and owner of the Cleveland Browns football team), released a statement saying he believed there was no wrongdoing. Later, he said the matter was about rebates involving an "insignificant" number of customers. (A review by auditors showed that about 250 trucking companies out of 400 may have had problems with their rebates.

The company faced multiple lawsuits.)

Today, in a crisis, speed wins. It's not unusual for the news media to call or show up—sometimes within 15 minutes—looking for information. So it's understandable that a company spokesperson will want to have something to say in a timely manner. The challenge is to avoid saying anything that will later turn out to be inaccurate.

How about these errors:

Early on in the Deepwater Horizon oil spill crisis in the Gulf of Mexico, BP CEO Tony Hayward downplayed the incident, describing the amount of oil being released as "relatively tiny" in comparison with the "very big ocean." He said, "I think the environmental impact of this disaster is likely to be very, very modest." (The oil flowed for 87 days with a total discharge of 4.9 million barrels.)

And in 2007, the Crandall Canyon coal mine in Utah collapsed, killing six miners and three rescue workers. At a news conference, Robert Murray, president and CEO of Murray Energy, the mine operator, insisted that he could prove the mine collapse was caused by a 3.9-magnitude earthquake. Later, Murray's claim was flatly rejected by a study which showed that pillars in the mine collapsed, causing giant slabs of sandstone above the mine to shift. The mine collapse was so powerful it registered as an earthquake.

At one time, company spokespersons had the luxury of time when responding to crisis-related media inquiries. Newspapers, which generally came out in the morning, had late, previous-day deadlines. Local TV news was at 6PM and 11PM (Eastern time zone). All-day news radio? It didn't exist. Ditto the internet. So, depending on the time of day the crisis occurred, reporters could often wait hours for a company response. Those days are gone.

People are used to instant news. And they (and reporters) have come to expect an instant response from a company spokesperson. But that doesn't mean that you have to sacrifice accuracy for speed. Here's how you can balance those two elements:

- Make sure your organization understands that a quicker media response is required today. If your mindset is that reporters can wait, your company runs the risk of being perceived as uncaring or unprepared, or as hiding something.
- Most news outlets value accuracy. But some take the approach that being first is better than being accurate. They feel they can quickly correct their inaccuracies—for example, by placing new information on their website (all traditional news outlets also have websites). You, on the other hand, must be accurate—especially from the onset.

- In the early moments of a crisis, information is often limited and sketchy. Politely challenge those who are providing you with the details. Ask them how they have come to know what they are telling you. For example, have they actually seen something with their own eyes? Or did they get it second- or third-hand? Be skeptical. Before sharing anything, verify. Separate facts from conjecture.
- Don't feel you need complete information before talking to the news media. (Lawyers are notorious for wanting every "t" crossed and "i" dotted before letting their company speak publicly.) It's okay to brief the media when you have only partial information. You can always hold follow-up press briefings or news conferences as additional information is available.
- Even when very few of the 5Ws and 1H (what, when, where, who, why and how) are known, you can talk to the news media and tell them you're gathering information, you're concerned about the situation (especially people), etc. Initial press briefings don't need to be lengthy; they can last just a few minutes, and you don't need to take questions.
- Resist the temptation to speculate. Get comfortable with telling reporters you don't know, but that you'll try to get answers to their questions.

Mark Twain once said, "A lie can get halfway around the world before the truth can even get its boots on." The same can probably be said about errors in today's world of instant news. Most crisis communication experts consider the first hour of response the "Golden Hour." In many breaking news events, initial news reports take place in this first hour. Make sure you're prepared to share accurate information during that period.

COMMUNICATING EMPATHY (THE RIGHT WAY) DURING A CRISIS

The Crandall Canyon Mine, an underground coal mine in Utah, made headline news in 2007 when six miners were trapped after a collapse. Ten days after the event, three rescue workers were killed by a second collapse. Rescue efforts were eventually called off.

Robert Murray, owner of Murray Energy Corporation, which operated the mine, shocked many in the media and general public when they saw his poor media skills. Chief among his mistakes was his failure to understand that in a tragic event—loss of life or serious injury—the primary message must center around the dead or injured. Other messages are secondary, and some have no place at all in post-accident communications.

Murray began his press briefing by mentioning that he built the company by mortgaging his home and cited that accomplishment as proof that "the United States is a great country." Then he delivered a passionate and lengthy defense of the coal industry, pointing out that low-cost coal accounts for fifty percent of America's energy production, and that it's essential to the American standard of living, including American manufacturers' ability to compete globally. He added, "…every one of the global warming bills that [have] been introduced in Congress today to eliminate the coal industry will increase your electric rates four-to-five-fold."

Murray even invited the media to join him at a later date to go underground in one of his coal mines, "so that you can see for yourself what we do that is essential to the American economy."

During just about every press briefing or media interview, Murray assumed the role of coal industry pitchman, hammering home the pro-coal message and giving short shrift to the nine men who perished and their families.

No doubt, Murray genuinely cared about the men. When he spoke about them, he did so with what seemed like heartfelt grief. But those comments most likely rang hollow, overshadowed as they were by his commercial messages, his attacks on certain union officials and his lectures to specific media outlets such as Fox News and the Associated Press.

Eight years later, Ohio State University showed a somewhat different, but also unfortunate, lack of empathy. Kosta Karageorge, who played football for the school, had been missing for several days before his body was found in a trash bin near his apartment. Cause of death was a gunshot wound to the head, and investigators believe his suicide was concussion-related.

The university issued this press release: "The Ohio State University Department of Athletics was shocked and saddened to learn today of the death of student-athlete Kosta Karageorge, a senior from Columbus. Our thoughts and prayers are with the Karageorge family, and those who knew him, during this most difficult time."

That press release sounded like it had been written from a template found in some file drawer. Boilerplate language heard almost daily. Clichés that have lost their value through overuse (e.g., "shocked and saddened," "Our thoughts and prayers"). And where is a quote from then head coach Urban Meyer? In short, a failed attempt at empathy.

Here are some tips for communicating empathy during a crisis:

- Don't wait too long to communicate. Queen Elizabeth II waited too long to communicate following the death of Princess Diana, and was severely criticized for it by the British people. The public often perceives silence or a delayed response as indifference. Even if you have very little information, quickly issue a statement or conduct a press briefing (it could be as short as a minute or two), if only to express concern and share the few details you have at that point.

- If your crisis involves loss of life, describe it as a "tragedy," not as an "unfortunate incident."
- Avoid talking about the economic consequences of the crisis in tandem with comments about injuries or deaths. Or at least don't lead with a discussion of damage costs, impact on sales or profits or adequate inventory levels. Treat such items as a footnote to your primary statement.
- Put a human face on your organization. Issuing a press release is preferable to saying nothing, but having a real person talking on camera is the best way to make your communication personal. Also, avoid words such as "the corporation" or "the company." Instead, use your company's name in conjunction with "our company" or "we."
- Never use humor—even as an icebreaker—in matters involving health, safety or the environment.
- When reading from a prepared statement, look at the audience, a reporter or the camera at the point when you express concern. Speak from the heart rather than read verbatim.
- Although expressing concern or showing emotion is acceptable, losing composure (e.g., crying) is not. In a crisis, your role often requires you to communicate strength. Spokespeople who cry don't inspire confidence.
- Remember that you can also express empathy when people are inconvenienced (e.g., temporary road closures or evacuations, shelter-in-place orders, etc.).
- During a tragic event, if you have responsibility for speaking to the media, assess your ability to keep your composure. If necessary, take a few moments before you speak, or consider having someone else do it (make sure he or she has been media trained).
- Expressing empathy, caring or concern does not imply accepting liability. There is a difference between accepting responsibility and accepting blame.

YOUR FIRST LINE OF DEFENSE IN A CRISIS

When an explosion at a Houston-area forging plant killed eight workers and injured another two, reporters quickly arrived on scene in search of information. One of the first individuals they approached was a fire department volunteer. The young man's instincts told him to be careful about how much he said, prompting him to comment, "I know you guys are trying to get it out of me." The reporters simply remained silent, so the firefighter continued, "It reminded me of Hollywood in there…It's pretty bad. I've never met a plane crash before, but I'm sure some of the situations in there are similar." He then went on to talk about "many bodies" and "body parts."

What those reporters did was right out of Journalism 101: They got the firefighter to "fill the silence." Most of us are uncomfortable with silence, so if reporters simply keep quiet, chances are the interviewee will start talking—and may say something quotable…something damaging…something that can be aired on the news or printed in the paper.

Today, most crisis-prepared organizations have identified and trained spokespersons who can interact successfully with the news media. These are the PR folks, executives and "content experts"—the people with primary media relations responsibilities.

But crises can occur in inconvenient places and at inconvenient times. So the first contact a reporter may have could be with a front-line employee—a security guard, shift supervisor, receptionist. It's critical that these individuals know the "rules of the road" so they too can have a successful encounter with a reporter. Although these employees might not serve as your primary spokespeople, they should be trained to understand the reporter's role in an operational crisis. Your company's image is at stake, and all it takes is one bad interaction to damage your company's reputation.

In a crisis, there are three likely roles for front-line employees who encounter the media:

One is "meet and greet." In this role, the employee lets the reporters know that the organization is aware of their presence. (It's not uncommon for reporters to show up—only to be ignored—intentionally or unintentionally.) This individual also escorts the reporters to an appropriate location such as a conference room, or asks them to remain in the lobby, parking lot or wherever else they might be. The primary message is that a designated spokesperson is on the way. If possible, front-line employees should also provide an estimate of when the spokesperson will arrive.

Reporters are usually quite skillful in getting front-line employees to provide some of the information they're looking for. They do this by being friendly and starting out asking easy questions, such as, "What does your company do?" or "What happened?" But then the questions become more challenging and potentially damaging. And once the employee begins to answer those initial questions, it's tough to know when to stop. So it's critical that they know their mission: be polite and affable, but not be a source of any sensitive information.

Because reporters may decide to "wander around" in search of information while waiting for the spokesperson, front-line employees may also want to keep an eye on the media. And if appropriate, they can offer the reporters coffee or other refreshments.

What if it will be some time before the spokesperson arrives? Reporters work on tight deadlines, so they are unlikely to wait passively while their competitors file their stories. So, another role for these employees could be serving as a temporary spokesperson. The idea here is for them to provide some basic information about what has happened. The best approach is to read a short statement (which can be drafted with the help of others in the company) but take no questions afterward. Quickly meeting some of the informational needs of the media can help prevent reporters from concluding that the event is worse than it really is or reporting incorrect information.

Reading from a prepared statement keeps you from speaking extemporaneously—perhaps saying something you shouldn't or leaving out something important.

A third possible role for the front-line employee may be to conduct a press briefing, including answering a few questions. This happens when there's a very long delay before the primary spokesperson will arrive or when that person will not be able to arrive.

Any interaction with the news media can be a challenge but having a game plan that includes front-line employees can make the encounter less stressful and more successful.

AFTER A CRISIS, DO THE FOLLOWING:

Twenty-first century crisis management (CM) involves a number of components. Among them: having a crisis management plan, a crisis management team, and a crisis management center (today, it's usually virtual). CM best practices also include being prepared to provide different kinds of assistance to people impacted by a crisis and conducting drills and simulations.

Another component—one that is frequently ignored or given short shrift—is the post-crisis review—sometimes known as the "post-mortem" or debriefing. It's easy to understand why companies want to move on after a crisis—especially one that was prevented or well handled. They have other work to do. Or, managing the crisis required substantial time, effort and resources, so the last thing the company wants is to revisit the nightmare.

But the crisis management process doesn't end once the problem has been resolved. There are some best practices to follow when conducting a post-crisis review:

- Make the review a standard, mandatory part of your crisis management efforts. Let team members and any others involved in managing the crisis know that you plan to seek their input when the crisis has passed. That way, they can begin to record their observations during the event.
- Timing is critical. Hold the review "after the smoke has cleared." Many organizations wait a few days. This gives your team an opportunity to reflect on what happened and gain perspective. It also allows you to see if any crisis-related developments surface shortly after the event (e.g., community anger, sustained media coverage, etc.).
- Review participants should include all members of your crisis management team and any "seconds" to those individuals, appropriate executives (even if they weren't on the team) and any others who contributed to managing the crisis. Reviews can be opportunities to observe and learn and for team-building. Top executive participation is especially important. If your leadership is too busy to attend, think of the message that sends out to others in the company.
- Allow enough time for a meaningful review. For example, arbitrarily allotting thirty minutes for the meeting is probably a mistake. Depending on the nature of the crisis, the number of review participants and the scope of the response, you might need several hours.
- Cultivate good will. Thank everyone in the organization who participated in managing the crisis. And don't forget those outside the organization, such as emergency responders, government officials, etc. Reach out to them as well.
- Agendas for these reviews will vary, but generally have these elements worth focusing on:

1. Briefly review the event or issue, along with the key developments that accompanied it.
2. Examine whether the crisis was preventable (e.g., warning signs?). Was there anything that could have or should have been done differently (e.g., operational, technological, procedural, etc.)?
3. Evaluate the team's performance in managing the crisis. That involves looking at the two inseparable aspects of most crises—operations and communications. For example, did the team follow established procedures

as outlined in the company's crisis management plan? No finger pointing—just a candid assessment of what worked and what didn't work.

4. Identify the changes (e.g., in policies, procedures, plans, etc.) that should be made. In other words, what should the company stop, start or continue doing? Establish timelines for their implementation.

- Consider restitution. Identify what actions, if any, may be required to help you regain public trust. For example, should you seek public input? Should you hold a public meeting? Is it appropriate to donate to a particular cause or organization? Are any management changes in order (this is a form of "paying a price")?
- For a period of time, monitor whether anything is being said about your company in the media—both traditional news and new media.
- Prepare a written report or summary of the key findings. Distribute that document to everyone who participated in the review, as well as to any other appropriate individuals.

Post•crisis reviews have their roots in debriefings which originated in the military as a way to learn from a mission and to correct mistakes or make adjustments to a plan. Both are structured learning processes that lead to better performance. And that's important not only in the military, but also in business.

CHAPTER 4

COMMUNICATING WITH INVESTORS AND THOSE WHO INFLUENCE THEM

Communicating with investors and those who influence them is not for lightweights. Listen to just about any quarterly earnings call or analyst presentation and you'll quickly realize how complex the subject matter is. The primary goal of investor relations is to tell a company's story. That important but daunting task requires some special skills in communicating with no-nonsense analysts, investment bankers, individual and institutional shareholders, prospective shareholders and business reporters. In short, investor relations is a marketing and communications function, designed to increase awareness and understanding of a company and what makes it an attractive investment option.

DEVELOPING AND SELLING YOUR COMPANY'S STORY

For most publicly traded companies, the annual or biennial analyst presentation is a financial communications staple—an important tool to reach analysts and investors. The time, effort and money some companies invest in these presentations can be staggering. For example, one of my clients provided extra compensation to about a hundred select employees to come to work on a holiday to serve as an audience and pose questions during an analyst presentation practice session. No doubt an expensive investment, but also a smart one.

If analyst presentations are part of your financial communications efforts, make sure those presentations are generating solid returns. Here's a six-point plan to help you do that:

1. KNOW YOUR AUDIENCE

So, what's to know? You're talking to analysts—people whose job is to know your industry and company inside out, right? Sure, but your audience may also include institutional and individual investors, employees, business reporters and others. Rather than thinking of your audience as a homogeneous group, view them as a collection of individuals with varying levels of interest and knowledge about your company and different information needs and wants. This more diverse audience can impact the content of your presentation as well as how you communicate that content. For instance, you may have to cut back on the jargon and other shorthand that have become part of your vocabulary.

2. HAVE A STRONG OPENING

Most analyst presentations begin in a predictable way—with a profile of the company, including such things as its mission statement, business divisions, facility locations, number of employees, senior management, etc. Not only is this approach boring, it's self-centered. Instead, right at the start, tune in to the audience's frequency by answering this question they are asking themselves: "What is it about this particular company that will benefit me or my client?" The one part of any presentation guaranteed to get audience attention is the opening. But most audiences will give you only about a minute to show them you have something important or interesting to say. Don't squander this moment on the ordinary, the mundane, the expected. Deliver a message they can use—one that's simple, concise and memorable.

3. GO BEYOND A LITANY OF FACTS

Businesspeople love data, which explains why so many business presentations are loaded with it. Analysts love data. But they want and need something more—meaning.

Let's say you're a U.S. international energy company that's been aggressively acquiring hydrocarbon assets in the energy-rich region of Queensland, Australia. You have permits in five million acres in a state with more than nine billion barrels of oil-equivalent reserves and an amazing 42 percent exploration success rate. Great! Make sure your audience knows that.

But that's only part of your message. Here's the rest: China is now the second largest economy and has surpassed America as the world's biggest energy user.

But China has exhausted its domestic oil reserves and its coal reserves will be depleted by 2032. So the country is importing vast amounts of liquid natural gas (LNG).

LNG comes from unconventional sources such as coal seams—found in abundance in Queensland. Gas from this coal can be liquified and transported in ships—to China. And China is buying more energy from Australia than from any other country. All of this makes our hypothetical energy company a very attractive investment.

As a presenter, you must do more than merely share data; you must provide the insight and meaning associated with that data.

4. USE POWERPOINT SPARINGLY

PowerPoint is a great tool, but it's frequently misused—i.e., overused. Most presentations today incorporate mind-numbing visuals—large numbers of slides, multiple points per slide, and too many words. A better approach is to use PowerPoint for such things as pie charts, bar graphs, diagrams and photos, but minimize or even eliminate "word" or "copy" slides. Projected images are competing with you for the audience's attention. Just as you can be only in one place at a time, your audience can process only one incoming message at a time. They are either listening to you or viewing your visuals. Powerful presenters rely on themselves rather than on projected images to reach an audience.

5. HAVE SOLID PLATFORM SKILLS

The best ideas are no better than ordinary if they aren't well delivered. Among the most important delivery skills to master are high energy, minimal reliance on notes and sustained eye contact.

6. NAIL THE Q&A

The most valuable part of nearly all investor presentations is the question-and-answer segment. In one study, buy-side analysts said that 45 percent of the time spent on earnings calls should be devoted to Q&A. Presenters sometimes use too much of their allotted time for their prepared remarks. So the Q&A segment is either scrapped or the session runs overtime. Treat Q&A, not as an afterthought, but as an integral part of your presentation.

Anticipate questions by using the audience analysis you conducted when developing your presentation. Enlist the aid of some trusted colleagues to help you predict the questions and to critique your planned answers.

Answer questions succinctly. Shorter answers have greater staying power. If you listen to any of the news talk shows, think about how you react to an expert who drones on and on with an answer—making it nearly impossible for you to remember a takeaway. Less is more.

Most speakers end their presentation with their response to the final question. Avoid this. Instead, wrap up the Q&A segment with a brief comment tied into the key idea of your presentation.

If you want your company's story to stand out, you must stand out among the many other presenters analysts will hear. And that may mean eliminating comfortable, but outdated and self-defeating communication skills.

TEN EARNINGS CALL MISTAKES TO AVOID

Not all executives are conference call savvy. When Steve Wynn, former CEO of Mirage Resorts, held his first investor conference call, it didn't go very well. At one point, he attempted to hold a group discussion, but there was only silence when the listen-only participants couldn't contribute. In another call, he addressed a female analyst as "honey." Ouch!

Then there's Jeffrey Skilling, former Enron president (and convicted felon). During a conference call, an analyst chastised the company for not providing a balance sheet and cash flow statement in time for the call. Skilling responded with a sarcastic, "Well, thank you very much. We appreciate that," then added an expletive.

If conference calls are part of your investor relations efforts, you want to generate the best possible return on that investment. Here are ten mistakes to avoid:

1. **Poor scheduling.** Hold your conference call shortly after you release your earnings. But be sure to give analysts enough time to review the information and prepare for the call. The best days are Tuesday through Thursday. Mornings are best; avoid late-afternoon calls.

2. **Insufficient preparation.** Busy executives often end up "winging it" during conference calls. Avoid this self-inflicted mistake. Plan your work, then work your plan. In other words, carefully script your remarks or your notes—then follow them. Practice those remarks several times—aloud. One segment that usually gets short shrift during preparation is Q&A. Develop a list of the questions you expect, and answer them—again, aloud. Call-prepared companies frequently review the kinds of questions asked in previous calls and can usually anticipate specific questions from specific analysts.

3. **Inappropriate length.** Analysts sometimes have to participate in several calls per day—perhaps as many as six—a real challenge to their stamina and con-

centration. If your call is too long, analysts will begin to multi-task, have one of their associates take over for them, or they may even disconnect from the call early. Try to keep your call to about an hour, including Q&A.

4. **Too many company spokespersons.** Don't confuse or overwhelm your audience with a "cast of thousands." Your CEO or president should be the featured speaker and should lead off. There should be no more than three or four other senior execs, including the CFO and the head of IR, who usually serves as moderator.

5. **Lots of facts, but no key message.** Conference calls provide you with an opportunity to review the financials, discuss recent or upcoming developments and answer questions. But you should also have a specific message. State it clearly and repeatedly; don't expect your listeners to infer it. Help them see the big picture. Ask yourself, "What one or two things do I want my audience to know and remember after the conference is over?"

6. **Boring delivery.** Most executives read from a prepared script. There's nothing intrinsically wrong with that. Analysts are used to it (though usually bored by it) and doing so can keep you out of trouble with the SEC. Daily, you see news anchors reading from a prepared text. But they do it in a way that makes you forget that they're doing it. You must achieve that same skill level. Practice, but don't sound "canned." To increase your energy and project more authority and enthusiasm, consider standing up while participating in the call (be sure to use a wireless mic). Also, incorporate stories, examples and anecdotes into your remarks or responses. Stories are more easily remembered than facts. But don't read the story; tell it—to add a note of spontaneity to your delivery.

7. **Not enough time for Q&A.** In an hour-long earnings call, try to limit prepared remarks to about 15 minutes. That will leave ample time for Q&A. Be sure to monitor the number of calls in the queue. If time limitations prevent some analysts from being able to ask questions, revisit or establish guidelines (e.g., limit the number of questions per analyst) or consider shortening your answers.

8. **One-way communication.** Who says information has to flow one way in a conference call? Analysts follow and talk to a wide range of companies and industry experts. If you hear something of interest, don't be afraid to ask a few questions of your own.

9. **Technology problems.** You cannot afford, and should not tolerate, technical glitches of any kind. They speak volumes about your company and are not easily forgotten. Whether you're conducting the call over phone lines or streaming it via the internet, make sure your service provider is delivering a trouble-free service. If you're one of the growing number of companies incor-

porating PowerPoint visuals or video into your conferences, make sure those visuals are appropriate and well crafted. And that they work!

10. **No follow-up.** Your conference call is not over when it's over. The executives who participated should collectively review how the call went. Individually, each executive should listen to the archived call—identifying his or her own strengths and weaknesses. In addition, your IR professional should occasionally seek feedback from a few analysts.

THE DAY AND TIME YOU HOLD YOUR EARNINGS CALL MATTERS

Although earnings conference calls are optional rather than required by the Securities and Exchange Commission, estimates are that 98-99 percent of publicly traded companies hold them quarterly. Moreover, studies indicate that the accuracy of earnings forecasts by analysts increases when earnings announcements are accompanied by conference calls.

The best days for earnings releases and conference calls are Tuesday through Thursday.

As it turns out, there's another compelling reason to schedule your call carefully. Research reported in the *Harvard Business Review* shows that physical and mental fatigue cause irritability and a decline in executive function, especially right before lunch and late in the afternoon. For example, one study showed that parole boards' rulings on similar cases varied significantly according to whether a case was heard just before or just after lunch.

With this in mind, Jing Chen, a PhD candidate, and Baruch Lev, a professor at New York University's Stern School of Business, along with Elizabeth Demers, an associate professor at the University of Virginia's Darden School of Business, wondered whether a similar phenomenon might apply to earnings calls. So they analyzed 26,585 earnings calls of 2,113 publicly held U.S. firms based in the Eastern and Central time zones.

Using linguistic algorithms to measure positivity, negativity and uncertainty during the Q&A portion of the calls, the researchers found that negative tone increased as the morning progressed, dipped slightly after lunch, and then rose again until the market close. The researchers also found that the more negative the tone, the more negative the stock returns over the five trading hours after the call. Those negative stock returns associated with negative calls continued downward for up to 15 trading days.

The lesson? Even if top executives are not "morning people," it may be best for them to avoid late-afternoon conference calls in order to convey a positive, resolute tone.

EARNINGS CALLS: A BEST-PRACTICES CHECKLIST

Scheduling:
- Best days: Tuesday through Thursday
- Remember to factor in various time zones of primary analysts
- Avoid right before lunch and late afternoon
- Know your key competitors' earnings call schedule to avoid day/time conflicts

Length:
- 1 hour
- Q&A should be longer than scripted material

Delineate roles:
- Avoid "cast of thousands," but show bench strength. Also avoid "one-man shows"
- IR head: first words audience hears are yours; don't squander this critical opening
- CEO: "30,000-foot" view (provide only those numbers required to make your case)
- CFO: review the numbers, but convey what is significant and why
- Other execs: provide detail/color for your area of responsibility, plus significance

Open with a characterizing statement…then provide 3-4 highlights backing up that statement:

For example: "This was a quarter that we began to see some positive results from our turnaround plan. Sales are up. Inventories were reduced significantly. Cost-cutting initiatives began to produce results."

Aim for simplicity:
- Know what to exclude
- Prioritize relentlessly
- Avoid the "curse of knowledge" (telling everything you know)
- Less is more

Avoid a mere recitation of facts:
- Analysts already have key numbers (earnings release)
- Provide significance
- Numbers alone don't provide perspective or demonstrate your vision or command of a situation

Bolster key points with "sparklers" (use both analytical + emotional content):
- Analogies
- Stories
- Examples
- Anecdotes
- Illustrations
- Memorable (quotable) lines
- Compelling data

Repeat and reinforce:
- Have an opening "headline"
- End with a closing summary

Consider including "bad news":
- Transparency/credibility is enhanced when you appropriately share negative info
- Better in the script than raised during Q&A

Writing style (script):
- Tight and to the point
- Simple, straightforward language ("language of the living room")
- Write for the ear, not for the eye
- Minimize complexity (clauses, compound-complex sentences, "fifty-dollar words," etc.)
- Avoid clichés, jargon
- Use smooth rather than jarring transitions occasionally between ideas (e.g., "So, how do our margins compare to those of our competitors?" vs. "Now let me talk about margins."

Tone:
- Similar to business casual dress
- Conversational, friendly, relaxed vs. stiff, formal
- Use contractions (e.g., "I'd like to …" vs. "I would like to …")
- Use analysts' names

Delivery:
- OK to read script, but do so effectively
- Take ownership of the script if it's written by someone else (change phrasing as needed)
- Practice 3x, aloud, sitting/standing
- Increase energy
- Use a few "detours" (going off script briefly) to add a note of spontaneity

HOW TO PRESENT VIA TELECONFERENCE

Most quarterly earnings conference calls today are conducted via teleconference. (Video conference technology such as Go to Meeting, Cisco Webex or Zoom will one day become the preferred tool for these calls.)

As a reminder, in a teleconference:
- Those representing the company can be heard but not seen by the audience.
- These company reps can hear but not see the audience.
- Presenters frequently use PowerPoint or even video.

And while these teleconferences remain a valuable way to reach a distant audience, they pose some challenges. Presenters often seem to lack energy and sound flat—especially if they are reading a script. This bores the audience and they may begin to multi-task—checking and sending emails and texts, surfing the internet, etc.

To minimize or eliminate these and other problems, consider the following:

INCREASE YOUR ENERGY

One of the biggest disadvantages of presenting via teleconference is the inability to see the audience, and therefore, feed off their energy. So you must take other measures to generate energy, which the audience uses to remain engaged. Aim for about a fifty percent increase over your normal energy level. Here are some ways to do that:
- Speak louder. Increasing volume is one of the easiest ways to raise vocal energy.
- Deliver your presentation while standing. Doing so will allow you to breathe more deeply, become more animated and add more inflection to your voice.

- If you remain seated, lean forward about twelve inches; doing so will increase energy.
- Use a good-quality, wireless lavaliere or headset microphone. These mics deliver consistent sound and allow you to move around, something that also increases energy.

In a teleconference, of the three communication components that connect you with the audience (visual, vocal and verbal), one of them is missing—the visual. So the vocal element takes on added importance—contributing some 86 percent to making that connection.

KEEP THE AUDIENCE ENGAGED

In a face-to-face presentation, a solid presenter can usually hold an audience's interest for about 20 minutes. Audience attention wanes more quickly in a teleconference, so use these strategies:

- Stick to the most important information. Don't wander or get sidetracked. Be disciplined with your content. Less is more.
- Consider incorporating short video or audio clips, if appropriate.
- Use analogies, stories and examples to bolster your messages.
- Provide occasional brief reminders of what was covered (i.e., repeat and reinforce).
- During Q&A, incorporate the analysts' names in your responses.

AVOID READING FROM A SCRIPT

You're at a concert. The performer plays or sings every song without once using sheet music…for the entire two hours! You're impressed…even if you weren't consciously aware of it. Do likewise when presenting via teleconference. Don't read a script because you know the audience can't see it. They can hear it. Research shows that script readers are viewed as less knowledgeable. They also sound less interesting. Instead, use notes but speak conversationally. (This advice is somewhat unconventional, but try it.)

SHARE YOUR VISUALS PROPERLY:

In most teleconferences involving visuals (usually PowerPoint), the audience is listening by phone or streaming audio while the visuals are being projected online. There are several approaches you can take. Here's the best one:
- Avoid sharing your visuals beforehand. Audiences can read faster than you

can talk, so they are likely to read ahead—causing you to lose control of the flow of information.

- Use technology that lets you, rather than the audience, control the progression of your slides. That way, all viewers are synchronized. Plus, you won't constantly need to tell your audience what slide you're on (e.g., "Now, turning to slide number 5 … ").

- Give the audience access to the visuals after the conference call. Archive them on your website. Research indicates that 75 percent of long-term investors want a company's earnings calls to be available on the website for a full year.

Being an audience member in a teleconference requires little effort. Not so if you're the presenter. Presenting effectively via teleconference requires you to shift gears a bit and use some techniques that differ from conventional presenting.

INVESTOR & ANALYST ROAD SHOWS: A BEST-PRACTICES CHECKLIST

BEFORE THE EVENT

- **Lead time:** Two months is ideal to develop and rehearse thoughtful content.
- **Know your audience:** Don't be afraid to inquire about their specific information needs and wants.
- **Schedule:** Hold the first few presentations with the least-important audiences. Save the most important for the middle and the end of the road show.
- **Anticipate questions:** Develop a list of questions most likely to be asked, along with those you hope no one asks. Then develop and vocalize suggested answers.
- **Rehearse:** Ensure that every presenter has practiced his/her presentation, including recording and critiquing it. Have a "dress rehearsal."
- **"Platform" skills:** Assess the communication skills of the execs who'll be involved. Is some one-on-one communications coaching necessary?

DURING THE EVENT

- **Length:** Limit your prepared remarks to 15 minutes (non-deal road shows).

- Maximize dialog, Q&A.
- **Road show purpose:** Communicate your business plan:
  - Background of the business
  - Management team
  - Company products/services (+ features)
  - Current state of the business
  - Competitive environment of the company
  - Expected results
- **Avoid data dumps:** Instead, engage in dialog and relationship-building. Focus on providing insight, perspective, meaning.
- **Messaging:** Incorporate analogies, stories, examples—the three most powerful tools of persuasion.
- **Communicate your company's "investible idea":** Before investors will purchase, or analysts will recommend, a particular stock, they ask this question: "What is it about this particular investment that will benefit me or my client?" What makes you different? What's your value proposition? State it in a couple of sentences.
- **Have a strong opening:** Don't squander this important moment on the ordinary or mundane. Deliver a message that's simple, concise, memorable.
- **Use PowerPoint sparingly:** Powerful, persuasive presenters rely on themselves rather than on projected images to reach an audience.
- **Don't "read" to your audience:** Avoid the script reading associated with most earnings calls and analyst presentations. Instead, "talk" the audience through your material.
- **Props work:** If possible, bring product samples, demos, etc.
- **Leave-behinds:** Provide the detailed version of your PowerPoint visuals. Also, consider a clever, high-quality gift that represents the company's products, services, industry.

AFTER THE EVENT

- **Send a handwritten thank-you note** to every investor/analyst with whom you met.
- **Seek feedback** from some of the attendees.
- **Conduct a "post-mortem"** to assess the success of your event.

WHAT'S YOUR COMPANY'S INVESTIBLE IDEA?

Let's do some word association. You know how this game is played: Someone gives you a word, and you respond with a word you associate with it. In this case, I'm going to list the names of some companies. What word or words do you associate with the following companies:

Southwest Airlines...Nordstrom...The Walt Disney Company.

It's fair to say that those three companies do a good job of telling their story. Maybe you know them through their ads or commercials, or through the news coverage they get. Maybe you've had first-hand experience with one or more of them—as a customer.

Here's how these companies see themselves: Southwest: The low-fare airline. Nordstrom: Compelling shopping experience. The Walt Disney Company: Imagination and wholesomeness.

Most companies have a story or core idea. It's their reason for existing—what they do best (better than their competitors) and why they do it (beyond just making money). Their core idea addresses the Who? What? Why? (Who they are. What they do. Why they do it.). These things don't change—or at least shouldn't change. But analysts and investors want to know the "How?"

How is Southwest Airlines going to become and/or remain the low-fare airline? How is Nordstrom going to give customers the most compelling shopping experience?

Financial communications is primarily about the "How?" That's where the "investible idea" comes in. It addresses the "How?"

One of the first questions investors ask themselves is: What is it about this company that makes it an attractive investment option among all the other options out there. And there are a lot of them. What makes this company tick? What's the investible idea that's going to make me or my client prosper?

Most companies fall short in communicating their investible idea (if they have one).

One approach some companies take in their corporate financial communications is to highlight their strong, past results—going back five, maybe ten years. I call it the "rising bar graphs" approach. The problem with this approach is that the past may be fine, but for the future, you're asking someone to buy on faith. Investors and analysts generally are not faith buyers. They want to know <u>how</u> a company plans to achieve results.

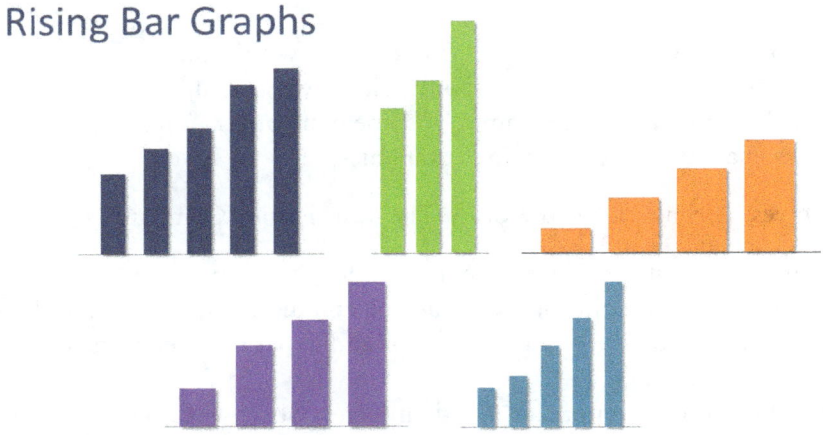

Highlighting strong, past performance can be impressive, but what about the future? Don't expect analysts and investors to buy on faith.

Another approach some companies take is to provide massive amounts of data. They assume that analysts will take it, evaluate it, compare it with other data, and develop the appropriate selling message.

It's like Procter & Gamble saying to Walmart: "Here's some Vicks NyQuil. Here's what it contains. Here's what it does. We'll leave it to you to figure out how to sell it."

Companies spend enormous amounts of time, effort and money generating data that analysts, investors, business reporters and others are not always able to absorb or correctly interpret. Companies assume these individuals will go on to develop the right positioning or message. (Think of analysts writing their reports—sometimes literally while they're attending the company's analyst presentation or listening to its earnings call.)

Numbers alone don't provide perspective or insight. A better approach is to have a compelling investible idea—and to communicate it repeatedly in analyst presentations, earnings calls, press releases and the annual report.

Let's look at an investible idea:

Convenience is becoming increasingly important to customers, especially millennials who make up a large portion of the consumer population. This demographic wants their favorite foods whenever and wherever they want. In fact, consumers in general are increasingly ordering food to be delivered:

- Restaurant delivery traffic (not including pizza) has risen 33 percent since 2012.
- 51 percent of Americans use delivery services to purchase meals from casual dining restaurants.
- 26 percent of Americans order takeout or delivery at least once a week.
- Digital ordering and delivery are growing 300 percent faster than dine-in traffic since 2014.

Grubhub is a leading online and mobile food-ordering and delivery service with the largest and most comprehensive network of restaurant partners. It operates in more than 4,000 U.S. cities, features more than 300,000 restaurants, serves more than 30 million active diners and generated $1.3 billion in revenue in 2019 (a 30 percent year-over-year increase from 2018). When you consider those facts along with the restaurant industry trends cited above, you have the ingredients for an investible idea.

How do you develop your investible idea? You've got to look at your company from the outside in—from an investor's point of view. Ask yourself, what is it about your company that could attract the interest of an investor? Your investible idea should involve a discovery. It's as if a lightbulb goes on in someone's head—revealing the reason why a particular company is notable, perhaps even unique.

Your investible idea might spring from the industry you're in. Or, as in the case of Grubhub, it could relate to a social or demographic trend.

Strip your investible idea down to its most critical essence. Eliminate the superfluous—ideas that are important, but not the most important. Express your idea in a few sentences. A successful salesperson will tell you that when he gets a prospective customer on the phone, he must get that person's attention immediately or risk losing the sale. If someone asks you why you shop at Home Depot, you tell him why in a couple of sentences. The same is true about stocks.

Imagine you're on a plane, talking to the person sitting next to you. The plane is about to land when your seatmate asks about your firm as a potential investment opportunity. You have just a few brief minutes to succinctly make the case why the stock is a good investment. What do you say?

Rob Tobin, a successful script doctor put it this way: "There's an old saying in Hollywood: If you can't describe your story in a sentence, there's something wrong with the story."

Expressing your investible idea with word economy makes sense. Analysts follow many companies; provide them with a succinct, compelling message, and they'll likely end up using it verbatim in the reports they generate. Plus, you'll find it easy to use during your quarterly earnings conference calls or if you're lucky enough to be invited to appear on CNBC or Bloomberg.

So, what's Grubhub's investible idea? Here's my take (in two sentences): Convenience is becoming increasingly important to customers—especially younger ones, who want their favorite foods whenever and wherever they want, and to pay with the click of a button. Grubhub, an online and mobile food-ordering and delivery leader with the largest network of restaurant partners, is well positioned to capitalize on the widespread popularity and growth of food delivery.

Once you have your investible idea, enhance it with other points that show why your company is an attractive investment—e.g., good management, including bench strength; solid safety record; impressive financial performance; etc.—the things you're probably already talking about. Remember to include both emotional and analytical content.

Your investible idea is not a slogan. And while it's close to what some companies call their mission statement, it's not a mission statement. (Your mission statement addresses the "Why?") An investible idea is concrete—not abstract—it's something that causes investors and those who advise them to take a closer look at you and what you have to offer. Work your investible idea into your analyst presentations, earnings calls, annual report and other financial communications.

CAUTION: ANALYST INTERACTION SLIP-UPS

Former professional wrestler and outspoken Minnesota Governor Jesse Ventura created a furor when the following quote attributed to him appeared in an interview in *Playboy* magazine: "Organized religion is a sham and a crutch for weak-minded people who need strength in numbers. It tells people to go out and stick their noses in other people's business." Ouch!

Afterward, in a CNBC interview, Ventura confirmed that he uttered the quote, but explained that he had spent many hours over several days with the *Playboy* interviewer, and that his comment about religion was not made during the actual interview.

Off-the-record comments to reporters have damaged or destroyed many a career or reputation. These and other mistakes can also occur when investor relations professionals and executives interact with analysts during earnings calls, road shows, presentations, as well as in more informal settings—during cocktail hours, lunches and dinners, tours and other events. Every analyst interaction entails a degree of risk. Here are the most common and damaging mistakes made, especially during those informal moments:

Off-the-record:

Like reporters, analysts are never "off the clock" when it comes to gathering information. Don't share information in confidence or let your guard down with an analyst. Assume everything you say in the presence of an analyst will be used.

Personal opinion:

It's tempting to respond when asked your opinion about something. But remember that you represent your company. You cannot publicly (or privately) separate yourself from it. Avoid offering a personal opinion.

Rumors:

Steer clear of commenting on rumors—heard or invented—by analysts. The best response is to say that your company's policy is to not comment on rumors.

Speculation:

Engaging in hypothetical or speculative banter with an analyst is dangerous. Hypothetical questions often begin with, "What if…?" and are followed by a layered set of fictional circumstances. Don't play a game you cannot win. Limit your responses to what is known.

Third-party discussions:

In this trap, the analyst attempts to get you to discuss an organization other than your own—a competitor, former employer, customer, supplier, etc. When you engage in third-party discussions, you waste an opportunity to convey information about your own company.

"No comment":

This phrase implies that you are evading the issue, hiding something damaging, or that you are guilty of wrongdoing. There are many ways to say you can't discuss the issue without seeming to take the Fifth Amendment as your protective cloak. One way is to give sound reasons why you will not or cannot answer a question (e.g., proprietary or material information, current or pending litigation, don't know, etc.).

Repeating words or phrases:

Most correspondents on the TV news magazine *60 Minutes* have mastered the skill of getting people to deliver the exact sound bite they need. Case in point:

> Anderson Cooper: "And that's essentially a commercial for GoPro."
> GoPro CEO: "Essentially a commercial for GoPro."

Sometimes the goal is to get a juicy sound bite. Other times, the journalist is trying to help the interviewee say something interesting. Don't allow analysts to put words in your mouth—words that could end up in the reports they issue. Instead, choose your words carefully and stick with them rather than parroting back what you just heard.

So, should you talk just about football or the weather when you're with analysts in informal situations? Not at all. Have one or two key messages and find a way to work them into the conversation. Stories, analogies, examples, compelling data and memorable lines are especially appealing to analysts.

Analysts and reporters have a lot in common. Both have competitors out to best them. Both are in search of information—often, information that's difficult to obtain. So they use the tools and techniques of journalism to get it.

There's a saying in corporate media relations: "Be friendly with reporters, but remember that they are not your friends." Similar advice applies in investor relations when it comes to analysts.

TOUGH EARNINGS CALL QUESTIONS ... AND HOW TO HANDLE THEM

Most quarterly earnings conference calls today are one hour in length, with the majority of that time devoted to Q&A. That's a good development. An ideal mix is 15 minutes of prepared remarks, followed by 45 minutes of Q&A.

Listen to most execs respond to questions during earnings calls and analyst presentations, and you can't help being impressed with their company and industry knowledge. But then there are those occasional out-of-left-field questions—a little tougher to handle. Here's something that can help. Most tough questions can be distilled into several types. Here they are and how to handle them:

QUESTIONS THAT FALL OUTSIDE YOUR AREA OF EXPERTISE OR RESPONSIBILITY

Strategy: Don't feel pressured to respond. Defer to the appropriate person, either immediately or later.

Example: Q: I understand you recently had a fatality at your facility in Alabama. What happened?

A: I don't have all the details, but that's correct. We had a tragic accident—something that's very unusual for us. We're conducting a thorough investigation and are providing support to the victim's family. If you need more information, I can put you in touch with someone else in the company.

HOSTILE, IMPOLITE, NEGATIVE QUESTIONS. QUESTIONS WITH AN EDGE

These are decidedly unfriendly questions, perhaps asked by individuals who are upset with you or your organization.

Strategy: Don't show discomfort. Don't reinforce by repeating negatives. Neutralize by rephrasing.

Example: Q: Why is the management of this company so **incompetent** that it had to **slash** the dividend?

A: Let me explain the reason why we decided to lower the dividend.

QUESTIONS YOU SHOULD NOT ANSWER
(MATERIAL, PROPRIETARY OR CONFIDENTIAL INFORMATION. PENDING LITIGATION. RUMORS.)

Example: Q: I've heard rumors from a number of sources that your company is about to make a sizeable acquisition in Brazil, perhaps as early as next quarter. Is this true?

A: Our policy is that we don't comment on rumors. What I can tell you is that our company, like many others, is always looking for growth opportunities.

MULTIPLE

Someone may ask you a series of questions—often in a rapid-fire manner. If the questions are related, responding is usually not difficult—if you can remember them. The difficulty usually comes when there's no common thread among the questions. Also, standard operating procedure is to allow analysts to ask one question and a follow-up; some analysts violate this guideline.

Strategy: Manage multiple questions by handling them one at a time. Choose only one of the questions—the first, the last, the easiest, the most important, etc. You decide. Then say to the questioner, "You had another question." Also, don't feel you need to answer every question in the series; select one and then move on to another questioner. Politely remind the audience of the two-question limit.

STATEMENTS

These are not questions at all, merely views—perhaps charged and strongly voiced.

Strategy: Many people are thrown by statements; they say nothing and look weak or appear "bested" by the audience member. Have a response. Convert statements into questions you can answer or simply provide your perspective.

Example: Statement: I listened to your March 13th presentation in New York, and I think you're seriously underestimating the negative impact China will have on your company.

Response: China has certainly increased its production of what we manufacture. But there are a few factors people need to keep in mind...

LIMITED-OPTION QUESTIONS (MULTIPLE CHOICE, EITHER/OR, YES/NO).

In this type of question, the questioner provides a limited number of possible answers, forcing you to select one.
Strategy: Don't accept the questioner's limited options.
Example: Q: Was the accident a result of employee error or equipment failure?

A: We don't know the cause of the accident yet. We're looking at a number of possibilities.

DIDN'T HEAR OR UNDERSTAND THE QUESTION.

Strategy: Ask for clarification or for the question to be repeated.

PERSONAL OPINION.

Strategy: Remember that you represent your organization. You cannot publicly separate yourself from it. You are not being questioned for your private views. Avoid offering a personal opinion unless it tracks with the company position.

Example: Q: Recently, executives of major oil companies testified in Congress about obscene profits and high energy prices. As someone who is knowledgeable about the oil and gas industry, do you think such hearings are worthwhile?

A: I'm not in a position to judge such things. What I can tell you... (bridge to one of your key points).

WHAT TO DO WHEN IT'S EARNINGS SEASON AND THE NEWS IS BAD

Four times a year, publicly traded companies have the pleasure (or pain) of reporting their financial performance to shareholders and to the analysts who advise them. At some point, nearly every company may have to deliver bad financial news. It's not easy, but it's critical to get it right. Here are some ideas for communicating disappointing results in your quarterly earnings conference call:

Communicate more, not less.

Some executives tend to pull back on their internal and external communications when their company experiences difficulties. And while quarterly earnings calls are not mandated by the Securities and Exchange Commission, it's unlikely that a company that's been conducting these calls in the past will suspend them during difficult periods. However, some companies temporarily change the format of their calls. The call may be shorter, have one or two fewer executives participating, or less time may be devoted to Q&A. These and other changes that depart from the format previously followed are readily noted by those listening to the call—especially analysts—and can raise concerns.

Another change sometimes prompted by disappointing results (or the belief that there will be bad results to report in the future) involves ending the practice of providing earnings guidance (management's view about what the company will earn in the next quarter). The decision whether to issue guidance is a complex one, but not doing so may send this message: the company is not doing well so its management finds it hard to forecast. Another downside of providing less information is that it can create the perception that management is not being held accountable. And in light of corporate scandals, disclosure has taken on added importance. In short, more information generates greater confidence and understanding.

Don't bury the lead.

There's an expression in journalism that says, "Don't bury the lead." In other words, the most important information should appear in the headline and in the first paragraph, not be buried somewhere later in the article. One mistake some execs make is to downplay the bad news by mentioning it (almost as an afterthought) later in the call or by trying to neutralize it with phrases that are at odds with the actual results (e.g., "We are well positioned." "We are pleased with … " etc.).

Open with a statement that characterizes the quarter. If the results are disappointing, say that. Doing so enhances credibility. (Warren Buffet, one of the most credible and plain-spoken business executives, once told investors, "I made one particularly egregious error, acquiring Dexter Shoe for $434 million in 1993. Dexter's value promptly went to zero. The story gets worse: I used stock for the purchase...")

Next, explain what's behind those disappointing results—in specific and concrete terms. Then, discuss your action plan to address the problem. For example, if you lost a major customer, talk about what you're doing to get new customers or keep existing ones.

At one time, I was coaching a number of executives at a company that owns and manages shopping centers throughout the United States. The goal was to help them improve their quarterly earnings conference calls. For several quarters, the company's financial results had been disappointing because of the recession. During the coaching session, the CEO mentioned that there were signs that things were starting to improve. Then he relayed a story about a phone call he recently received from an executive at Target, the giant retailer. The call was a "heads-up" that in the coming months Target planned to build a number of new stores which would serve as anchors for several new shopping centers. When I asked the CEO if he planned to tell that story in his upcoming conference call, he said no. I convinced him to do otherwise—even if he couldn't reveal the name of the retailer.

Simply telling analysts that things were starting to look up would have lacked impact. It's a cliché. Analysts have heard it many times before and probably wouldn't have believed it. But when you tell them that a national retailer is planning to expand and that the expansion will positively impact your company, that resonates and enhances credibility.

Transfer energy and enthusiasm.

Communication is selling. And successful selling involves transferring energy and enthusiasm from speaker to listener. Although content is king in the quarterly earnings conference call, powerful messages can fall flat if they aren't delivered well. Every executive who speaks during the call (including those who are there simply to respond to questions) must be able to communicate in a confident and compelling manner. No low-energy, boring (and therefore, not credible) speakers!

Most conference calls are conducted via teleconference. Listeners hear the executives, but don't see them. This poses some special challenges when communicating. A spoken message contains three components: verbal (the words you say), vocal (how you sound) and visual (what people see). With the visual element absent in a conference call, the vocal element takes on added importance. Research shows that it constitutes 86 percent of your believability (with verbal contributing 14 percent). Think about the amount of information communicated in a single word when someone says, "Hello" when answering the phone. Have you ever listened to the greeting you recorded on your phone and thought about what signals it's sending? Your voice conveys both logic and feeling.

A few suggestions:

- Try not to read from a prepared script (audiences view "readers" as less knowledgeable), but if you do, be sure to sound like you're talking, not reading.
- Your delivery must be fluid—not "halting." Avoid too many "non-words" ("uh," "um," etc.).
- Just as people naturally gravitate to individuals with outgoing personalities, they are inclined to listen to ideas presented with energy and conviction. To help sell your message, increase your normal energy. Try standing up while talking; volume and inflection tend to increase when we're on our feet. If you're sitting, lean forward to raise energy.
- Practice your remarks several times. Use your smart phone to record; then critique. Identify the questions you'll probably be asked and know how you'll answer them.

End on a positive note.

Your closing remarks should reference the most important idea or ideas discussed during the call. Closing remarks are defined as what the CEO says right before the Q&A segment and some final words right before the call ends. It's okay to acknowledge the disappointing earnings, but that's not the takeaway. The last words listeners should hear should be what your plans are going forward. And those comments should be delivered with impact and authority.

STORYTELLING: THE SECRET WEAPON IN YOUR INVESTOR COMMUNICATIONS

Analyze the content of most investor communications (annual reports, earnings calls, analyst presentations) and what you usually find is a lot of analytical content—facts, data, documentation, evidence. But analytical content alone is not enough to make the case why your company is worth looking at, perhaps as an attractive investment option.

One way to make that case is through stories. Effective storytelling is critical if you're going to reach analysts, investors, reporters and others who follow your company.

MACRO-LEVEL STORYTELLING

First, there's storytelling on a macro level. Every company has a story—a core idea that differentiates it from its competitors.

The Starbucks story is all about "your third place." There are several important places in our lives. Our home is one. Our workplace is another. Starbucks wants to be your third place—somewhere you want to go to relax and spend time—regularly. Oh, and have a cup or two of coffee.

For Panera, the story is "clean," healthy, fast food served in a pleasant environment.

Southwest Airlines? The low-fare airline.

Successful companies have a laser-like focus on their core idea or story. Anything that doesn't relate or contribute to that key idea is superfluous and a potential distraction that should be avoided. Successful companies also communicate their story—repeatedly—to achieve awareness and understanding. Repetition and reinforcement are powerful tools, and a company's story needs to be told and retold at every appropriate opportunity.

The other type of storytelling occurs at the micro level.

MICRO-LEVEL STORYTELLING

On a daily basis, amazing things occur throughout most companies. Nordstrom is a department store known for providing outstanding customer service (its macro story). You've probably heard of some of the things Nordstrom employees have done for customers: One employee ironed a new shirt for a customer who needed it for an afternoon meeting. Another employee gift wrapped items a customer bought... from Macy's.

Investors and those who advise them need to hear such stories. But you need to find them. That means developing a network of employees to help you unearth those gems. If you're the head of investor relations for your company, part of your job involves talking to engineers, plant managers, supervisors and others on the front line who can provide the stories that will bolster the facts and other analytical content you plan to convey. Other sources for good stories are your company's PR, marketing and sales professionals.

But you might be thinking, "Wait a minute, analysts are a special breed. They're 'numbers' people—perfectly happy with loads of data. They don't want stories." Wrong! They are human beings who have an emotional side as well as an analytical side. And human beings are hard-wired to pay attention to (and remember) stories.

When you develop the content for your next investor communication, be sure there's a reference to your company's macro story, along with a micro story or two.

HOW ONE COMPANY HITS HOME RUNS IN ITS ANALYST PRESENTATIONS

Analyst presentations probably rank among the most important events a publicly traded company hosts. Typically, the CEO, CFO and usually several additional executives are the individuals involved. The presentations are often held in New York and may run a half-day or more in length. In short, they're a big deal.

I'm keenly interested in these presentations—in part, because many of my clients conduct them and I'm frequently involved in the preparation process. Some companies give scant attention to their analyst day efforts. And the results are often predictably disastrous. Others have figured out the why and how of good preparation.

One of my clients, in particular, stands out as a model of effective analyst presentation preparation and execution. I won't identify the company by name, other than to say it's a Fortune 500 energy company. Several of its executives participate in the company's yearly analyst day event in New York. Here's a look at what this company does to prepare:

First off, it recognizes the importance of the event and is willing to commit the necessary resources—time, effort and money—to ensure that it's a success. As with most successful efforts within a corporation, the CEO is the driver. And in this firm, the CEO leads by example—meaning, he himself takes an active role in the preparations. No "Do as I say, not as I do" here!

LEAD TIME

One of the most common mistakes associated with analyst presentations is that companies don't start to prepare early enough. So, a few days before the event, they're scrambling to cobble together some remarks. The content is neither thoughtful nor well rehearsed. In contrast, my model client wisely starts the process more than a month before the event. The process has a number of elements:

MESSAGE DEVELOPMENT

Understandably, individual presenters (there have been as many as eight) are responsible for determining the content of their presentations. They're assisted by staff members within their function who understand the big picture, but also can track down facts and other details that make their way into the presentation. Two other individuals play an important role in developing the messages.

One is the head of investor relations, who tends to focus on factual content. The other is one of the company's communications professionals assigned to the presenter; this individual is typically the advocate for "emotional" content (e.g., analogies, stories, examples). Together, all these individuals craft the key messages. A separate resource then develops the PowerPoint visuals that support the presentation.

In a survey conducted by Distinction, only 25 percent of executives surveyed said they invest more than two hours preparing for very high-stakes presentations. My client understands that quality presentations take time and planning.

CEO REVIEW

When each presentation is complete or nearly complete, a session is scheduled so the presenter can get feedback from the CEO. Several other individuals are usually present at this review: the CFO, head of IR, general counsel, head of communications and any of the presenter's staff involved in developing the presentation. Rather than deliver their presentations, most presenters "talk the reviewers through them." This is an opportunity to ensure that the overall message is on target, that the facts and other details are accurate, and that the presentation meshes well with the other presentations.

Also, I participate in this review and provide the client with an outsider's perspective on such things as messaging, organization and idea flow, length, use of PowerPoint, and whether the presentation captures and holds audience attention.

These reviews take place over a number of days and are conducted in person or sometimes via video conference (for executives who are based in various regions around the country).

ONE-ON-ONE COACHING

The best messages are less than effective if they are poorly delivered. So this client arranges for a series of one-on-one coaching sessions with the presenters (including the CEO) to be conducted over several weeks. The sessions typically run a half-day (for new presenters) to several hours (for returnees or stellar performers). The focus is on delivery or "platform" skills. In this particular company, the execs do not read a prepared script; instead they use notes and their PowerPoint visuals as an aid to discussing their material. This approach, which is atypical of most companies, can be very engaging, but it takes skill to make it work. Several other skills addressed during the sessions include having a powerful opening (in terms of both content and delivery), using a few "sparklers" throughout the presentation (e.g., stories, anecdotes, examples, memorable lines, etc.) and some tips for fielding questions.

These sessions vary greatly—depending on the presenter. But the sessions always include recording and critiquing the delivery. Some presenters request a second coaching session.

DRESS REHEARSAL

The day before the event, all presenters gather together at the hotel where the event will be held to run through their presentations. It's one final practice and sometimes an opportunity to fine tune their comments, based on suggestions from the other presenters. These presentations are not recorded, but each presenter gets an assessment of his delivery skills and some last-minute reminders or suggestions. There's real benefit in having all presenters hear this feedback; they pick up a wide variety of presenting tips. The rehearsal is also an opportunity for the presenters to get a look at the room where they'll be speaking, and familiarize themselves with the lectern, monitors and other equipment they'll be using.

FOLLOW-UP

This client requests that I attend its analyst day event. I do, and afterward, submit a detailed written critique of all aspects of the event, including each executive's performance (including during Q&A) and audience reaction. That report is distributed to the presenters and usually resurfaces the following year during preparations for the company's next meeting with analysts.

Great presentations don't happen by accident. They require effort. Make that effort and you can hit a communications home run for analysts who follow your company.

CHAPTER 5

SOCIAL MEDIA

Social media has become an important—some might say, vital—tool in professional communication. But just like most anything of value, along with it come some potential problems. Knowing how to navigate the tricky waters of social media is a must for every business leader.

SOCIAL MEDIA MISSTEPS ... AND HOW TO AVOID THEM

A 16-year-old high school junior—let's call her Samantha—goes to a party where alcohol has somehow made its way into the home. Peer pressure being what it is, Sam has a few drinks. Later, she takes a few "selfies," showing off her latest dance moves, drink in hand. The next day, she posts those photos on her Facebook page and sends a few pics to her friends via Instagram.

Fast forward one year. Sam submits an application to her "dream" college, where the school's admissions officer conducts a background check. What surfaces? You guessed it. Those Facebook party photos. Not good.

When most of us think of social media faux pas, the young and inexperienced—people like Samantha—come to mind. But adults, including savvy business executives, are not immune to social media missteps.

Remember when clothing designer Kenneth Cole decided to piggyback on the trending topic of riots in Egypt? He sent out this tweet: "Millions are in uproar in #Cairo. Rumor is they heard our new spring collection is now available online at..." His tweet generated viral outrage on the internet, resulting in #boycottKennethCole hash tags.

Then there was former Uber CEO Travis Kalanick who was caught on a dashcam video arguing with an Uber driver who claimed to have lost $97,000 because Uber lowered fares. "I'm bankrupt because of you," said the driver. Kalanick shot back, "You know what? Some people don't like to take responsibility for their own s---. They blame everything in their life on somebody else. Good luck," as he got out of the car and slammed the door. Kalanick's performance got worldwide negative media coverage and social media exposure.

Social media, a collection of some amazing tools, can pose potential problems. Just ask the fifty million Facebook users whose profiles made their way to Cambridge Analytica, the British political consulting firm that harvested personal data and used it for political advertising purposes.

Most likely, you probably have a presence on social media through platforms such as Facebook or LinkedIn. But regardless of your social media use (or non-use), you'll find the following suggestions beneficial:

Don't Be a Technology Dinosaur.

If you're in today's business world, you must familiarize yourself with social media—the various networks or platforms, their language and how they work. This is especially important for people in the latter stages of their careers. (Does the phrase, "early retirement" ring a bell?) For example, even if you've never sent out a tweet, you better have at least some familiarity with Twitter.

Personal, Professional, Public or Private?

If you decide to use social media, determine the strategy that's right for you. For example, on Facebook you could have a personal or professional presence, or both. Also, you could limit your audience to family and friends (private) or widen it to include the public (customers, etc.). In part, your decision should be driven by whether you have the time or access to other resources to maintain that presence. By the way, using a ghostwriter is a bad option when it comes to social media. Remember, the whole point of social media is authentic, transparent communication. In short, there are practical considerations to weigh, including whether you're willing or able to devote time to this form of communication.

The Pause That Refreshes.

For many people, one of the most appealing features of social media is its immediacy—instant communication. Write a letter and send it by "snail mail?" No way! Send multiple emails? Too slow and time consuming!

Social media seems tailor made for our fast-paced society. But before hitting that "send" button, users of social media need to pause—something that seems to conflict with what the technology is all about—namely, rapid response.

Many of the mistakes associated with social media use in business stem from poor judgment—saying something you shouldn't have said. Fast food restaurant Chick-fil-A learned a hard lesson when one of its top executives sent out a tweet criticizing same-sex marriage—igniting a firestorm. The tweet was eventually deleted, but not until after it had already been archived.

Most of us know that after we've written an angry letter or memo, it's best to "sleep on it" awhile before sending. If you find yourself wondering if you should say something, you probably shouldn't.

Take the Bad with the Good.

I once worked at a company whose media relations manager always reminded executives who wanted to clam up during bad news that his title was not, "Manager, Good Media Relations." In other words, you can't communicate just when the news is good. This guy's advice also applies to social media. If you think you can use social media when times are good, but can pull back or "go silent" when problems arise, think again. You're better off not to get involved at all. Inherent in social media is direct, candid, credible, two-way communication.

Monitor What's Being Said about You.

Not only does social media provide you with low-cost platforms to communicate with a wide variety of audiences, this tool also lets you learn from the instant communication it generates—what's being said about you and your organization. What you don't know can hurt you.

Steve Martin, an accomplished comedian and banjo player, delivered this humorous line to the audience during one of his concerts with the bluegrass band, Steep Canyon Rangers: "Well, it's been about 45 minutes now since I have Googled myself. And I think you understand the kind of anxiety that can create in a person like myself. And I'd like you to get to know the Rangers a little bit better. I've asked them to do a song on their own. Do you guys [the band] think you can handle that?" Google yourself—regularly.

Beware of Citizen Journalists.

Today, everyone is a potential reporter. Anyone armed with a smart phone can instantly use social media to pass along news, photos and video. You see it every day in the news—the name of some citizen who provided the media with a photo that appears on screen or in print. Remember the US Airways plane that landed on the Hudson River? News of that event was first reported by a man who happened to be nearby on a ferry and had a Twitter account. Being discreet in what you say around others has taken on added importance with the emergence of social media.

YIKES! HAVE YOU SEEN WHAT'S ON YOUTUBE?

It had to be one of the company's worst nightmares: Some years back, Domino's Pizza learned that two of its employees in North Carolina posted videos of adulterated food on YouTube. The employees, who were bored working on Easter Sunday, decided to amuse themselves by uploading vulgar videos, one of which showed an individual putting mozzarella cheese up his nose and then blowing the cheese onto a sandwich. Some one million people saw these videos before they were removed from the site several days later. The North Carolina store where the videos were shot eventually had to be closed.

Organizations today operate in an environment loaded with new threats to their reputations. Those threats can come from a variety of new media and social media sources: text messages, blogs, protest sites, digital videos, tweets, etc. As two *Harvard Business Review* authors once wrote, "Today, anyone armed with a $100 digital camera and Internet connection is a potential Spielberg or Riefenstahl." (Leni Riefenstahl was a German film director and alleged propagandist for the Nazis.)

The way in which large and small companies, other organizations and even individuals respond during a crisis has changed—with the advent of Facebook, Twitter, YouTube and the like. That's not to say the traditional ways of communicating during a crisis (e.g., press briefings, news conferences, media interviews, letters to the editor, advertising, etc.) are no longer important. It's just that these tools may not be enough. To protect yourself from new threats, you need to use new strategies as well.

KNOW HOW TO USE SOCIAL MEDIA

While briefing a company's top executives on crisis management, I asked how many of them were familiar with LinkedIn, Facebook or Twitter. Some responded with blank stares. Others said they thought Facebook was for their teenagers.

Social media are now mainstream in business, and business leaders must understand how these new tools of open, transparent, non-hierarchical, interactive and real-time communication work. Social media represent a significant shift in the way people—especially the younger generation—communicate. Therefore, you should learn the basic social media networks, their language and how they work. In crisis management drills, fictional, damaging videos are being incorporated into scenarios to test a company's ability to respond quickly and effectively to this new element of crisis management.

MONITOR SOCIAL MEDIA

Odds are that an unhappy customer, a disgruntled employee or even a contract worker intending no harm will say or show something on social media that can prove damaging to you or your business. You need to know about it. So it's critical for you to be monitoring what's being said about you. This is especially important if you don't yet have (or plan to have) an active social media presence. (Domino's was first alerted to the disturbing viral video mentioned above by the consumer watchdog organization, GoodAsYou.org.) Some companies have a social media function; its responsibilities include monitoring. You can also hire PR and other firms that specialize in social media monitoring.

SET EXPECTATIONS WITH EMPLOYEES

Research shows that about thirty percent of corporate crises are caused by employees. So the widespread use of social media makes employee-related social media mistakes more likely. The best way to prevent problems is to develop a social media policy for employees. These policies vary by company, but generally consist of guidelines or rules governing social media use. The goal is not to prevent or discourage employees from using social media (that's neither legal nor practical), but to help them understand what constitutes inappropriate behavior. For example, sharing customer information, discussing proprietary technology, and "trash-talking" the company are all unacceptable—even if they are done while off the job. It's also a good idea to let employees know that the company has the right to monitor employee use of social media, and if appropriate, take disciplinary action against offenders.

In a world where joint ventures, intercompany partnerships and significant use of contract workers are standard fare, it also makes sense to ensure that everyone "representing" your company understands the proper use of social media.

RESPOND WITH SPEED

No longer do victims (or villains) have the luxury of time—responding days or sometimes even hours after a crisis surfaces. Just as today's public is used to getting "instant" news, it also expects an "instant" response from the party or parties involved in a crisis. Too often, while a company's PR and legal departments are carefully crafting, reviewing and re-crafting a response, the public is tweeting, emailing or otherwise communicating about the issue or event. In today's world, speed wins, and social media enable you to engage rapidly and simultaneously—directly with your audience.

FIGHT VIRAL WITH VIRAL

Many executives have tunnel vision when it comes to social media. They just see it as a tool that can be used against them by their critics. But they fail to realize that they can use that same tool to help manage a crisis. For example, in the Domino's Pizza video that went viral, the company's U.S. president used YouTube rather than a traditional press release to apologize for the rogue employees' behavior. This approach made sense because the best chance of reaching those that saw the disturbing video on YouTube was through YouTube. (Initially, Domino's used the internet to upload a video response on its corporate website. However, the number of people who viewed the response was a fraction of those who saw the employee prank videos on YouTube.)

Southwest Airlines did something similar after one of its followers on Facebook posted the following: "How about those twins that got bumped for being overweight? Not very good for SW that claims to be customer service oriented on all those ads! Shame." Rather than responding with a disproportionate show of force through the traditional news media or ignoring the posting, the airline provided an explanation on its Facebook page—targeting those who might have read the criticism.

Crises have become a growing, prominent and permanent feature of life in the business world. The paradox of social media is that it has made them both more challenging and more manageable.

CHAPTER 6

SPECIAL SITUATIONS

Executives and managers often find themselves in situations where their ability to communicate is put to extraordinary tests. A plant manager may need to go to a hospital to talk to the family of an employee seriously injured on the job and now in intensive care. A top executive may have to face several hundred concerned, angry or even verbally abusive citizens who oppose the facility his company wants to build or expand. Testifying at a public utility commission or Congressional hearing is another possible responsibility. Knowing what to say and how to say it in these kinds of situations is critical…and these high-stakes communications may even have career implications.

THE LANGUAGE OF TRUST

The issue of trust frequently occupies center stage. In particular, the spotlight is usually on the decline in trust that has occurred in some of our best-known and most important institutions—such as government, journalism, organized religion and business—especially big business.

As our parents taught us, trust is earned, and once lost, is hard—though not impossible—to regain. When it comes to trust, actions speak louder than words. Someone who lies, cheats or steals is a liar, cheater or thief, respectively.

And no words—however effectively delivered—can change that fact. But words matter. And honest people with poor communication skills sometimes undermine their credibility. Perception is reality. Language and trust are linked, and communicating trust is a skill that can be learned. Let's begin class:

THE SCIENTIFIC SIDE OF TRUST

The starting point of any communication is to establish trust. If your audience doesn't see you as trustworthy or credible, you won't get all or some of your message across or be able to address their concerns. Trust, credibility or believability is overwhelmingly determined in a specific part of the brain—the non-rational or emotional part (the brain stem and limbic system).

Think of this emotional part of the brain as a door or gate. It may be closed, wide open, or partially open. Your goal is to make sure that door is open so that what you say can pass through and make its way to the thinking or rational part of the brain. Put another way, communication is a two-stage process—getting your message to the rational part of the brain, but first having it make its way past the emotional part.

When most people communicate, they're focused on that rational brain—using logic, reason, common sense to reach it. Technically trained individuals are especially prone to believe all they need to do when trying to inform or influence someone about a complex issue is to rely on science. But, for example, having an engineer at a school board meeting to explain why power lines near an elementary school pose no health threat to children is no guarantee that parents will listen or believe.

As Bert Decker says in his book, *You've Got to be Believed to be Heard*, "The emotional judgment that is formed in your preconscious mind about the speaker determines whether you will tune in to his or her message—or tune out. If you don't believe in someone on an emotional level, little if any of what they have to say will get through. It will be screened out by your distrust…Even if the facts and content are great by themselves, they are forever locked out because the person delivering them lacks believability."

COMPONENTS OF TRUST

Research provides some valuable insight into trust or credibility:
- Empathy/caring accounts for half of a person's credibility and is assessed in the first thirty seconds. That's why, for example, it's critical for a company spokesperson to express sorrow or regret when there's been an injury or loss of life in an accident. When delivering a business presentation, a speaker demonstrates empathy/caring by addressing the information needs and wants

of the audience. Unlike the other three components of trust (discussed below), there are no degrees of empathy/caring as far as the audience is concerned; to them, you are either empathetic/caring or not. There's no in between.

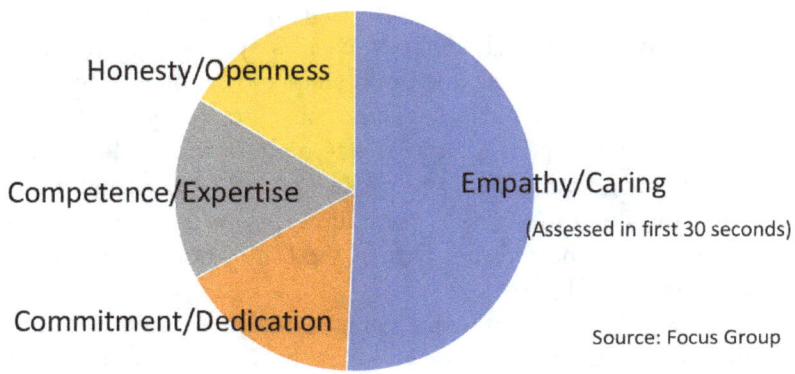

- The other three components account for 15-20 percent each. Competence/expertise: What is your knowledge level? Honesty/openness: Are you truthful, accessible, forthcoming? Commitment/dedication: Do you care about or believe in what you're discussing?
- Technical training tends to drive out communicating empathy/caring. (Hence, all the stereotypes about engineers and computer geeks.)
- Women tend to be perceived as having a high degree of empathy/caring, and a willingness to communicate it. Male communication patterns generally don't exhibit empathy/caring. It's not that men don't care, it's that they are less likely to communicate it.
- When trust is low and concerns are high, non-verbal cues will override verbal cues (what an audience sees says more than what you say).

PITFALLS THAT UNDERMINE TRUST

JARGON

If you're a football fan—and a knowledgeable one at that—even you probably get frustrated when a former player, now a football TV analyst, describes a play using terms only the pros can understand: "Red Right 30 Pull Trap." Say what? Audiences are generally wary of people who lapse into jargon. Those who fail to explain things in layman's terms rarely inspire confidence and often engender suspicion.

Kansas Senator Bob Dole sought the Republican presidential nomination in 1980. While he was on the campaign trail at a middle school in New Hampshire, a student asked him about his plans to combat acid rain (a serious problem in New England). He told her, "That bill's in mark-up." How many students, or even adults, do you think understand the mark-up process? (Dole eventually dropped out of the race.)

Use language that can be understood by an eighth grader or is four grade levels below the average educational level of your audience.

PERSONAL ATTACKS

Argumentum ad hominem—using race, gender or sometimes the character of a person is never a legitimate argument, and it destroys the credibility of the person using it. Organizations, not just people, can also be the target of a personal attack. Address the issue, but don't attack the person or organization. For example, you may view Greenpeace as an extremist organization, but when you talk about the group publicly, stay away from phrases such as "tree huggers." Instead, describe the organization as one whose tactics and proposed solutions are well intentioned but misguided.

IMPERSONAL COMMUNICATIONS

Some experts cite the decrease in face-to-face communication (and the increase in less personal forms of communication, such as texting and email) as a contributing factor in the erosion of trust. When possible, meet face-to-face with employees, customers, vendors, analysts and other key constituencies. Video conferencing is sometimes an effective substitute.

UNINTENDED MESSAGES

Certain cues—tone, volume, gestures, posture, eye contact—often tell us whether to trust someone. For example, halting or slow speech raises red flags, as does failing to make eye contact.

HOW TO INTRODUCE A SPEAKER

It's a familiar story: You've been asked to deliver a presentation or speech at some meeting or event. You've prepared your remarks. Practiced your delivery. You're ready to score a touchdown (or at least a first down).

And then it happens: The person who introduces you fumbles the ball. The introduction is too long (or too short). It contains inaccurate (or irrelevant) information. It's read verbatim by someone who doesn't know you very well (or at all), including how to pronounce your name, and has made little or no attempt to prepare for this assignment. What's more, the delivery is halting and boring.

In short, you're off to a bad start. The audience is already turned off...and you haven't even said a word!

Introducing a speaker is something few of us prepare for very well (or at all). Yet, an introduction can play an important role in getting the audience's attention and helping to create a connection between them and the speaker. It's the equivalent of the opening act that warms up the audience for the headliner at a concert or other performance.

Here are some techniques you can use to create a powerful introduction—one that generates audience interest in the speaker:

- The key to an effective introduction is to give the audience a reason why the speaker was asked to be there. This usually has nothing to do with where the speaker went to school, where he lives, his hobbies, his spouse or how many children he has. Unfortunately, most introductions involve someone merely reciting a litany of degrees earned, positions held or honors achieved. Audiences find this information irrelevant and boring. A better approach is to point out the link between the speaker's professional background and the audience's reasons for being there.

    For example, if you are introducing a political consultant, tell the audience they're about to hear from an expert on political campaigns. Point out that the person has worked on more than twenty state and local campaigns, and that she herself has won (or lost) elective office.

- An exception to this "logical reason" approach is the "testimonial" or "award" introduction. In this case, where the honoree or recipient is going to give an acceptance speech, the introduction is a mini-speech itself. Get a detailed resumé from the person. If you don't know the person, interview him or her by phone to get some additional interesting material. Better yet, interview one or two acquaintances of that person.

- Be different. Consider starting out with the speaker's name. "Bill Stewart is not only a key executive at Pinnacle Software, he's a leading authority on virus protection." Chances are the audience already knows the name of the speaker, so why make it appear you're building to a surprise by waiting until the end of the introduction to give the speaker's name? Another approach is to begin with a brief, compelling story about the speaker.

- Double-check information on resumés and bios. Facts change—including job titles and responsibilities, education, memberships, etc. Check out the speaker's Facebook or LinkedIn page.

- If you are introducing a colleague who is well known to most of the audience—such as an executive in the same company—use the opportunity to say something new about the person. Remember, part of your job is to get your speaker off to a good start, and even old friends appreciate thoughtful introductions.

- Avoid saying, "Our guest speaker needs no introduction," "Without further ado…" and other such clichés.

- As a speaker, consider providing your own written introduction. The person introducing you will appreciate it, and you'll know it's accurate and appropriate for your talk because you decided what information to include.

- Your introduction (like the speaker's presentation) is a performance—an important one. Avail yourself of the best-kept secret to a comfortable and effective delivery: practice it three times, aloud, on your feet, into a recording device.

TO READ OR NOT TO READ

Two questions some people in business frequently ask: "Is it okay to read a prepared statement at a press briefing or news conference?" And: "Is there anything wrong with reading a prepared speech word for word?"

The answers to those questions are respectively, "Yes" and "No." There's nothing intrinsically wrong with reading a prepared statement or speech aloud to an audience. Here's why:

First, some perspective: There's no question most audiences prefer to have a speaker talk to them in a natural, conversational style. (Most speakers prefer to communicate this way as well.) The more extemporaneous or "off the cuff" something sounds, the better the audience likes it. No one likes to be read to (other than young children at bedtime). Also, speakers who read are usually judged to be less knowledgeable and authoritative and are harder to connect with emotionally.

But there are times when reading from a prepared script makes sense. For example, when briefing the news media or conducting a news conference (especially in a crisis), sometimes you simply don't have time to hone your delivery. That's where reading a statement will serve you well. Reading a statement ensures accuracy, and in some communications to the news media, it's especially critical to get word choice exactly right. If you're not using a script, you're either ad-libbing (a definite "no no") or you're speaking from notes or bullet points. Either way, you run the risk of leaving something out, saying too much or saying too little.

In most press briefings and news conferences, reporters and the audiences they are trying to reach are primarily concerned about getting information. How it's delivered is less important to them than what is said. In other words, content trumps delivery. (The one element of a press statement that should never be read, but instead should be spoken conversationally, is the expression of empathy or concern—for example, in the event of injury or death. Picture a spokesperson doing the following—reading these words: "Our company is very concerned…"—then pausing briefly to turn the page before continuing, "…about the three employees who were injured in the accident." Think about how that will look and sound. Not good.)

What about a speech? Here too, reading verbatim can be perfectly fine. When you craft and then read a speech, it's like saying to the audience, "I cared enough about you to prepare these remarks." Every day, you see news anchors reading to the audience from a prepared text. We think nothing of it—as long as it's done with skill. Moreover, some individuals (executives, for example) deliver a lot of speeches—so many that working from notes or bullet points is not practical. (President Obama frequently read from a prepared script—via TelePrompter—and was criticized for it, but just imagine how many speeches he had to deliver in a given week.)

If you opt to read a prepared speech, read your script aloud during the preparation stage; this will help you make sure it sounds conversational.

Reading a speech verbatim effectively is a skill worth having, especially if you plan to end up in the executive ranks. To achieve that skill, keep in mind some of the tips discussed in **How to (Correctly) Use a TelePrompter**, found on p. 52.

BRIEFING LESSONS FROM TOM CLANCY'S JACK RYAN

Tom Clancy was a prolific author who wrote more than eighteen #1 *New York Times* best-selling novels, including *The Hunt for Red October*, where Clancy's best-known fictional hero Jack Ryan first appeared.

Clancy was known for his incredibly detailed and technically accurate espionage and military science plots. But there's a scene in *The Hunt for Red October* that shows Clancy also knew a thing or two about effective communication—specifically, how to conduct a successful briefing—something most of us in the business world need to be able to do.

In the scene, CIA analyst Jack Ryan is at the White House to convince the President and others that the Soviet Union's newest submarine with their most trusted and skilled naval officer at the helm is attempting to defect to the United States. Ryan argues that this explains why nearly the entire Soviet Atlantic fleet is on the move—to find and destroy the sub.

Tom Clancy's Jack Ryan knew a thing or two about conducting a successful briefing.

THE LESSONS

Know the room:

Ryan's briefing would take place in the Situation Room, and Ryan was shown the room before the briefing began. He'd be speaking from a lectern, and his slides (yes, 35mm slides were used in the 1980s) were already set up. At the lectern were a wireless control for the projector, his choice of pointers and a glass of water.

- Get a first-hand look at your room before presenting. If this isn't possible, have someone describe it in detail for you or send you some photos.
- Don't be afraid to use a lectern. It gave Ryan, and it can give you, instant authority. And although it can be a barrier between you and your audience,

you can occasionally move from behind it to get closer to your audience (e.g., during Q&A).

- Test the equipment. If there's a technical glitch during your briefing, most audiences will give you about ten minutes to correct the problem; after that, their patience turns to frustration. Have Plan B ready.
- Be careful with pointers: Presenters sometimes "play" with the older, telescoping variety or use laser pointers for no good reason (e.g., simply circling words that appear on screen).
- Have water on hand. (Caution: some environmentally conscious audiences react negatively to water in plastic bottles, so be careful.)

Control anxiety:

Right before the briefing started, Ryan was asked by the CIA Director whether he was nervous. "Yes sir, I sure am," he replied.

- Most presenters experience some anxiety. That's okay. The goal is not to eliminate it (that could lead to a flat, uninspired delivery), but to control it. Channel that nervousness out in the form of energy (gesturing is one way to help you do that).
- Practice your delivery three times, aloud, on your feet, into a recording device.
- Engage in positive "self-talk." Most people approach their presentation thinking about all the things that can go wrong. Instead, tell yourself that you are there to share your knowledge, ideas and expertise with an audience that is eager to hear you and will benefit from listening. That's a different mindset.

Plan your work, and work your plan:

Ryan's notes "were full of errors and scribbled corrections." That was a "no-no."

- Last-minute changes are rarely delivered as effectively as material you've practiced. President Clinton was known for changing his remarks as he walked from backstage to the lectern (it drove his staff crazy), but he could pull it off. Most of us can't.
- Avoid handwritten notes. Stick with typewritten material.

Know your audience:

Ryan knew who'd be in the audience. In some cases, he also knew their reputations. More importantly, many in the audience knew of him through his impressive past reports on terrorism. And it didn't hurt that the CIA Director made sure some audience members were aware of some of Ryan's other accomplishments.

- Analyze your audience: Who are they? Why are they there? What is their interest in, and knowledge level of, your topic? What are their information wants and needs? Are there any sensitivities in the audience you ought to be aware of?
- Leverage credibility transference. Get a respected colleague—someone you know and who knows you—on board ahead of time with what you're saying or proposing.

Nail the content:

After stating his name and the reason for the briefing, Ryan provided some background information—details about the sub, including its unique features and capabilities, along with a profile of its captain. Then he focused on his theory on what the captain of *Red October* was attempting to do, which in turn explained the unprecedented movement of Soviet ships. The briefing was clear, concise and compelling. Excluding Q&A, it lasted 15 minutes.

- Have a strong opening. Don't squander this critical moment on the ordinary or mundane.
- Be explicit. Communicate directly, not indirectly. Don't expect your audience to "read between the lines" or infer your message.
- Analogies and stories are among the most powerful tools of persuasion. Use them.
- Beware the "curse of knowledge"—having too much information and sharing it all.
- Should your most powerful arguments come first or last? It usually doesn't matter (unless you're interrupted or time becomes an issue). But consider voluntarily addressing opposing viewpoints; it's a way to bolster credibility.

MISSION POSSIBLE: TURNING ENGINEERS INTO EFFECTIVE COMMUNICATORS

One of the things I often hear from industrial companies such as utilities and those in energy, chemicals and technology is this:

"We have engineers who are very capable of identifying critically needed, capital-intensive projects at our facility. But they can't seem to effectively communicate the rationale and details for those projects to plant or corporate management in a clear, concise, compelling manner. They have good ideas but can't sell them."

Can these engineers become more effective communicators? You bet they can! Communication is a skill, and skills can be taught, learned and applied.

The stereotype of engineers and other technically trained individuals is well known: They're nerds. They are uncomfortable around other people. You'll find them holed up in a lab or workshop—probably staring at a computer screen. They dress funny and wear pocket protectors. And so on. Over the years, I've worked with enough engineers to question the accuracy of that stereotype.

That said, many engineers have a communication style that often works against them. Here are three of the most common problems…and how to correct them:

FAILING TO CONNECT

Typically, engineers and other left-brain thinkers are not well acquainted with how critical it is to establish a human connection in order to communicate more effectively. Engineers are trained to approach communication from the vantage point of, "Let's get to the facts, and the facts will carry the day." There's a tendency to believe that messages are sent directly to the logical side of the recipient's brain. But that isn't the way it works. Messages must first pass through the brain's emotional gate. In other words, before you can reach someone on an intellectual level, you must first connect with them on an emotional level. Before an audience will listen to, hear, understand and act on what you said, it must see you as credible, believable, trustworthy, even likeable.

At one point in my career I attended a public meeting being held after an accidental release occurred at a nearby chemical plant. A woman in the audience stood up to say she believed that two miscarriages she suffered resulted from the plant's emissions over the years. The plant manager responded by citing a Johns Hopkins University study that showed no connection between the plant's emissions and any ill effects on human health. What he first should have done was to express empathy for her situation, and then talk about the science.

Suggestions:

- The better you understand your audience, the better you can connect with them.
- Whenever possible, use face-to-face meetings for high-stakes presentations, especially where persuasion is involved.
- Be sure your presentation goes beyond analytical content (e.g., data, facts, examples, etc.). Include emotional content (e.g., stories).
- Avoid overuse of PowerPoint. Minimize or eliminate "word" or "copy" slides. Your visuals should support your presentation, not be your presentation.

USING JARGON OR TECHNICAL LANGUAGE

Most professions, especially highly specialized fields such as science and engineering, have their own language. People in those professions use that language with ease, but the rest of us are left scratching our heads. One sure-fire way to lose an audience (or get it to ignore your ideas) is to confuse them.

Suggestions:

- Gear your communication to the level of sophistication of the audience—remembering that there's been an erosion of scientific and mathematical literacy in this country.

- Regardless of your audience's level of expertise, you'll do well to eliminate or explain jargon.

- "Doing simple" requires a tremendous amount of thought and effort, but the audience will thank you for it.

NOT BEING BRIEF

Audiences rarely complain because a presentation was too short. Some presentations fail because the speaker tries to say too much. In their book, *Made to Stick: Why Some Ideas Survive and Others Die*, authors Chip Heath and Dan Heath refer to this as "the curse of knowledge"—wanting to share everything you know. Engineers are particularly guilty of this—in part because they are logical, sequential thinkers. They can't bear leaving out all the details.

Suggestions:

- Technical talks are not the same as technical papers. Don't dwell on detail. Hit the key points.

- Even though your subject matter is technical, you are still talking to human beings—people who get bored, even during serious, important presentations. Keep your presentations fast-paced and brief.

- When presenting to executives—especially top execs—remember this: They have limited time, short attention spans and are quick studies.

Conventional wisdom has it that engineers are poor communicators, but are analytical, strategic thinkers. If that's so, what makes them good thinkers can also make them better communicators, because effective communication is about approaching communication strategically.

NOTE TO WOMEN: FORGET GENDER-SPECIFIC COMMUNICATIONS ADVICE

There's no shortage of books and articles offering women in business advice on how to improve their communication skills.

Some experts encourage them to adopt a more masculine communication style—direct, hard-hitting, data-driven—the kind used by Margaret Thatcher, Geraldine Ferraro and Jean Kirkpatrick. (Okay, I'm showing my age, so how about Hillary Clinton, Christine Lagarde and Angela Merkel?) Others tell women to embrace their innate feminine style of communicating—empathetic, non-combative, self-revealing. Think: Oprah and Katie Couric.

Most of the advice is skewed toward the masculine: Avoid sentiment and emotion. Use more facts and figures; don't round off numbers. Wear suits and tone down the makeup and jewelry. Use sports references. Steer clear of weak, unnecessary qualifiers, such as "I think..." and "It might..." Lower your voice so it's more resonant. Don't touch your hair.

There may have been a time when such recommendations were justified—say, two or three decades back—when many women may have been receptive to them. Before GenXers and millennials.

I once coached a female engineer who worked in an engineering company predominantly made up of (you guessed it)—male engineers. She was convinced that she needed to adopt a communication style similar to theirs in order to fit in and move up within the firm. My advice to her: Don't do it.

Sure, some gender-specific advice makes sense—for both women and men. For example, most men need reminding to avoid the default "front-fig leaf" stance they assume when standing in front of an audience (hands clasped in front, below the waist)—it's weak. And they need to get more comfortable with storytelling.

But much gender-specific advice—especially for women—misses the mark. For one thing, most women already possess some traits that make them effective communicators:

- Women are more instinctively collaborative. This makes them more likely to consider what an audience wants or needs to hear, rather than focusing on what they want to say. Also, watch how effortlessly most women engage an audience by asking questions and seeking feedback.

- They have a much higher comfort level sharing emotion. Ask a man to incorporate a story (especially a touching one) into a speech or presentation, and you'll get pushback. Most women do it with ease.

- They know what to do with their hands when they're in front of an audience. You rarely see that "front fig leaf" stance. Women gesture easily.
- Behavioral scientists tell us that when we encounter and assess others (especially in business situations), we first judge them on two characteristics—their warmth or trustworthiness and their strength or competence. Research suggests that it is better to project warmth before strength. Most women do this. And it can serve them well at high-emotion public meetings or in a media interview or press briefing where it's critical for a company to apologize or express sorrow over an accidental injury or death.

Women imitating male communication patterns is a charade, and it insults both women and men alike. It reminds me of the salesman who doesn't golf but puts a borrowed set of clubs in the back of his SUV so his potential client (an avid golfer) is sure to notice them as they drive to a restaurant for lunch. At some point, the prospect will likely discover the deception. Women who communicate in a way that's not genuine will probably be found out as well.

Another reason to avoid most gender-specific advice is that it usually fails to address the most serious communications mistakes made—regardless of gender. Here's what matters:

First, have a clear, compelling message. And don't expect the audience to infer it; state it directly. Whether delivering a presentation or speech, or talking to reporters, know what you want to convey. Ask yourself, "What do I want my audience to know, think, feel or do after I finish speaking?" Messages that are personalized, evoke emotion and come from trusted sources resonate best with audiences.

Second, the audience must see you as credible. During every presidential election cycle, the American public is sizing up the candidates, looking to see if any of them are not who they say they are. How the candidate communicates is a primary signal. What a shame for a woman who is naturally engaging, humorous or who knows (and can tell) a good story, to suppress her natural style of communicating.

Third, speak plainly. Most people incorporate the specialized vocabulary of their profession into their communication. Define all technical terms and acronyms. Use language that can be understood by a 12-year-old and avoid jargon or "corporate speak."

Fourth, make a personal connection with the audience. When most people see and hear someone interesting and personable, they are receptive to what that person says. Ask yourself why you watch a particular local or national TV news channel. In general, news programs all report the same news. Your choice of channel is based on a connection you have with the reporters or anchors. In other words, you like them.

Fifth, communicate with energy. Much fun was poked at former Secretary of State Henry Kissinger's accent. But it was actually a minor part of his problem as a communicator. The real culprit was his lack of visual and vocal energy. There's a sameness to the sound of his voice; he speaks in a monotone. Also, there are some eighty muscles in the face, capable of generating 7,000 different facial expressions. Kissinger uses very few of them.

And sixth, watch TV. Today's audiences judge a speaker by what they see on television. If the speaker appears uncomfortable, unprepared or uncaring, people will tune out. Many people in the business world assume the information they are sharing is inherently interesting, and that they don't have to infuse it with excitement. They are wrong. Watch the morning shows, news and other programs that rely heavily on narrative and storytelling, and use the techniques of the entertainment industries to capture and sustain attention.

For the foreseeable future, communication skills will remain one of the most important contributors to success in the business world. Women (and men) who have something to say and a creative way of saying it—those who can communicate confidently and competently—will enjoy much success.

IMPORTANT NEWS TO COMMUNICATE? HARNESS THE POWER OF AN INTERVIEW

When Baker Hughes Inc. and BJ Services Co., two worldwide oilfield services companies (with combined revenues of more than $17 billion) decided to merge in 2009, there was a lot of information that needed to be communicated—quickly—to a variety of internal and external audiences. Among the tools the companies used to reach those audiences was one that's often overlooked—the sit-down, recorded interview.

The day the merger agreement was signed, the chairman of each company sat down together and responded to questions by a seasoned former journalist. After two, short 15-minute takes, the interview was quickly edited and made available to the 57,000 employees of the combined companies and to anyone else via a link on each company's website.

If your organization is planning a major acquisition or faces some other significant event, don't overlook the power of an interview. To paraphrase from a once-popular commercial, "They're not just for reporters anymore." Here are some guidelines for developing a first-class product:

Determine your key messages:

Every successful communication effort starts with knowing what key points you want to make. Write them down. If the interview is designed for multiple audiences, factor that into your messaging.

Develop a script:

This is an outline containing the topics or questions that will be explored in the interview. Some execs like help identifying key points; others prefer to respond without any coaching. In any event, the scripting process should not include developing complete responses that are meant to be delivered verbatim.

Review interview essentials:

Use the same techniques that work in media interviews: Short, crisp responses rather than long-winded, rambling answers. Powerful soundbites (e.g., stories, analogies, examples). No jargon. High energy instead of a business poker face (if the subject lends itself to a more animated delivery).

Practice:

Find time to prepare. Most executives are under time crunches, but they're quick learners. However, try to do a practice run before the camera rolls. Your goal is to respond conversationally. Think in terms of talking to a relative, friend or neighbor.

Aim for high-quality production values:

This probably means hiring an outside crew to handle camera, lighting, sound and even make-up. Remember, audiences who will watch the interview will be judging its quality based on what they saw the previous night on television. Don't do it on the cheap.

Use a skilled interviewer:

Successful interviews don't just happen. The person asking the questions plays a critical role in making the interview work. Skillful journalists spend years perfecting their craft, including learning how to frame questions and sift through answers to develop follow-up questions. They set the tone of the interview. If there's no one in your organization who has those skills, go outside to get them. Find a retired reporter or a working journalist who moonlights on the side.

Think marketing:

How can you use the final product? Ask yourself whether the interview is appropriate for multiple audiences. For example, in the past, such interviews were often produced exclusively for employees, who watched the video at employee meetings. Today, technology exists that enables a variety of external audiences (e.g., shareholders, analysts, customers, suppliers, etc.) to get immediate access to the information contained in those interviews.

LOST IN TRANSLATION: COMMUNICATING WITH NON-NATIVE SPEAKERS

Remember that scene in a *Seinfeld* episode where an American businessman (who happened to have a cold) told a Japanese executive that he didn't want to shake hands so as not to pass on any germs? The Japanese executive, who was in New York to purchase the American's struggling publishing company, misunderstood, took the remark to be a snub, and called off the deal. Such misunderstandings don't just occur in Jerry Seinfeld's bizarre world.

In today's global business environment, chances are you've had to communicate to an audience made up of at least a few individuals who were not native speakers of your language. Or perhaps you've been that non-native speaker in an audience.

Either way, the communication process can be tricky. But communicating with people who are not native speakers of your language is a skill that can be developed over time and with practice. Here are some adjustments that are typically necessary:

- **Speak a little slower** than you normally do. It takes the audience more time to process your language, so give them time to do that. But be careful not to allow this slower delivery to lower your energy level.

- **Enunciate clearly,** but don't overemphasize each word. This can cause confusion and may even be seen as insulting.

- **Use shorter, simpler sentences** (generally avoid compound, complex, and compound-complex sentence constructions). The more elaborately you speak, the more difficult it will be for the audience to understand.

- **Summarize your point(s) frequently,** and when necessary, repeat key points. Don't be afraid to make your presentation somewhat redundant by using synonyms and rephrasing.

- **Use more pauses** (between sentences, paragraphs, sections of your presentation).

- **Use more gestures** than you normally use. Sometimes it's possible to understand just by catching a few words and seeing the gestures.

- **Use visuals** when appropriate—especially charts, diagrams and photos. Some speakers even incorporate more "copy" slides (visuals containing words that summarize what you're saying).

- **Face the audience and don't cover your mouth.** Listeners will want to watch you as you pronounce your words. This can help them figure out what you're saying.

- **Avoid using "fillers" or nonwords** (e.g., "um," "ah," "like," "you know," etc.). The audience may become confused, thinking this language is vocabulary they don't possess. Or these fillers may make it harder to process what you're saying. In other words, remove the "noise" from your speech.

- **Avoid the temptation to speak more loudly.** Today's audiences are much more accustomed to listening to speakers who have a different mother tongue. So there's a greater comfort level and proficiency in hearing and understanding what's being said. That said, remember that your audience must work a bit harder to understand you. Be sure to make their job a little easier.

LOGIC 101: ANTIDOTE FOR MUDDLED THINKING

For some parents, hearing their college-age son or daughter declare philosophy as a major often produces this silent or vocal reaction: "What are you going to do with that?"

Back in the '70s when elective courses in high school came into vogue, I developed a semester course in philosophy for seniors. When that subject resonated with a student who decided to pursue it in college, I always wondered whether the parents held me responsible.

Philosophy is generally considered a complex, esoteric subject. Some of the terms associated with it—metaphysics, logical positivism, categorical imperative—are enough to send people running. Moreover, philosophy is not viewed as relevant to life in the "real world." After all, what are we to make of a discipline that readily admits to offering more questions than answers to those who study it? No wonder most Americans, practical people that we are, say, "Thanks, but no thanks."

In truth, philosophy, like algebra and some other subjects that appear to so rarely apply to our lives, is an important tool. The examination and evaluation inherent in it help us to determine whether our views and the views of others are rationally defensible.

Logic, one branch of philosophy, is particularly valuable in that process. If you've never studied logic or if you need a refresher, here's a brief tutorial on the fallacies of reasoning most of us regularly encounter or use.

Argumentum ad Misericordiam:

"Running from Mexico" was a story that aired on National Public Radio. It was about a college student who came to the U.S. illegally—fleeing violence in Mexico. He became a talented runner, but feared deportation. The content and tone of the story strongly implied that the student should be allowed to remain in the country because of his difficult past. Today, many people who advocate a "hands-off" approach to illegal immigrants commit this fallacy where pity or a similar emotion such as sympathy or compassion is used to get a conclusion accepted.

Argumentum ad Hominem:

This fallacy is an attack directed at a person, rather than against what that person says. Few people can trump Rush Limbaugh when it comes to stinging certain individuals: "Info babe" (select female journalists). "Pencil neck" (California congressman). "Pocahontas" (Massachusetts senator). "Plugs" (Joe Biden—who had a hair transplant). Ad hominem attacks produce a negative shift in the audience's mental representations—how they see a person, and by extension, that person's positions or beliefs.

Non Sequitur:

This Latin phrase can be translated as, "Does not follow." Michael Flynn was a campaign aide to Donald Trump. When reports surfaced that some of Hillary Clinton's aides had been granted immunity by the government in exchange for sharing information with the FBI about Clinton's private email server, Flynn said, "When you are given immunity, that means you probably committed a crime." Oh really? Requesting or being granted immunity doesn't necessarily imply guilt. Individuals often seek immunity to avoid being prosecuted for saying something they normally wouldn't utter. In other words, immunity is an alternative to invoking their Fifth Amendment privilege against self-incrimination.

The fallacy in Flynn's quote was exposed when Flynn himself was the subject of an investigation, and his attorney indicated that the former national security advisor would cooperate with congressional investigators in exchange for immunity.

Fallacy of Emphasis:

Admit it, try as you might, you've never been able to read all of the small print that briefly appears at the bottom of the TV screen on certain commercials. And that's just how advertisers like it. Pharmaceutical companies are particularly fond of this fallacy in which some of the claims touted in the prominent portion of the communication are walked back elsewhere.

Arguing from Authority:

Most of us are taught from birth to respect and believe authority—parents, teachers, law enforcement officials. It's been shown that an expert opinion cited in a *New York Times* news story can generate a two percent shift in public opinion. But the truth or falsity of a statement cannot be established simply on the basis that an authority says it. The 2016 presidential election probably did more than anything else in recent memory to remind us that even experts can be wrong.

"Everyone Knows":

It's an often-heard phrase that ignores the fact that people differ in knowledge and opinions. Here's Bill O'Reilly, journalist, author and former television host: "There's little desire on the part of the liberal city government here (New York) to lift people out of welfare. Liberal politicians actually want dependency. For example, if the city were to investigate disability claims, they'd find many of them are bogus, frauds; it's a racket. Everybody knows it." Actually, it's unlikely that every person "knows" that. And Bill O'Reilly, a former high school teacher, should know that.

Post Hoc, Ergo Propter Hoc:

"After this, therefore because of this." When former Secretary of State Rex Tillerson publicly stated that the United States would no longer work to oust Syrian President Bashar al-Assad, many in the American media suggested a cause and effect relationship between that shift in policy and a Syrian chemical attack on civilians that occurred five days later.

Glittering Generalities:

"Yes We Can." "Stronger Together." "Make America Great Again." You recognize the slogans. Even your local TV news station tells you, "Channel 5 is on your side." When someone uses words or images that reinforce values you hold dear but offers little or nothing in the way of specifics, he or she is serving up empty calories.

Mistakes in logic are on display daily in politics, on TV, in advertising and in many other arenas, including business. The best antidote? A solid grasp of what constitutes clear thinking. It's worth remembering the admonition of one of the greatest philosophers that ever lived—Socrates:

ὁ δὲ ἀνεξέταστος βίος οὐ βιωτὸς ἀνθρώπῳ ("The unexamined life is not worth living").

HOW MILLENNIALS COMMUNICATE... AND WHY YOU NEED TO KNOW

Just about any discussion of the millennial generation (generally considered those born between 1982 and 1994) is likely to include something about their communication style. For example:

- **Millennials don't like talking on the phone.** They grew up as email and texting were coming into vogue, and they readily embraced those technologies. Interestingly, one telecommunications company conducted a study that showed that smartphone apps that enable you to make phone calls ranked fifth among apps used by the public.

- **They prefer text messages.** Millennials like the instantaneous nature of texting, plus the fact that they can send or receive messages anywhere and at any time. Also, unlike phone calls or face-to-face conversations, text messages give the sender a bit more "thought time" to figure out what to say.

- **They still like emails... for less urgent communications.** Emails give users more time to respond (i.e., a few hours). Plus, they can say more when there are fewer space or other formatting limitations.

- **Millennials value open and honest communication.** They like "straight shooters"—people who tell the truth, are direct, and avoid "corporate speak" and words and phrases that sound disingenuous.

- **They value brevity.** Long-winded communications are seen as time and money wasters—something that should be avoided. So, 280-character tweets, abbreviations such as lol ("laughing out loud"), tl:dr ("too long; didn't read") and similar shortcuts are likely to find their way into business communications.

This style of communication is likely to become more common in the business world as millennials assume leadership roles formerly held by the baby boomers. In fact, millennials now comprise half of the workforce. So it's not surprising that there's no shortage of articles, books or workshops offering advice on how to better communicate with millennials.

Without a doubt, baby boomers and Generation Xers will need to adapt. But it's also important for millennials to understand and master more traditional styles of communication—the kind used by those "still in charge." So, let's tackle a topic rarely, if ever, addressed by those "how to" articles on the internet and in business publications and other sources—namely, what can be done to expand and enhance the communication skills of millennials.

LOOK FOR MENTORING OPPORTUNITIES

For instance, if you spot a younger employee whose writing skills are sub-par (e.g., he or she cannot write a clear, compelling or even grammatically correct proposal or report), pair that individual with a colleague who has mastered that skill. Make sure the mentor knows that his or her primary role is to help cultivate a specific communication skill. Millennials want feedback—in part because of their desire to move up through the organization. They are incredibly receptive to assessments and advice given by supervisors and others who have achieved success.

CULTIVATE FACE-TO-FACE COMMUNICATION OPPORTUNITIES

It takes practice to master the art of in-person conversation. Some millennials don't get much practice. Because of their extensive reliance on online communication, many of them have missed out on the face-to-face interactions previous generations have benefitted from—benefits such as learning how to speak in a professional manner, listening attentively and reading body language. It's been said that younger workers would rather send an instant message than walk down the hall to speak directly to a colleague. If that's true, they are missing out on more than physical exercise.

When appropriate, invite them to certain meetings or presentations—as observers rather than as participants—so they can see the many aspects of face-to-face communication. Also, walk down that hall; seek them out in person—even if you're tempted to send an email or text about something. Most learning is observational, and observing your approach may make them less awkward in face-to-face conversations.

INVEST IN TRAINING

All generations of employees value it. Millennials are no different. But keep some things in mind:

- **Be sure it's meaningful.** In other words, make it clear not only what skill is important, but also why it's important. Telling a millennial that he needs to change his "too casual" style of communication (e.g., too terse, informal, slang, etc.) is not enough. You need to tell him why it needs to change (e.g., that it's inappropriate to use with a particular colleague, client or customer he's communicating with).

- **Provide training in smaller chunks.** Forget two-day or even one-day workshops. Think: half-day or several hours. When providing training opportunities for millennials, think in terms of multiple, but shorter sessions.

- **Beware of lectures.** The best training is interactive or includes such things as on-camera practice or other learning-by-doing activities. (Millennials are especially into gaming—perhaps an outgrowth of their fascination with video games.) Millennials are among those in the "TV generation." They are quite comfortable seeing themselves practice on video.

- **Address blind spots.** Most companies assume their employees know how to communicate effectively—that they learned these skills in school or at a previous company. Wrong! Consider the following: Have you ever been taught how to craft a powerful, effective presentation? What about PowerPoint? Most people misuse it, so it's unlikely they've ever had a tutorial on it. Handling Q&A? Managing presentation stress? Unless someone seeks out <u>accurate</u> information on these topics (few people do), he or she must rely on what they see inside the company.

Help your millennials expand their horizons by offering them new and different approaches to communication. And be open to their approaches to communicating as well. If you do, you'll find that your baby boomers, Gen Xers and millennials will make a great team.

DEALING WITH PUBLIC ANGER: NEW APPROACHES TO AN OLD PROBLEM

Across the country, battles are frequently being waged between citizens' groups and a variety of companies and other organizations. Helping fuel that anger are groups such as Sprawl-Busters, which show communities how to mobilize against corporate behemoths. Today, the NIMBY (not in my backyard) syndrome encompasses opposition to more than just power plants, landfills or factories. And it's not just the private sector that's under attack. Angry parents and residents are challenging all sorts of decisions made by school boards and city councils.

Public anger is not new. But it is more common, more newsworthy and more damaging than it used to be. It is also more preventable and more manageable. In recent years, much has been learned about what causes public anger, and what works and what doesn't work when dealing with an angry public.

Here's some practical guidance on how to deal with individuals who are upset, angry, aggressive or verbally abusive in public. These techniques are based on case studies, behavioral models and proven psychological principles.

People who are angry hold two primary beliefs: One, that something is unfair, and two, that something is out of their control or that they are losing control. They believe that by expressing their anger they will restore fairness or get or regain control. About sixty percent of angry people say they behave aggressively in order to repair a damaged self-image or to enhance their self-esteem. If you are confronted by an angry person, you must defuse that anger and get the person to return to his or her "normal" level of functioning. How do you do that?

Prepare for stressful encounters.

Begin with a self-audit. Ask yourself how you typically react to difficult people and stressful situations. Do you withdraw or "clam up?" Do you retaliate or escalate? This self-awareness can keep you from giving in to feelings or reactions that are counterproductive. You may even want to prepare for potentially difficult encounters by rehearsing with a neutral friend.

Take preventive action.

You can significantly reduce aggressive, disruptive behavior by making it easier to identify individuals, and by holding them personally responsible for their anti-social actions. For example, at a public or any group meeting, use nametags, have people identify themselves before speaking or testifying, and call on people by name whenever possible. This removes the anonymity that encourages people to behave angrily. If practical, greet audience members—shake their hands—as they arrive. This may be uncomfortable when you anticipate a hostile audience, but it could pay dividends in the form of audience cooperation, because people are less likely to lash out when they've made physical contact with you.

Years ago (when pay phones were commonplace), researchers conducted this study: They put a quarter in the coin return of a pay phone. After someone used the phone, found the quarter and began to walk away, the researcher approached them and said, "Excuse me; I used that phone a moment ago and forgot to take my quarter. Did you happen to find it?" In nearly every instance, the person denied taking the quarter. However, when researchers conducted the same experiment but introduced themselves by name and shook the person's hand, just the opposite happened; the person handed over the quarter. Human contact facilitates honesty. (By the way, the ideal handshake lasts three seconds. Any longer than that causes heightened levels of anxiety in those receiving the gesture.)

Also, never leave a public meeting early.

Ensure realistic expectations.

Provide people with a road map of the meeting. Describe the agenda or sequence of events. Review the ground rules, including the topics to be discussed (or not to be discussed), time limits for speaking, etc. In particular, assure people that they'll have an opportunity to speak.

Sometimes a good offense is the best defense.

If you know that people are upset, begin the meeting or conversation by verbally acknowledging that you're aware that a problem exists or that people have concerns, and that you're eager to hear those concerns.

Stay calm.

Although the angry person may not be thinking clearly, you must be able to think clearly. For that to happen, proper breathing is critical. When confronted by an angry person, immediately make a conscious effort to breathe in through your nose and out through your mouth. Take a deep breath—fill your lungs entirely, hold it for a few seconds, and then exhale. This will slow your breathing, lower your heart rate, relax you and enable you to think clearly and respond calmly. Keep your neck, hand and shoulder muscles relaxed and don't clench your teeth or jaw.

Allow acceptable venting.

Rather than trying to stop an outburst, it may be helpful to allow the angry person to let off some steam. A good rule of thumb is to permit 1-2 minutes of uninterrupted venting. People tend to run out of steam after a few minutes. During this venting period, don't offer advice or feedback. And don't tell the person to calm down; that's a request that requires a rational response when the angry person is operating in an emotional mode. Plus, that request is likely to be seen as a "second assault" (the first assault is what caused the initial anger).

Interrupt only if someone is verbally abusive. Respond politely but firmly. One possible response: "I want to help you, but I find it difficult to do that when you use that kind of language. Please don't." Another strategy for dealing with verbal abuse is to ignore it the first time, responding calmly. Sometimes the angry person will begin to mirror your response as he or she recognizes what constitutes appropriate behavior.

Find common ground.

If you've ever debated in high school or college, you'll recall that one very effective debating tactic is to agree with something your opponent has said. This tactic is equally effective when facing an angry person. Even if you are unable to agree with most of what was said, chances are you can say you share the person's goals but disagree with the solution.

Demonstrate empathy.

One of the most effective ways of calming someone down is by empathizing with them or their situation and showing that empathy. According to research, expressing empathy accounts for fifty percent of your credibility, and is assessed in the first thirty seconds. One way to empathize with an angry person is by recalling an anger-generating experience of your own. Then respond succinctly and in an even, non-dramatic tone, with words that show concern and caring.

Express concern, but avoid the often-said, but ineffective statement, "I understand how you feel." No one—including psychiatrists—can fully understand another person's feelings. Instead, consider a response such as, "I know someone with a similar problem, and I can only imagine how you must feel."

Listen actively.

Most of us spend 70-80 percent of our waking time communicating; nearly half of it—some 45 percent—is spent listening. But we are poor listeners. We listen at an efficiency rate of only 25-50 percent. One reason for this is that the average person speaks at a rate between 150-200 words per minute (WPM), but we can hear at a rate of at least 600 WPM. That leaves a lot of time for our minds to wander. Another reason is that when someone is talking—especially someone who's angry—most of us are thinking about how we're going to respond. Resist this impulse. Pay close attention to what the angry person is saying (or not saying).

Listening is hard work. When you listen actively, your pulse goes up and you breathe faster. To listen effectively, and to show that you are listening, do the following: Take notes. Repeat or paraphrase what the speaker has said. Ask questions. Ask the speaker to clarify or elaborate on what was said. Don't interrupt. Look at the speaker.

If the angry person begins to "withdraw," here are five words guaranteed to get and keep that person talking: "Tell me more about it."

Admit mistakes.

A straightforward acknowledgment of error and sincere apologies go a long way toward changing the behavior of angry people. When appropriate, provide a prompt, verbalized, public admission that a problem occurred or that something could have been handled better. And remember that there is a difference between accepting blame and accepting responsibility.

Focus on solutions.

Quite often, people who are angry are willing to spend a lot of time rehashing the problem. Your role must be to help shift the discussion from the problem to the solution. You can do so by providing guided problem solving. Ask future-oriented questions: "If you could have the ideal situation, what would that be?" Offer suggestions of your own: "Here are some other possible options to consider."

Anticipate...and plan for problems.

I once saw a chemical industry CEO "freeze" when a group of demonstrators (wearing animal costumes) stood up and silently held up signs and banners during his presentation at a conference. He was so rattled he didn't know what to do, so he kept on speaking. Not surprisingly, no one in the room heard or cared about a word he said once the theatrics began.

Unlike that executive, you should know exactly what you'll do if an audience turns hostile. The time to develop a strategy for dealing with an angry public is not during the meeting, the event or the encounter. Have a plan clearly in mind before arriving:

First off, keep your composure, no matter what. If you're interrupted, politely ask the individual to hold his or her question or statement and allow you to finish your remarks. Address that individual; don't direct your response to the entire audience. Let people know the consequences of disruptive behavior: "I'll call security if you don't stop yelling."

Appeal to the audience's sense of fair play. Tell them you're trying to share information or that people have invested valuable time to attend the meeting, and that interruptions are unfair. Politely, but authoritatively, explain that nothing can be accomplished when people are rude or fail to cooperate.

Be prepared to temporarily jettison prepared remarks, PowerPoint presentations or the agenda, and seek input from the audience.

If the situation becomes extremely intense, call for a short break. Then appeal directly to those who are angry for their cooperation.

If you cannot regain control, indicate that perhaps the best approach is to adjourn and reschedule the meeting after tempers have calmed down. This is a better approach than allowing the meeting to spiral out of control.

Heed warning signals.

We live in a different world today—a more violent one. So watch for visible signs of anger: a red face; a change in voice—louder or softer, slower or faster;

standing up, perhaps invading your personal space (3-6 feet is generally a safe distance). Never touch someone or physically try to force someone to leave. If you hear threatening language, don't respond by saying, "Is that a threat?" Instead, say, "That sounds to me like a threat, and I take threats very seriously."

Most people are practical—problem solvers. When faced with a problem, we want to resolve it quickly and move on. But keep in mind that where anger and problems co-exist, no problem can be resolved until the anger is addressed. So, when encountering an angry public, your initial objective may simply be to address the anger—and not the problem.

COMMUNICATING CHANGE TO EMPLOYEES

It's been said that the one constant in life is change. Another one of life's constants is that people are uncomfortable with change. So, to help employees cope with it, companies need to make communication a priority.

Here are some suggestions for communicating during a time of change:

Ramp up your communications.

Communicate more, not less. In many firms, change makes management more tight-lipped. One reason is that they are busy—managing the change. Communication is put on the back burner. Another reason is that talking about change or knowing what to say is difficult. Avoiding the subject is easier.

Ironically, just as communication from management drops off, communication among employees takes off. The rumor mill shifts into overdrive. And today, social media make it easy for employees to share speculation about what's happening or what's likely to happen. Digital technology has made us all much more connected, and that means information and misinformation are more frequent and powerful than ever before.

If the change you have to communicate involves unpleasant news, take comfort in knowing that research shows employees would rather get bad news than no news. And it's likely that employees may already know or suspect that something has changed and have begun to prepare for its impact.

Use appropriate tools.

We've all heard horror stories such as the boss who used email to notify employees that their jobs were being eliminated. Whether due to ignorance or insensitivity, that approach was wrong.

Most employees prefer to get information from their immediate supervisors, senior executives and small-group meetings—in that order. Recognize that employees need a balanced communications diet, so make sure the method you use to communicate fits the message. The fastest or easiest way to communicate may not be the best. One size does not necessarily fit all.

Direct and clear.

When a difficult message has to be communicated, some people adopt an indirect or subtle form of communication. It usually requires the audience to "read between the lines" to figure out the meaning of what's being said. Euphemisms frequently find their way into such communications. For example, a supervisor who's uncomfortable telling a subordinate that his performance is unsatisfactory might casually mention that there's room for improvement rather than address the performance issue head on—identifying the specific problems and what's needed to fix them.

Studies show that direct communication—explicit statements, conclusions or recommendations—are more effective. So, when communicating change to your employees, speak plainly and openly—knowing that they can be resilient in the midst of change.

Allow for feedback.

The best kind of communication is two-way, so when communicating change, be sure to include a feedback mechanism. This will give your audience a chance to raise questions and concerns, and that feedback can help you determine whether your messages are being heard and understood.

When Hillary Clinton ran for the New York Senate seat, she first embarked on a "listening tour." In the aftermath of the Jerry Sandusky sexual abuse scandal, Penn State held a town hall meeting with students to allow them to share their opinions and concerns. Seeking input and feedback is part of a smart communications strategy.

There are many ways to get feedback: in person, online, in writing, anonymously, etc. Use the method that works best for your particular organization, situation or issue.

A word of caution: If you're communicating your message in person, be sure to devote enough time to the Q&A segment. Don't knowingly or unknowingly cut is short—something that frequently happens when the going gets tough. At the onset of the meeting, reassure the audience that there will be plenty of time to comment or ask questions. Take a lesson from school districts that understand the importance of not curtailing input: Some evening school board meetings continue well into the morning hours.

HAVE A PLAN

All too often, communication is an afterthought when a company embarks on a change initiative. In some cases, it's because the firm has no communications function, or its communications professionals are not consulted or not consulted early on in the planning process.

Just as a company must have a well-thought-out plan for how to implement the change, it should have a well-thought-out plan on how it will communicate that change. A solid communications plan should address the following:

- **Strategy:** Your overall plan for communicating
- **Messaging:** The specific messages about the changes, including rationale
- **Tactics:** The tools that will be used to communicate with employees (e.g., speeches, written materials, intranet, employee meetings, etc.) and who will use those tools
- **Training:** The training or practice provided to those who will deliver the messages
- **Timetable:** Specific dates by which information will be developed and communicated
- **Measurement:** How you will determine the success of your effort (e.g., Were messages understood? Are the desired employee actions/behaviors being observed? Etc.)

The centuries-old proverb, "For want of a nail the shoe was lost" reminds us that seemingly unimportant acts or omissions can have serious consequences. When your organization is facing change, be sure your communications are planned and announced in a way that helps facilitate that change.

THOSE ANNOYING "UHS," "UMS," "LIKES" AND "YOU KNOWS"

One of the most frustrating communication problems some people have is excessive use of non-words such as "uh" and "um." These annoying filler words can make their way into speeches, presentations, media interviews and even everyday conversation.

Back in 1986, after a U.S. retaliatory air strike on Libya, Secretary of Defense Caspar Weinberger held a press conference. He spoke for three minutes. Tens of millions in the United States were watching and many millions more in other parts of the world. Believability was crucial, but it was sorely lacking. Not because of what was said; the facts sounded plausible. It was the delivery. Weinberger had 59 "ums" and "uhs." His halting delivery made us wonder whether we could trust him.

"Uh," "um," "like," "you know" and similar utterances are called non-words or filler words. They drain energy out of communication. They're also a distraction for the audience. (Come on, admit it—you found yourself counting the number of times someone uttered those sounds.)

So, if you have this problem, how do you correct it?

- The first step is to determine if there is a problem. Record yourself (preferably during a practice session), and then listen to your delivery. Many people are clueless that they have the problem unless someone else has the courage to tell them.

- Using a few filler words is perfectly fine. It's one characteristic of conversational speech. So it's a plus, not a minus. Listen to most speakers and you'll hear a few non-words.

- Using too many non-words usually happens, not because the speaker lacks knowledge of the material, but because he or she has not practiced. For most people, the antidote is simple: practice your presentation three times, aloud, on your feet, into a recording device.

- If you don't know your material well enough, and you notice that you're using a lot of non-words, becoming more familiar with the material is the likely way to address the problem.

- If you suffer from serious presentation anxiety, your problem with non-words may be related. In that case, you may need to seek professional help. There are specialists, including therapists—some of whom use virtual reality—to help people who have an unnatural fear of public speaking.

- Some people use non-words because they are uncomfortable with silence. Occasional pauses are an important part of all presenting, but those pauses can be awkward. So the speaker fills them with non-words. (A sound—any sound—is preferable to silence.) Practice this technique: after a sentence, a paragraph or an idea, force yourself to stop talking for a moment. Remain silent for a few seconds. Then resume speaking. You can re-program yourself to feel more comfortable with brief periods of silence.

- With some speakers, non-words serve as transitions. In other words, when moving on to a new idea, section or PowerPoint visual of their presentation, people simply utter a non-word. The better approach is to use some powerful transition words. For example, if you are transitioning to a discussion of safety, say something like, "So, what is our company's track record on safety?"

Eliminating excessive non-words is possible. But it may take time and effort. Remember, you may be trying to change a pattern that has existed for many years. You won't correct it overnight. But in most cases, this problem is correctable.

There's a lot to be learned from Mark Zuckerberg's two-day Congressional testimony.

WHAT WE CAN LEARN FROM MARK ZUCKERBERG'S TWO-DAY CONGRESSIONAL TESTIMONY

Mark Zuckerberg spent nearly ten grueling hours over two days responding to questions from almost 100 Senate and House lawmakers. (I watched the entire two-day marathon while recovering from hernia surgery.) The issue was whether his social network company was doing enough to protect user privacy.

So how did the young founder and CEO of Facebook do? More importantly, what can the rest of us learn from his performance? A lot!

By any measure, what Mr. Zuckerberg had to endure was daunting. Unlike many Congressional hearings where the witness might find support or an open mind from at least one side of the aisle, Zuckerberg was challenged by Democrats and Republicans alike. For the most part, he handled himself well. I'd call his performance a success. But let's take a closer look and grade that performance.

MESSAGING

Zuckerberg went to the hearings with specific, clear messages. And he delivered them—in his opening statements and throughout Q&A. No doubt, he and his team put much effort into determining what they wanted people to hear and remember. For instance:

- He repeatedly acknowledged mistakes (e.g., being slow to identify Russian intervention in the 2016 presidential election through fake ads) and personally accepted responsibility for them.
- He referenced changes that have been, and are being, made to improve Facebook's platform. One key message was that by year's end, Facebook would have more than 20,000 employees devoted to security and content review.
- He continually reminded the audience that users already have a great deal of control ("ownership") over what they share, and that the control is not hidden, but is prominently displayed.

I'd give Mr. Zuckerberg high marks for his ability to speak plainly and avoid jargon (or at least explain it). He frequently had to explain (to non-tech-savvy ears) how Facebook operates, and he did so effectively, without annoyance or condescension. When former Utah Senator Orrin Hatch wanted to know how Facebook makes money when its service is free, Zuckerberg simply responded, "Senator, we run ads." Duh!

An area where Mr. Zuckerberg fell a bit short was with powerful soundbites or "sparklers"—forms of expression that jump out and grab you. While he gave lots of examples, illustrations and compelling data, he was short on stories and analogies (two of the most powerful tools of persuasion) and memorable lines. One of his few memorable lines was, "This is an arms race," a reference to Russian hackers who are paid to use Facebook for nefarious purposes.

Messaging grade: A-

Q&A

I'll cut him some slack here—based solely on the sheer number of questions he had to field. But overall, a solid job. He paused briefly before responding (shows thoughtfulness) and his answers were succinct (short answers are mandatory since lawmakers interrupt mercilessly). When he was interrupted or accused of filibustering, he did not become confrontational.

He skillfully used what's known as a "bridging" technique. In other words, not only did he respond to the question, he occasionally used it as a springboard to add a point of his own (i.e., his key messages). Perhaps the technique used most frequently by the questioners was to instruct Mr. Zuckerberg to answer, "yes or no." He knew to avoid this trap and politely explained why he could not respond in such a manner. Even when pressed, he would not back down. Similarly, he was very comfortable in acknowledging when he did not know the answer, and committed to following up—a solid approach, but difficult for some people to do.

Clearly, Mr. Zuckerberg and his team anticipated most of the questions, and undoubtedly he practiced his responses (hopefully aloud). He did less well with zingers and questions out of left field (e.g., "Would you be comfortable sharing with us the name of the hotel you stayed in last night?") Although it's not possible to anticipate every question, he needed to think more quickly on his feet, and learn the skill of showing no discomfort. That will come with age and more experience.

A major mistake on his part was prefacing too many of his responses with the questioner's title (e.g., Senator, Congressman, Congresswoman, etc.). This is polite, standard procedure, but he used it excessively—which "weakened" him—made him a subordinate. Also, it was annoying. While the questioners addressed him as "Mr. Zuckerberg," they did so less frequently throughout their allotted time—creating the perception of superiority.

Q&A grade: B+

DELIVERY SKILLS

In his opening remarks at both the Senate and House hearings, Mr. Zuckerberg read a prepared statement—and he did so powerfully and with significant audience eye contact. A great start!

But beyond those few minutes, while he is smart, articulate and speaks with word economy, he looked and sounded "robotic." There's little, if any, change in the sound of his voice (i.e., inflection). So he comes across as somewhat distant, detached, remote. In short, he lacks warmth. He's difficult to connect with. Indeed, Louisiana Senator Kennedy said, "I'm a little disappointed in this hearing today. I just don't feel like we're connecting."

In those few instances where the opportunity to use humor (and flash a smile) surfaced, he missed most of those opportunities. Even when one senator who greatly admired what Mr. Zuckerberg created playfully quipped, "Only in America," he could not get Zuckerberg to play along and agree.

Note to Mr. Zuckerberg: Before we can reach someone on an intellectual level, we must first connect with them on an emotional level.

Delivery skills grade: C

APPEARANCE

Mark Zuckerberg has a "boyish" look. As he gets older, he'll appreciate that part of his DNA. But now, it can be a disadvantage. Thankfully, he now wears his hair shorter—since his curly hair makes him look even younger. Also, thankfully, he eschewed his standard tee shirt or hoodie in favor of a suit. But it looked like something parents buy when their son is ready for his first suit. His shirt collar looked one neck size too large, and his tie was not tight and crisp. Appearance counts, and he should have consulted a fashion professional—not to turn him into someone he isn't, but to help create a more polished, seasoned, executive presence.

Not wearing a wedding ring was a mistake. Trust increases when we see a wedding ring on a man. Another mistake was sitting on a booster cushion during Day 1 (removed for Day 2). It was easy to spot, and some media quickly picked up on it and reported it. Let the jokes begin... and they did.

Finally, Zuckerberg left his notes opened on the table during a break in his Senate hearing. That allowed an Associated Press photographer to snap a picture of his talking points. A real rookie mistake—that one of his aides should have caught.

Appearance grade: C

While it's not every day that an executive is asked to appear on Capitol Hill, it can happen. What can happen more frequently is a request to testify at a public utility commission hearing, give a legal deposition or serve as a trial witness. Today's executives would be well advised to know how to handle such situations.

SOME BAD NEWS ABOUT COMMUNICATING GOOD NEWS: IT'S TOUGHER THAN YOU THINK

Layoffs. Benefit cuts. Slumping sales. Accidents. Communicating bad news isn't easy. Which is why some companies avoid doing it or do it in an untimely or ineffective manner.

On the other hand, communicating good news is a "no brainer," right? Wrong. Sharing positive information can be just as tricky. And some companies fail at it or fail to get full benefit from that news.

Here are some things to consider when you have good news to share:

HOW "GOOD" IS YOUR GOOD NEWS?

The sender and receiver of a message may have different perspectives on what's being said. For example, when a company announces that it's acquiring a competitor, and as a result will double in size, that's usually good news—to the acquiring company. But analysts and shareholders who focus on the debt incurred to buy that competitor may see it very differently. Also, what about that competitor's employees who wonder about their jobs?

Or when employees learn that their company has landed a major new customer, all they may see is the added workload.

When determining what to say about your "good news," remember that your audience will be thinking, "What's in it for me?" Be sure to frame your news so that the "mental picture" your audience creates (i.e., how they see it) is positive. For example, landing that new customer could mean promotion opportunities, wage increases, etc. Make sure those kinds of messages find their way into your communications with the appropriate audiences.

BE CREATIVE

Effective communication is clear and concise. But it's also compelling. Share the good news, but don't waste it on the run-of-the-mill.

One of my clients was an oilfield services company that held one of its analysts' meetings at its research center. The event included a number of displays showing some of the new technology being developed to find and produce oil and gas. In his presentation, the company's head of research referenced hockey great Wayne Gretzky, and reminded the audience of Gretzky's famous quote: "I skate to where the puck is going to be, not where it has been." The research exec then went on to say that the developing technology on display will pay dividends down the road by addressing future challenges faced by oil and gas companies.

I liked the comparison but recommended one other thing—that the company give each analyst a hockey puck (with the company's name and logo on it, of course). Those hockey pucks have probably ended up in offices, serving as paperweights—a constant reminder of the company's forward-thinking approach to research.

Given the large amount of information all of us are bombarded with daily, even good news can use a boost.

CREATE AN EVENT

Some good news almost demands to be communicated with pizzazz—something other than in a straightforward, "just the facts" manner.

When Steve Jobs introduced the MacBook Air, he said it was "so thin it even fits inside one of those envelopes you see floating around the office." Then he walked to the side of the stage, picked up an inter-office envelope and took out a MacBook Air.

Is your company launching a new product? Building a new facility? Has it made it to the *Fortune* 500 or *Fortune's* list of most admired corporations? Why not consider doing something more than just issuing a press release or sending something out on the internet? Oh, and by the way, props, which seem to have fallen into some disuse, are clever ways to grab attention.

CHOOSE THE RIGHT SPOKESPERSON

Most of us have seen it: Some manager or executive is tasked with sharing some exciting news with employees at a company meeting. He (or she) begins by saying, "I'm excited to be able to tell you that..." The only problem is he looks and sounds like someone's just died. The message isn't in sync with the low-energy, business-poker-face delivery. Before he can even share the news, the audience is already turned off, and may even start multi-tasking. Audiences want the sizzle along with the steak.

So, what do you do if your spokesperson is a sub-par communicator? In some cases, it might be possible to select a different spokesperson to deliver your good news.

True story about the research executive mentioned above: Top management knew he was not a dynamic presenter. But with more than a hundred analysts expected to be in the audience, the company needed a homerun. So, the exec was told someone else might have to deliver his remarks if his performance at the dress rehearsal wasn't what it should be. (By the way, his dress rehearsal performance was a hit and he remained on the roster.)

While some may see the company's willingness to yank that speaker as brutal, it underscores the importance of practice. Communication is a skill, and skills can be taught, learned and applied. The key is coaching and practice. Most companies instinctively know the importance practice plays in delivering bad news; not so for delivering good news. Be sure the folks who are delivering your good news get some coaching and invest the time to practice.

One other thing: Instruct your spokesperson not to read the good news to the audience. Doing so weakens the message. Share the information with minimal or no reliance on notes. Would you tell your wife what you love about her by reading from a prepared communication? Enough said.

CREATE FEEDBACK OPPORTUNITIES

The best communication is two-way. It gives the audience a chance to participate, and the speaker an opportunity to get feedback from the audience. Most companies know how important it is to seek feedback or to let people vent when the news is bad. (That's one reason for the "open mic" segment at shareholder, city council, school board and other meetings.) What's less understood is how important it is to allow audiences to comment and ask questions when the news is good.

If you share your news in person, make sure there's ample time for audience feedback. If you're communicating through technology (e.g., email, intranet, social media, etc.) be sure people can ask questions—whether privately or publicly through a chat function.

As with any important communication, the key to success is having a plan and executing it flawlessly.

IMPROMPTU REMARKS: YES, THERE'S A KEY TO SPEAKING EXTEMPORANEOUSLY

It's probably happened to you: You're at a meeting when your boss unexpectedly puts you on the spot and asks you to elaborate on something being discussed. Or you're told your colleague who was scheduled to say a few words at a new employee orientation just called in sick. You need to pinch hit—now.

Most of us have had to deliver impromptu remarks of some sort. Few of us like it, but it's a fact of life in business. The good news is that there's a formula to help you get through it with minimal discomfort and maybe even with some success. Here it is:

There's no question that the ability to "think on your feet" is a valuable asset for anyone who has to deliver impromptu remarks. If you possess that ability, congratulations; you may be able to coast. If quick thinking is not your strong suit, there are still some things you can do.

First of all, be aware if you work in a company, department or environment where being asked to speak off-the-cuff is a common occurrence. Maybe your boss has a tendency to ask people to speak extemporaneously—especially in certain situations. Observe what those situations usually are. Anticipating can reduce anxiety as much as it can increase it.

Don't panic. When you're asked to speak, immediately begin taking several deep breaths to lower heart rate and counteract other physical changes happening with your body. Re-programming yourself to breathe properly (in through the nose and out through the mouth) takes only a few seconds, and it enables you to think more clearly.

Have realistic expectations. Early on in my career, I was a speechwriter. Most of the time I had plenty of lead time to research and write the speech I was assigned. But every once in awhile, a speech was needed immediately—tomorrow! In those situations, I always reminded myself not to expect that speech to be my best work. Don't beat yourself up if the impromptu remarks you deliver are not your best work. Cut yourself some slack.

In some situations, you may have a few minutes to gather your thoughts (and even jot a few key points onto your smart phone, tablet or even on a napkin) before you have to speak. For example, maybe your boss has a few more things to say before passing the baton. Or, you're on right after a break.

In other situations, you may have to speak immediately. In either case, draw upon this formula: Every presentation has three parts: the opening, the body and the ending. Think of that structure and apply it to your impromptu remarks. The trick, of course, is to do it quickly.

Let's say you've been asked to describe your company's culture. (Remember those three parts of a presentation: opening, body, ending.)

Begin by mentioning that every company has its own culture. Enron's was toxic—"dog-eat-dog." Southwest Airlines: customer-focused and employee empowerment. Sometimes, current events can provide you with a launchpad. Can you recall seeing anything in the news recently that might be useful?

Then, transition to the body—your company's culture. What is it? How does your company characterize it (most companies do this), or what's your own perspective? Perhaps relate a story, anecdote or example that illustrates that culture. Regardless of the topic, a good strategy is to limit the body of your remarks to no more than three key points; your brain can easily remember three items.

End with a brief recap—repeat the key characteristics of the culture (i.e., "tell them what you told them"), and mention how those characteristics will help employees in their career.

Delivering impromptu remarks is much less daunting than most people believe—if you follow this format. It eliminates the problem of how to organize your remarks, and lets you focus on the content of those remarks.

COMMUNICATION: A STRATEGIC TOOL FOR SUCCESSFUL PROJECT MANAGEMENT

"Last count, I figured I've got somewhere between six and seven thousand landowners in the United States that have my cell phone number...I'm very proud of the fact that I can send out widespread communications to thousands of people and say, 'If you have any questions, if you have any concerns, feel free to call me at any time.' And that is my personal cell phone number; that's the same number that my wife calls me on."

So said Andrew Craig, land manager with TransCanada Corporation, owner of the Keystone Pipeline System. Mr. Craig has put his finger on a frequently ignored or underrated element of successful construction project management—effective communications.

Construction projects often face opposition by environmentalists, government officials, landowners and citizen groups. The result can be delays, project changes, increased costs and even project cancellations. One way to minimize or handle that opposition is by communicating to a variety of audiences before, during and after a project.

Here are some communication strategies for the three phases of any construction or similar project:

PLANNING STAGE

Involve your communicatios professionals.

In many companies, communication is an afterthought. The PR folks are called in when a news release has to be written or when a problem surfaces. Avoid this mistake. In the early planning stage of your project (well before word of it goes public), get your communications professionals involved. They can help you anticipate and manage opposition, identify critical audiences, and help develop and fine tune messages that need to be communicated. If you don't have a communications function, find an outside consultant or agency—preferably one with a track record of successfully managing issues or campaigns and one that understands both traditional and new media.

Maximize credibility transference.

The overriding goal of any communication is to establish trust and credibility. If your audience doesn't see you as trustworthy or credible, you won't get your message across or be able to address their concerns. You can enhance credibility by coordinating your project or forming alliances with other credible sources. (The Clintons did this during the Monica Lewinsky scandal when they vacationed in Martha's Vineyard with Walter Cronkite—and made sure they were photographed with "the most trusted man in America.")

For example, issue joint communications with others. Or quote supporting statements from credible sources, such as:

- Local citizens who are viewed as neutral, respected and well informed on the issue
- Professors (especially from respected local universities)
- Environmental and safety professionals
- Not-for-profit organizations
- Your own employees (hourly and middle- and lower-management employees are perceived to have more credibility than does senior management)

Seek out thought leaders.

Every community has its "influentials"—individuals or organizations busy people look to for guidance, especially on complex issues. Take time to brief them (preferably in person) on your project.

- Federal, state and local government officials
- Chamber of Commerce, Rotary Club, etc.
- Religious leaders
- Neighboring businesses
- News media (Most print and broadcast news outlets will give you an opportunity to conduct an editorial briefing for their editors and reporters who will be following your project—and perhaps commenting on it in an op ed.)

Communicate with the community.

One of the most challenging and time-consuming, yet critical, activities you'll face with any project is your communication with the public. Today, it's not just the government that gives you permission to operate, it's the public as well. Most companies keep quiet or delay talking when they are under attack. But those situations call for more, not less, communication. There are many ways to communicate with the various external audiences you need to reach: public meetings, open houses, one-on-one interactions, traditional news media, social media and more. Regardless of the strategies and tactics you use, first and foremost, communicate.

Develop messages that work.

Some companies try to win public support for their project by citing such lofty factors as job creation or other economic or patriotic issues. While these are important, they often fail to address what the public wants to know: Will I be safe? Inconvenienced? How will the project affect my property value or quality of life? What's the environmental impact? Tailor your messages to the particular audience you're trying to reach. When it comes to messaging, one size does not fit all.

People who speak plainly generate trust and credibility. They avoid jargon, abstractions, technical details and debates, and organizational identity (words such as "the corporation" or "the company," which reinforce the public's perception of large corporations and organizations as uncaring, faceless entities).

CONSTRUCTION STAGE

Keep stakeholders informed.

During construction, it's understandable that management's focus is on getting the project up and running. But during this phase, your critics don't necessarily become silent or inactive. Also, the public may have new concerns or questions you need to address. So keep communications flowing.

Utilize technology.

Back in 1982 during the Tylenol product-tampering crisis (seven people died from cyanide-laced Tylenol capsules), Johnson & Johnson, which owned the brand, had to rely on "snail mail" and mailgrams to notify thousands of doctors, hospitals, retailers and distributors throughout the country about the contaminated capsules. You have much faster and more efficient ways of reaching your target audiences—through social media. Ideally, your organization is familiar with and is already using Facebook, Twitter, YouTube, etc. These now-mainstream communication tools enable you to engage quickly and directly with large and small audiences.

Don't ignore traditional media.

Much is being made about the decline of traditional news media. But print and broadcast news outlets still play a role in reaching the public and shaping public opinion. Designate a knowledgeable, charismatic, media-trained individual in your organization as spokesperson for the project. Then have this person respond to media inquiries <u>and</u> seek out interview opportunities.

OPERATING STAGE

Communication-related activities are usually ignored or given short shrift once a project is completed. But while communication does wind down, it should not end.

Monitor the media.

Monitor whether anything is being said about your project (positive or negative) in the media, including social media, letters to the editor, op eds, news and feature stories, blogs, podcasts, etc. There are firms that provide this service if you need assistance.

Tell your story.

Don't miss the built-in fascination your completed project may have. For example, pipelines are engineering marvels, but most people don't know how they are built, operated and maintained. Reporters are always looking for story ideas, and the following may just capture their interest:

- How pipelines are controlled and operated remotely using sophisticated field instrumentation, data gathering and communication systems
- How pipelines are inspected and cleaned using pigging
- Technologies and strategies for monitoring pipelines, such as physically walking the lines and satellite surveillance

All of the above also make for great YouTube videos.

Contrary to popular opinion, communication is not a "soft skill." It's a critical skill—one that can "move the needle" when it comes to shaping the public's view on construction projects, especially those that might generate skepticism or opposition.

FIVE, FOUR, THREE, TWO, ONE. YOU'RE ON!

Some airlines show you a video of their CEO welcoming you aboard the flight. The video usually runs before the safety briefing, which might also be delivered by an airline employee. That CEO may be talking to you while walking through the terminal or standing in the aisle of the plane. He's good at it, even though he was never an actor or broadcast journalist. He probably studied accounting or law.

Other CEOs occasionally appear in TV commercials, pitching their company's products or services.

Increasingly, corporate execs and leaders in other organizations are addressing various audiences—both internal and external—through video in a conversational, "ad lib" fashion. This kind of communication is popular with today's audiences—especially younger audiences who have grown tired of "talking heads"—people who come across stiff, uncomfortable, over-rehearsed. And with more organizations using social media, websites and other forms of electronic communication, there's a need for executives to perform comfortably and effectively—like news reporters—speaking directly to the camera as if it were a person.

Success with this form of communication can be elusive—as some organizations are finding out when they try it. The challenges are many and varied:

- Although some people are naturals at this task, most are not. So the speaker must be highly motivated to master the skills needed for an effective performance. Skills such as moving with and/or for the camera, while delivering a message using few, if any, prompts (cue cards). And adding an informal, personal feel to that message.
- Some special technology and technical expertise are needed to produce a solid end-product. For example, a professional videographer is needed—

someone who can shoot the speaker while moving (including zooming in and out) and monitor audio at the same time. It's critical to record the picture and sound in a way that's not distracting and makes the most of the action. Few companies have the in-house capability to do this.

- Rehearsal is mandatory. Professional actors in movies and TV shows usually do many "takes" before the director declares, "That's a wrap." Businesspeople who choose this form of communication need to invest the necessary preparation and practice time.
- The paradox of this kind of video communication is making planned messages appear to be delivered extemporaneously. That requires work, including having powerful opening and closing lines, as well as some good stories, examples or anecdotes. And that usually means a communications professional (in-house or outside consultant) should be involved in message development, along with determining the location(s) of the shot.

If all this sounds somewhat daunting, there are firms that can work with your budding video star to show him or her the ropes. Those firms have the expertise to get your speaker ready for prime time. Before you know it, that individual will be walking down a hallway, emerging from an elevator or getting a cup of coffee—all the while, delivering messages that will resonate with the audiences who'll be watching the video.

LISTEN UP

Most of us spend 70-80 percent of our waking lives communicating, and nearly half of that time (about 45 percent) is spent listening. But we are poor listeners; we listen at an efficiency rate of only 25-50 percent.

Listening is hard work. When you listen actively, your pulse goes up and you breathe faster. There are a variety of strategies people can use to become better listeners, including concentrating intensely on the person who's talking, being alert to gestures and body language, and picking up on what's not being said.

Another way to improve listening skills is by sharpening questioning skills. Asking probing questions can be a way to unearth important information. Have a customer you're worried about? Want to know whether they plan to increase or decrease their purchases from you, or how they'll react to a price hike you're planning? Knowing the right questions to ask can help. Here are some common, but useful questioning techniques:

Closed questions usually get single-word or other short responses ("Will you be at the meeting?"). They can help you determine whether you or the other person understands something ("So, are you saying the project will be delayed?"). They're also good for ending a conversation or making a decision (Is everyone comfortable with a 9:00 am start tomorrow?").

Open questions typically get longer responses. "What?" "Why?" "How?" are good opening words, as are "Describe" and "Tell me." ("What happened at last week's meeting?") Use these words when you want to jump-start a conversation ("Tell me about that workshop you just attended."), obtain more information ("What do we need to do next?") or get someone's opinion ("What do you think about that new policy?").

Funnel questions: In this technique, you start with a general question, and then ask for more detail.
"How many potential vendors have you talked to?"
"Three."
"Are they all local?"
"Two of them are."
"Where is the third one located?'
"California."
"What are the strengths and weaknesses of these firms?"

Funnel questions help you obtain needed information. They can also help you increase (or decrease) the confidence you have in the person you're talking to.

Probing questions can help you get even greater amounts of detail. For instance, you might ask for an example ("Can you provide an example of a mistake the salesperson made with a customer?").

Leading questions: These are questions asked in a way that's intended to produce a desired answer ("Harvard is the most prestigious university in the world, isn't it?").

One final technique isn't a question at all. Barbara Walters is a former broadcast journalist and television personality known for her interviewing ability. One of the techniques she frequently used when interviewing celebrities was to reveal something very personal about herself right before the interview began. It was her way of getting them to reciprocate. They'd think, "Boy, Barbara just shared something touching with me; I guess it's okay to do that. I'll tell her about my difficult childhood." When the cameras were rolling, the interviewee would share something personal, and often get emotional and start to cry. It made for great television.

Knowing what to say (and when and how to say it) can prompt people who are reluctant to talk, to open up.

RAMP UP YOUR VIDEO CONFERENCING SKILLS

Video conferencing first appeared in 1964 when AT&T introduced Picturephone at the World's Fair in New York. This technology transmitted sound and images (one frame every two seconds) over analog telephone lines.

In the early 1970s, Picturephone was offered commercially, but it was cost-prohibitive for most people and the picture was small and blurry.

In the 1980s and 1990s, video conferencing developed and grew. Some readers of this book may remember the complex, expensive video conferencing systems found in some corporate conference rooms.

Today, video conferencing—much of it free—is available to just about anyone with a personal computer. Services such as Skype, GoToMeeting, Cisco Webex, FaceTime and Zoom are widely used. Zoom, in particular, has skyrocketed in popularity as a result of the COVID-19 virus which surfaced in 2020—forcing schools and businesses to shift to more online communication. It's likely that video conferencing use in business will become the "new normal" even after COVID-19 goes the way of SARS and the Swine flu. Some business travel and in-person meetings will surely remain replaced by virtual communication.

As you use this technology—from home or the office—to communicate with clients, prospects, colleagues or others, here are a few things to keep in mind:

EQUIPMENT

Webcams: Most laptops come with a built-in webcam, but for the most part it was an afterthought by the manufacturer and does only a fair job of streaming video and audio. If you're using a desktop or if you want to upgrade your laptop's camera and microphone, consider a stand-alone, high-resolution 1080p webcam, perhaps with a built-in mic.

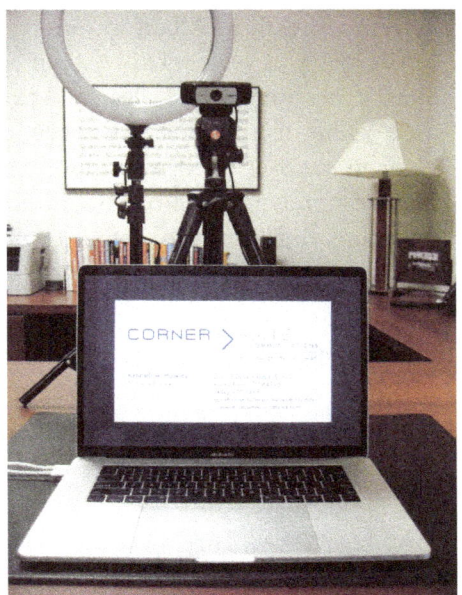

Microphones: People often complain about difficulty hearing others during video conferences. The culprit is usually a computer's built-in microphone. Solution: use an external mic which provides clearer, crisper audio. Choose a "plug and play" model; it's easy to install and delivers the best audio.

Headphones: While not the most fashionable devices, headphones can help minimize or eliminate background noise—especially important if you're working from home and you're not alone.

Ring lights: Good lighting is critical. Ring lights emit a soft, natural light. Set the light behind and above your camera, slightly off to one side or directly behind. To help hold the light where you need it, light stands are available.

DO'S AND DON'TS

Camera angle: You may have noticed that the built-in camera on most laptops sitting on a desk is below the user's eye level. The result? An unflattering view looking up at the user's nose. But when you look at people taking selfies, they are usually holding the camera up high and looking up at it. That's because it slims everything down, whereas sitting in front of a wide-angle webcam does the opposite—it makes things wider. Place your laptop on a stand or on a stack of books or boxes, and raise the camera until it's level with the top of your head, then tilt the screen down.

Lighting: Avoid excessive light (natural or artificial) behind you. Windows with the coverings open are especially problematic. Close the shades, blinds, shutters or drapes. Better yet, have a dark wall or something similar in the background. Light your face, not the back of your head. A lamp with its shade removed doesn't work very well, but you can set the lamp (shade on) next to your computer screen. An overhead light in a room will work, as long as you're not right underneath it. A better option is a ring light (discussed above).

Audio: You've probably seen photos of recording studios lined with sound-absorbing panels, designed to produce crisp, clean audio. Radio journalists working from home have been known to record their stories under a blanket or in a closet filled with clothes. To produce the best possible sound, avoid video conferencing in a room with little or nothing in it, including on the walls. Carpeting, drapes, upholstered furniture, wall artwork, etc. can greatly improve audio quality.

Setting: If you're video conferencing from home, select a quiet, appropriate environment. Be careful of background distractors—both visual and audio: kids, pets, lawn mowers, phones, etc. (Admit it, you've tried to read the titles of books found on shelves of some of the people you're talking to, or you were checking out their home décor.) Most video conferencing services allow you to choose from a variety of neutral, digital video backgrounds.

Appearance: Three words: business casual dress. Avoid patterns or stripes which may be distracting on camera. Also, wearing bright white or black may cause your camera to auto-adjust brightness and make it hard to see your face.

Wear a less extreme color. Position your laptop or camera so that your image includes the top of your head down to your shoulders or better yet, the desktop.

Software: Be familiar with the video conferencing software you or your host is using. Test it prior to the call. And have a fully charged device and strong Wi-Fi connection.

ON-SCREEN PRESENCE

Posture: While sitting, lean forward (it increases energy and shows engagement) with hands 8-12 inches on the desk in front of you. Avoid hands under the desk or on the edge (weak, tentative, unengaged). Have most of your forearms on the desk, but not elbows.

Gestures: Hand movements are more pronounced on screen than they are in person because you are framed within a limited area. Keep hands from getting too close to the camera (they appear larger than they are in proportion to the rest of your image). Too frequent hand movements can make you appear frenetic or nervous, and hands that flash in and out of the frame can be distracting. Use specific, well defined gestures that sync with a particular message you're trying to convey (e.g., two fingers when making two points).

Eye contact: Your camera is your surrogate audience. Over time, you'll get comfortable looking at this inanimate object, but don't constantly stare at it. Occasionally, look at your notes, glance down or to the side, or look at your screen (e.g., at a few audience members shown in thumbnails).

Put a priority on how you come across in video conferences. Most conferencing services enable you to record your session. Do it, and then take time to review and critique your on-camera image and performance. Audiences rarely notice when everything looks and sounds good, but they easily spot the distractions and glitches. Make sure what you say has greater staying power than anything else in the call.

EXIT LINE

Any company that's had to announce the abrupt departure of a top executive knows this can be a tricky assignment.

What if the executive was fired for poor performance? What if a power struggle existed…and he lost? What if there was some unethical or illegal activity behind the departure? What if the executive simply found greener pastures?

What do you say?

Even retirements can be hard to explain—especially early retirements. How many times have you heard that so-and-so left the company in order to spend more time with his family? Yeah, sure.

That explanation and its close relatives—"for personal reasons" and "to pursue personal interests" have become clichés. Their meaning is suspect—even if true.

Here's a different take on handling the changing of the guard:

First off, communicate. Remaining silent will only feed the rumor mill. And besides, if yours is a publicly traded company, depending on the position involved, the personnel change may be considered material information—something the Security and Exchange Commission requires you to disclose.

Speaking of rumors, be prepared to address them quickly. With today's 24/7 news reporting and the rise of the citizen journalist, rumors spread rapidly and can be accepted as fact.

Provide a short, honest, straightforward statement about the departure. This is especially appropriate when departures involve taking a new position, genuine retirements, or when there is a specific and non-controversial reason for leaving.

Where a relationship has broken down (e.g., a disagreement about the strategic direction of the company), simply acknowledge it. But also acknowledge the individual's contributions and service to the company. Remember, the executive may have enjoyed popularity with customers, investors, employees and others.

Avoid explanations such as, "to pursue other interests."

Situations involving wrongdoing can be a real challenge. On the one hand, some of the public may already have some idea about the real reason for the departure. So, being less than honest can damage the company's credibility. On the other hand, the terms of an executive's departure may have been negotiated (including what will be said publicly). In that case, the best strategy may be to say as little as possible—for example, simply that the executive has decided to leave the company. Unfortunately, this strategy often means that you may be bombarded with questions about the individual's health or other personal circumstances.

If possible, try to announce the departing executive's replacement concurrently or as quickly as possible. This tends to put the focus back on the organization rather than on the individual who left.

CHAPTER 7
THE END

Let's end at the ending…of a popular, award-winning film, *The King's Speech*. It's based on the true story of England's King George VI, who had to overcome a lifelong, debilitating speech impediment. To help him do that, his wife enlisted the aid of a quirky speech therapist.

Near the end of the film, we learn that Nazi Germany has invaded Poland, and once more, England is at war. The King must speak to his nation and rally the world. Standing in a small radio broadcast room, he says these words:

"In this grave hour, perhaps the most fateful in our history, I send to every household of my peoples, both at home and overseas, this message—spoken with the same depth of feeling for each one of you as if I were able to cross your threshold and speak to you myself.

"For the second time in the lives of most of us, we are at war. Over and over again, we have tried to find a peaceful way out of the differences between ourselves and those who are now our enemies. But it has been in vain. We have been forced into a conflict, for we are called to meet the challenge of a principle, which if it were to prevail, would be fatal to any civilized order in the world. Such a principle, stripped of all disguise, is simply the mere primitive doctrine that might is right. For the sake of all that we ourselves hold dear, it is unthinkable that we should refuse to meet the challenge.

215

Colin Firth as England's King George VI in *The King's Speech*. Effective communication can mobilize a nation at war. And it can propel your career.

"It is to this high purpose I now call on my people at home and my peoples across the seas who will make our cause their own. I ask them to stand calm and firm and united in this time of trial. The task will be hard. There may be dark days ahead. And war can no longer be confined to the battlefield. But we can only do the right as we see the right, and reverently commit our cause to God. If one and all we keep resolutely faithful to it, then with God's help we shall prevail."

As he speaks those words, we see a cross-section of British society listening intently to him on radio—religious and government leaders, men in pubs, people on the street, factory workers, soldiers, "upstairs" aristocrats and "downstairs" servants. Those scenes are incredibly moving…and they illustrate the transformative power of communication.

In September, 1940, a Gallup Poll found that only 16 percent of Americans favored providing aid to Britain. (World War I was still fresh in their minds, and most Americans wanted no part of another European war.) A month later, with the devastating effects of the Blitz better known—thanks in part to Edward R. Murrow's radio reports from London—52 percent of Americans favored aid.

Effective communication can mobilize a nation.

It can start a movement. (Think: Martin Luther King, Jr.)

It can attract supporters. (Think: Franklin D. Roosevelt, Ronald Reagan and Bill Clinton.)

It can sell products. (Think: Steve Jobs.)

And effective communication can propel a career. Best wishes on yours.

NOTES

INTRODUCTION

IX **In one survey:** Study conducted by Lamalie Associates (management consultants), New York.

IX **One executive who would probably agree:** From the documentary, "BP: $30 Billion Blowout," which appeared on BBC Two's *The Money Programme*, November 9, 2010.

CHAPTER 1. CRAFTING AND DELIVERING A TOP-FLIGHT PRESENTATION

3 **In addition, within 48 hours:** Research conducted by Dr. Lyman K. Steil (University of Minnesota), Chairman & CEO, Communication Development Inc. & Chairman, International Listening Leadership Institute.

4 **Research suggests that it is best:** Amy Cuddy, Matthew Kohut, John Neffinger, "Connect Then Lead," *Harvard Business Review*, July-August, 2013.

6 **Thomas Jefferson:** Lilyan Wilder, *7 Steps to Fearless Speaking*, (New York: John Wiley & Sons, Inc., 1999). Don A. Moore, *Perfectly Confident: How to Calibrate Your Decisions Wisely*, (New York, Harper Business, 2020).

9 **A book that's been around for quite awhile:** Ron Hoff, *I Can See You Naked*, (Andrews McMeel Publishing, 1992).

11 **Louisiana State University quarterback:** During a national championship post-game interview, ESPN's Maria Taylor asked LSU quarterback Joe Burrow what his ring size was. The question was prompted by a gesture Burrow made pointing to his ring finger twelve minutes before the game ended.

12 **Author and motivational speaker:** Zig Ziglar, *See You at the Top*, (Gretna, LA, Pelican, 1975).

14 **At one point in her remarks:** Barbara Bush, "Choices and Change: Your Success as a Family," Delivered at Severance Green, Wellesley College, Wellesley, Massachusetts, June 1, 1990, *Vital Speeches of the Day*, July, 1990.

16 **In his book:** Louis V. Gerstner, Jr., *Who Says Elephants Can't Dance? Inside IBM's Historic Turnaround*, (New York, Harper Collins, 2003).

19 **In an interview, band members Brian May and Roger Taylor:** 2003 interview with Queen band members Brian May and Roger Taylor, "Road to Wembley," *Live At Wembley Stadium*.

20 **One year to the day:** *Concert for George*, November 29, 2002, Warner Music Group.

21 **It's unconventional—not unlike in the James Bond movie, *Skyfall*:** *Skyfall*, Metro-Goldwyn Mayer Studios Inc. and Danjaq, LLC, 2012.

21 **Here's the non-traditional opening of a speech:** U.S. Supreme Court Justice John Roberts spoke at the Ronald Regan Presidential Library in Simi Valley, California on March 8, 2006—the first such public speech since he was appointed to the nation's highest court. C-Span Archives.

22 **At the end of his important speech:** "Money, Power and Wall Street," *Frontline*, 2012, WGBH Educational Foundation.

23 **The *Journal* used this analogy:** "Beltway Oil Drill," *Wall Street Journal*, November 9, 2005.

24 **Before the United States entered World War II:** Nicholas Wapshott, *The Sphinx: Franklin Roosevelt, the Isolationists, and the Road to World War II*, (New York, W.W. Norton & Company, 2014).

24 **It comes from the movie:** *Flash of Genius*, Universal Pictures and Spyglass Entertainment, 2008.

28 **In a TED Talk on malaria:** Bill Gates, "Mosquitos, malaria and education," TED, February, 2009.

29 **Here's one of them:** Talia Kaplan, "NJ FedEx driver picks up, folds fallen American flag: 'You have to do something whether people are watching or not'," *Fox News*, February 16, 2020.

31 **One of the most thoughtful commencement addresses:** Michael Ward, "Of Hills and Dales—2015 Commencement Address," delivered on May 9, 2015 at Hillsdale College, *Imprimis*, May/June 2015.

32 **When bestselling author:** Peggy Noonan, *Simply Speaking: How to Communicate Your Ideas with Style, Substance, and Clarity*, (Regan Books, 1998).

34 **But first, a few points:** Research on the use of visuals in presentations and marketing efforts was conducted by a 3M-sponsored study at the University of Minnesota School of Management in 1986.

36 **Nancy Duarte, who wrote a thoughtful book:** Nancy Duarte, *slide:ology: The Art and Science of Creating Great Presentations*, (North Sebastopol, California, O'Reilly Media, 2008).

39 **In 2003, the Space Shuttle Columbia:** Tad Simons, "Does PowerPoint Make You Stupid?" *Presentations*, March, 2004.

40 **PowerPoint's most vociferous critic:** Edward R. Tufte, *The Cognitive Style of PowerPoint: Pitching Out Corrupts Within*, (Cheshire, CT, Graphics Press, 2005).

42 **Adam Vinatieri, one of the greatest kickers:** Geoffrey Colvin and Ellen McGirt, "What It Takes to Be Great," *Fortune*, October 30, 2006.

42 **For example, how does a receiver catch:** Jeff Hawkins and Sandra Blakeslee, *On Intelligence*, (New York, St. Martin's Press, 2005).

47 **Sometimes, the toughest part of Q&A:** *Stop Making Sense* is a 1984 American concert film featuring a live performance by the rock band, Talking Heads. At the conclusion of one of the songs ("Life During Wartime"), lead singer David Byrne turned to the audience and jokingly asked if they had any questions. *Stop Making Sense: A Film by Jonathan Demme and Talking Heads*, Talking Heads Films, Inc.

48 **President Ronald Reagan and Soviet General Secretary Mikhail Gorbachev:** *Reagan* (from the American Experience Collection: The Presidents), WGBH Educational Foundation, 1998.

49 **Actor Sean Connery:** Diane K. Shah, *A Farewell to Arms, Legs & Jockstraps*, (Bloomington, Indiana, Red Lightening Books, 2020).

49 **Few things can do more:** Deborah Blum, "Face it!" *Psychology Today*, September 1, 1998.

50 **Have you ever found yourself gesturing:** Donna Frick-Horbury, "The effects of hand gestures on verbal recall as a function of high- and low-verbal-skill levels." *Journal of General Psychology*, April, 2002.

53 **He understood the importance of practice:** Adam Lashinsky, "The Decade of Steve," *Fortune*, November 5, 2009.

55   **Afterwards, Jobs said:** Walter Isaacson, *Steve Jobs*, (New York, Simon & Schuster, 2011).

CHAPTER 2. COMMUNICATING WITH THE NEWS MEDIA

75   **Long answers also bother TV viewers:** Robert Bellamy and James Walker, *Television and the Remote Control: Grazing on a Vast Wasteland*, (New York, Guilford, 2000).

79   **Bill Belichick, coach of the New England Patriots:** During the September 16, 2007 broadcast of the NFL game between the New England Patriots and San Diego Chargers on NBC Sunday Night Football, a portion of Bill Belichick's pre-game press conference was shown. During the press conference, reporters asked Belichick several questions related to the "Spygate" incident involving videotaping coaches' signals.

85   **Hypothetical questions are asked:** Sarah G. Moore, David T. Neal, Gavan J. Fitzsimons, Baba Shiv, "Wolves in sheep's clothing: How and when hypothetical questions influence behavior," *Organizational Behavior and Human Decision Processes*, September, 2001.

85   **Shortly after their son Newt Gingrich:** Connie Chung, anchor of a CBS program titled, *Eye to Eye*, interviewed the parents of Speaker of the House Newt Gingrich. The interview was broadcast on January 5, 1995.

89   **As part of a news investigation:** From an investigative report by Brett Shipp that aired on WFAA-TV/Channel 8 in the early 2000s.

96   **If you're an Indianapolis Colts fan:** From a joint press conference conducted by Peyton Manning and Jim Irsay. Broadcast by RTV6—The Indy Channel on March 18, 2016.

103 **Looking for an example:** *60 Minutes* episode titled, "Trouble Brewing," aired on CBS on September 26, 1982.

106 **In an interview with *Sports Illustrated*:** Richard Deitsch, "Man behind the mic: Fox NFL analyst Troy Aikman on broadcasting, more," *Sports Illustrated*, January 13, 2015.

CHAPTER 3. MANAGING A CRISIS

116 **Crisis Forecasting:** Ian I. Mitroff with Gus Anagnos, *Managing Crises Before They Happen: What Every Executive and Manager Needs to Know About Crisis Management*, (New York, AMACOM, 2001).

CHAPTER 4. COMMUNICATING WITH INVESTORS AND THOSE WHO INFLUENCE THEM

138 **Moreover, studies indicate that the accuracy:** Michael D. Kimbrough, "The Effect of Conference Calls on Analyst and Market Underreaction to Earnings Announcements," *The Accounting Review*, Vol. 80, No.1, 2005.

138 **As it turns out:** Jing Chen, Baruch Lev, Elizabeth Demers, "The Dangers of Late-Afternoon Earnings Calls," *Harvard Business Review*, October, 2013.

146 **Convenience is becoming increasingly important:** Citizens Restaurant Finance, "Restaurant takeout and delivery are taking a bite out of dine-in traffic," *National Restaurant News*. June 24, 2016.

147 **Rob Tobin, a successful script doctor:** Paul B. Brown, Alison Davis, *Your Attention Please. How to Appeal to Today's Distracted, Disinterested, Disengaged, Disenchanted, and Busy Audiences*, (Avon, Massachusetts, Adams Media, 2006).

CHAPTER 5. SOCIAL MEDIA

162 **"Well, it's been about 45 minutes now since I have Googled myself":** *Steve Martin and the Steep Canyon Rangers featuring Edie Brickell Live* (at the Fox Performing Arts Center in Riverside, CA), Rounder Records and Thirteen Productions, 2014.

CHAPTER 6. SPECIAL SITUATIONS

167 **As Bert Decker says:** Bert Decker, *You've Got To Be Believed To Be Heard*. (New York: St. Martin's Press, 1992).

168 **Components of trust:** Research conducted by Susan L. Santos, Focus Group.

173 **Tom Clancy was a prolific author:** Tom Clancy, *The Hunt for Red October*, (Annapolis, MD: Naval Institute Press, 1984).

204 **"Last count, I figured I've got…":** "Keystone XL Pipeline—Land Manager Craig on Landowner Relations," *Vimeo*, November 27, 2014.

CHAPTER 7. THE END

215 **Let's end at the ending:** *The King's Speech*, The Weinstein Company, 2010.

PHOTO CREDITS

Oh No! I Have to Give a Speech
GeorgiosArt/iStock by Getty Images

A Lesson from LSU
Todd Kirkland/Icon Sportswire via Getty Images

How to Craft a Winning Presentation
Rick Friedman/Pool via CNP

Presentations That Rock: What Business Leaders Can Learn from Rock Concerts
Corner Suite Communications

Hero in the Balcony
Reagan White House Photographs/U.S. National Archives

Please, Not Another PowerPoint Presentation
Glen LeLievre/The New Yorker Collection/The Cartoon Bank
Corner Suite Communications (Learning to Sail)

PowerPoint's Role in the Space Shuttle Disaster
Presentations

Q&A: Not as Hard as You May Think
Joseph Mirachi/The New Yorker Collection/The Cartoon Bank

The Presentation Genius of Steve Jobs
Siegle/Alamy

Why the Deck Is Stacked Against You
life_in_a_pixel/Shutterstock

Q = A+1
Eric Canha/CSM/Alamy Live News

Peyton Manning: Superstar ~~Quarterback~~ Communicator
Sylvia Buchholz/REUTERS/Alamy

Twenty-first Century Crisis Management: A Briefing for Executives
Corner Suite Communications

What's Your Company's Investible Idea?
Corner Suite Communications

The Language of Trust
Focus Group

Briefing Lessons from Tom Clancy's Jack Ryan
Steve Meditz/Berkley

Note to Women: Forget Gender-specific Communications Advice
Corner Suite Communications

What We Can Learn from Mark Zuckerberg's Two-day Congressional Testimony
Ting Shen/Xinhua/Alamy Live News

Ramp Up Your Video Conferencing Skills
Corner Suite Communications

The End
The Weinstein Company/Alamy

Back Cover Author Photo
Corner Suite Communications

ABOUT THE AUTHOR

Ken Haseley is founder and principal of Corner Suite Communications, a firm that helps leaders and aspiring leaders assess and improve one of their most important, yet frequently ignored skill sets – communicating effectively through the spoken word. His firm specializes in coaching executives on their communications with investors and those who influence them.

A graduate of Kent State University, Ken has a Bachelor of Science degree in communications and government. Additionally, he holds an MBA from the University of Dallas.

His corporate affiliations have included Diamond Shamrock, Occidental Petroleum and Tenneco, where he served as a communications director and worked in investor relations. During 1982, he was on loan to the Reagan Administration in Washington, DC where he served as a speechwriter.

His experience as a communications coach and trainer spans some twenty years and involved working with companies and other organizations in twenty countries. Ken has a loyal following among the C-suite executives he coaches.

He has lectured at MIT's Sloan School of Management, served as a visiting professor at Ivanovo State University in Russia, and developed and teaches Communications for Leaders in the Executive MBA program at the Bauer College of Business at the University of Houston.

After hours: In addition to business communications, Ken's other passions are sailing his 33-foot *Connecticut Yankee* and driving his '59 and '65 Corvettes. Those cars don't have names, but if they did, they'd be Tod and Buz – a tip of the hat to the two lead characters who traveled the country (in a 1962 Corvette) in the '60s TV show *Route 66*.

www.cornersuitecommunications.com

ken@cornersuitecommunications.com

www.ingramcontent.com/pod-product-compliance
Lightning Source LLC
Chambersburg PA
CBHW081305070526
44578CB00006B/810